PRAISE FOR WHAT THEN MUST WE DO?

"There can be neither peace, nor democracy, nor social justice until we change the system that underpins the American empire and policy-crippling maldistribution of wealth. For decades, Gar Alperovitz has been at the forefront of attempts to understand what could lie beyond our increasingly broken system of corporate capitalism. This book offers by far the most serious, intellectually grounded strategy for system-changing yet to appear. It could be the most important movement-building book of the new century—and, thereby, one of the most important political books as well."

—**Daniel Ellsberg**, author of
Secrets: A Memoir of Vietnam and the Pentagon Papers
and cofounder of the Freedom of the Press Foundation

"In this important new book, Gar Alperovitz is telling us there's something happening here in corporate-driven America, be it social enterprise, community land trusts, worker-owned businesses, or employee stock-ownership plans. We all know that the free-market economic system no longer works for the vast majority of citizens, and Alperovitz is showing us that there is a better, equally American way to spread the wealth and put more people to work, while making the nation a safer and healthier place to live. This is not a utopian fantasy or a call for social engineering, but a plain-spoken and easy-to-absorb analysis by one of our leading economists of what's gone wrong and how to make it better."

—**Seymour M. Hersh**, *The New Yorker*

"Gar Alperovitz, the intellectual leader of the economic-democracy movement, has produced the most compelling account yet of how we can move beyond the piecemeal, project-by-project transformation of our political economy to truly systemic change. A must-read for anyone who cares about the future of the United States and the world."

—**Juliet Schor**, author of *True Wealth: How and Why Millions of Americans Are Creating a Time-Rich, Ecologically Light, Small-Scale, High-Satisfaction Economy*

"Gar Alperovitz's new book is so plain-spoken and accessible that it takes a moment to appreciate the magnitude of his accomplishment. After examining new patterns of positive change emerging in America today—including many undernoticed changes that involve democratizing the ownership of wealth—he develops a brilliant strategy for the type of transformative change that can lead America from decline to rebirth. In giving a sense of strategic direction and honest possibility to the call for a new economy, Alperovitz has made an enormous contribution exactly where it is most needed."

—**James Gustave Speth**, author of
America the Possible: Manifesto for a New Economy

"A fresh take on how to reinvigorate democracy and civic life. An analysis that transcends labels and has a real blueprint for action."

—**Naomi Wolf**, author of
The End of America: Letter of Warning to a Young Patriot

"In this slender book, Gar Alperovitz does more than pack a tremendous amount of passion and wisdom about the structural ills of our society. He proposes a common-sense strategy for fixing them as well—grounded in local institutions that can construct a truly democratic economy. Every progressive should read this book and then start practicing what its author preaches."

—**Michael Kazin**, author of *American Dreamers: How the Left Changed a Nation* and coeditor of *Dissent*

"As Gar Alperovitz reaches an ever-larger audience, the cooperative and community-based economy he is encouraging will attract increasing numbers of consumers away from big business and its corporate state. *What Then Must We Do?* offers a powerful argument, written in a conversational style to prod you into the kind of meaningful discussions that lead to more equality and accountability in our political economy."

—**Ralph Nader**, author of *The Seventeen Solutions: Bold Ideas for Our American Future*

"If ever there was a time to consider new directions for our faltering economy, it is now! Gar Alperovitz's new book provides a comprehensive survey of the explosion of new cooperatives, worker-owned firms, city and state investment efforts, and dozens of other 'new economy' development strategies—and fashions them into a coherent strategy. Absolutely essential reading for anyone concerned with building the next Progressive Era."

—**Van Jones**, author of *Rebuild the Dream*

"Gar Alperovitz knows that we must look for new ways to create and sustain good jobs. In *What Then Must We Do?*, he has outlined a practical, common-sense strategy to improve our economy by making it more democratic. As the United Steelworkers has shown in its innovative partnership with Mondragon, combining employee equity with a progressive collective-bargaining process results in higher accountability, productivity, and efficiency because all workers have an equal stake in the company. Instead of measuring the value of a corporation only in profits, losses, and shareholder dividends, we must take into account how the enterprise serves its community."

—**Leo Gerard**, international president, United Steelworkers Union

"Gar Alperovitz is the rare economist who begins with the idea that economic activity should reflect the social aspirations of the community rather than merely the utilitarian interest of global enterprises. He has devoted his professional career to asking the critical question of how best to ensure a more democratic and participatory economy for everyone. *What Then Must We Do?* provides a much-needed, hopeful vision of how each community can take hold of its economic future and build a sustainable society."

—**Jeremy Rifkin**, author of *The Third Industrial Revolution*

"Alperovitz revives the tradition of political economy and spells out the institutional requirements and historical likelihood of moving the United States in the direction of a democratic community. An insightful and accessible book."

—**Herman Daly**, author of *Ecological Economics*

"If you're ready for hard-headed hope, here you go! Alperovitz's power is that he's no 'mere' theorist of democratic change. He is also a creator—practically engaged in demonstrating democratic-economic solutions that work. *What Then Must We Do?* is packed with mind-boggling facts, thoughtful insights, and practical steps."

—**Frances Moore Lappé**, author of
EcoMind: Changing the Way We Think, to Create the World We Want

"Alperovitz's latest is distinguished by clear, accessible, straightforward writing that dares to raise the *systemic* nature of today's problems in the United States and to show why *system change* is therefore the necessary solution. This call for the long-overdue 'next American revolution' will move system change forward on the agendas of many."

—**Richard D. Wolff**, author of *Democracy at Work: A Cure for Capitalism*

"The move to broadly participatory, locally rooted, cooperative ownership is essential to America's future. Gar Alperovitz presents a brilliant, accessible, and practical plan of action to make it happen."

—**David Korten**, board chair of *YES!* magazine and author of
Agenda for a New Economy: From Phantom Wealth to Real Wealth

"In this cooperative and democratic manifesto, Gar Alperovitz delivers his designs for a more harmonious society—a goal long dreamed of on these shores. May his ideas and ideals flourish."

—**James Galbraith**, author of *The Predator State*

"Gar Alperovitz continues to challenge us to recognize and assume responsibility for creating an America beyond capitalism."

—**Grace Lee Boggs**, author of *The Next American Revolution:
Sustainable Activism for the Twenty-First Century*

"With his latest book, Gar Alperovitz only adds to his status as one of the most creative and important thinkers of our time. Grappling with his arguments (even when we disagree) has been one of the chief intellectual pleasures of my reading life. For *you*, the immediate answer to 'What Then Must We Do?' is clear: *Read this book*."

—**Bertell Ollman**, author of *Dance of the Dialectic* and *Alienation*

"Gar Alperovitz brings some of the most lucid insight, deepest practical experience, and most compelling vision to the convergent transformation of politics and economy. Given radical climate disruption combined with arguably the greatest wealth inequity in the history of civilization, transforming the economy requires thoughtful and highly practical systems change. Alperovitz has produced a glimmering map guided by a compass of conscience. A must-read."

—**Kenny Ausubel**, cofounder of Bioneers, author of *Dreaming the Future*

"Alperovitz offers an approach to a movement for genuine structural reforms that may lay the foundation for deeper transformation. . . . These proposals stand in opposition to the inequities and injustices of neoliberal capitalism and offer the prospect for a progressive direction."

—**Bill Fletcher, Jr.**, author of *They're Bankrupting Us!
And Twenty Other Myths about Unions*

Gar Alperovitz

WHAT
THEN
MUST
WE DO?

STRAIGHT TALK

ABOUT THE NEXT

AMERICAN REVOLUTION

Chelsea Green Publishing
White River Junction, Vermont

Project Manager: Patricia Stone
Developmental Editor: Joni Praded
Copy Editor: Laura Jorstad
Proofreader: Nancy Ringer
Indexer: Margaret Holloway
Designer: Melissa Jacobson

Printed in the United States of America.
First printing March, 2013.
10 9 8 7 6 5 4 3 2   13 14 15 16 17

Chelsea Green Publishing is committed to preserving ancient forests and natural resources. We elected to print this title on 30-percent postconsumer recycled paper, processed chlorine-free. As a result, for this printing, we have saved:

12 Trees (40' tall and 6-8" diameter)
5 Million BTUs of Total Energy
997 Pounds of Greenhouse Gases
5,409 Gallons of Wastewater
362 Pounds of Solid Waste

Chelsea Green Publishing made this paper choice because we and our printer, Thomson-Shore, Inc., are members of the Green Press Initiative, a nonprofit program dedicated to supporting authors, publishers, and suppliers in their efforts to reduce their use of fiber obtained from endangered forests. For more information, visit: www.greenpressinitiative.org.

Environmental impact estimates were made using the Environmental Defense Paper Calculator. For more information visit: www.papercalculator.org.

Our Commitment to Green Publishing

Chelsea Green sees publishing as a tool for cultural change and ecological stewardship. We strive to align our book manufacturing practices with our editorial mission and to reduce the impact of our business enterprise in the environment. We print our books and catalogs on chlorine-free recycled paper, using vegetable-based inks whenever possible. This book may cost slightly more because it was printed on paper that contains recycled fiber, and we hope you'll agree that it's worth it. Chelsea Green is a member of the Green Press Initiative (www.greenpressinitiative.org), a nonprofit coalition of publishers, manufacturers, and authors working to protect the world's endangered forests and conserve natural resources. *What Then Must We Do?* was printed on FSC®-certified paper supplied by Thomson-Shore that contains at least 30% postconsumer recycled fiber.

Library of Congress Cataloging-in-Publication Data

Alperovitz, Gar.
    What then must we do?: straight talk about the next American revolution: democratizing wealth and building a community-sustaining economy from the ground up/Gar Alperovitz.
        pages cm
    ISBN 978-1-60358-491-3 (hardcover)—ISBN 978-1-60358-504-0 (pbk.)
—ISBN 978-1-60358-492-0 (ebook)
1. Capitalism—United States. 2. Income distribution—United States. 3. Democracy—Economic aspects—United States. 4. United States—Economic conditions—2009- 5. United States—Economic policy—2009- I. Title.

    HC106.84.A47 2013
    330.973—dc23

                    2013001701

Chelsea Green Publishing
85 North Main Street, Suite 120
White River Junction, VT 05001
(802) 295-6300
www.chelseagreen.com

MIX
Paper from
responsible sources
FSC® C013483

For Sharon

CONTENTS

A Note About What Can Be Talked About, and in What Ways   ix

Introduction   xi

PART I: THE SYSTEM PROBLEM

1. How to Detect a System Problem Without Really Trying   1
2. But Hasn't What We Normally Call Politics Done What Needs to Be Done in the Past?   6
3. Flies Number Two and Three in the Traditional Theory of Politics   11
4. The Fading Power of Traditional Politics   17

PART II: SYSTEMS OLD AND NEW: EVOLUTIONARY RECONSTRUCTION

5. A Note About Systems and History and Prehistory   25
   And Also About Just Plain Useful Change
6. An Initial Way to Think About System Change   28
7. Quiet Democratization Everywhere   35
8. Worker Ownership Redux   41
9. Cultural and Ideological Hegemony, Utopia—and Us   46

PART III: "CHECKERBOARD": EMERGENT MUNICIPAL AND STATE POSSIBILITIES

10. How the Conservatives Buried Adam Smith   51
    And What It Might Mean for Us
11. Everyday Socialism, All the Time, American-Style   58
12. Checkerboard Strategies, and Beyond   65

PART IV: HOT SPOTS: BANKING, HEALTH CARE, AND CRISIS TRANSFORMATIONS

13. Banking   75
14. Health Care   83
15. Beyond Countervailing Power   89
16. Bigger Possibilities and Precedents   93
    For Something, One Day, Possibly Even More Interesting

PART V: NARROW-MINDED EFFICIENCY, PUBLIC ENTERPRISE, AND ALL THAT

17. Public Enterprise Redux I   99
*And Just a Bit More on the Use and Misuse of
"Efficiency Talk"*

18. Public Enterprise Redux II   104
Airline Foolishness and Endless Growth

PART VI: THE EMERGING HISTORICAL ERA

19. The Emerging Historical Context   113
*And Why It's Critical to Your Theory of Change
and Your Strategy*

20. Two Dogs That Are Unlikely to Bark Again   119

21. Stagnation and Punctuated Stagnation   124

22. The Logic of Our Time in History   130
And What That Means for the Next American System

PART VII: CONCLUSION

23. The Prehistory of the Next American Revolution   139
Toward a Community-Sustaining System

Afterword   148
Acknowledgments   157
Notes   161
Index   197

A Note About What Can Be Talked About, and in What Ways

As is pretty evident, or will be in a few pages, this book is written in a very informal, conversational style—especially for someone like me, who is an academic and a former Washington insider (also an activist on things that matter).

The reasons are several.

First and foremost, I've been talking to lots of people the last few years about these things, all around the country, and I've found that it is possible, easiest, and best to discuss the really important points about our crumbling American system, and what to do about it, in language that is understandable and accessible.

Second, many of the really big issues covered in the pages ahead can't be handled in any way other than what is best termed informed speculation. In other words, judgments about what it makes sense to actually do politically all depend upon (usually unspoken and unacknowledged) assumptions about what is possible in the future.

And the problem—as historian Lewis Namier once quipped—is that we all tend to "remember the future." By which he meant that we don't and can't document what will happen in the future. Instead, most of us unconsciously project forward assumptions about what is possible based on our actual experience of the past. We "remember" forward that which we unconsciously take for granted.

This works most of the time, but it works terribly in times of great change.

Most academics and Washington insiders—like most people, including most activists—aren't much better than anyone else about avoiding this pitfall. They also tend to "remember" the future, projecting (often telling us, with seeming academic or political authority!) what is and is not possible.

So a really big reason to write the way folks talk when they're relaxing over a couple of beers or a cup of coffee is to break out of this particular foolish spell.

I'm from Wisconsin. I recall the 1950s when Senator Joe McCarthy had everyone trembling for fear of being called a Communist. It was pretty dark in Wisconsin in the 1950s. And accordingly, at the time ordinary citizens and academic scholars alike knew that if you remembered the future, nothing could ever really change.

Then, of course, came the 1960s—and the explosion of the civil rights movement, the feminist movement, the environmental movement, the anti–Vietnam War movement. All largely unpredicted, and especially by those who claimed academic or political-insider authority to forecast what is, or was, possible.

So not only is it more enjoyable to try to write the way we talk, and even to play with the language—especially when we're facing a pretty dire and profound set of issues—but doing so is a not-so-subtle hint that it is time to stop taking seriously the people economist Paul Krugman wryly calls "Very Serious People." These are the people who by tone and language and a seemingly knowing stance try to contain and constrain what can be talked about in polite circles . . . and what we really shouldn't say.

(And for those of you who do like academic references, see the endnotes and the afterword.)

What Then Must We Do?

I've borrowed my title *What Then Must We Do?* from Tolstoy, and the profoundly disturbing 1886 book he wrote once he began to dig below the surface of what was happening in late-nineteenth-century Russia—a time when the system was in decay, the aristocracy enjoyed extraordinary luxury, and the peasants endured lives of hunger and pain. As a person of privilege he began to understand something deeper about his time in history: "I sit on a man's back, choking him and making him carry me," he wrote, "and yet assure myself and others that I am very sorry for him and wish to ease his lot by all possible means—except by getting off his back."[1]

Most of us do not literally sit on men's backs, making them carry us. We do, however, often uneasily look the other way, satisfying ourselves with modest changes that reassure us all is well while millions are in despair. "We've done the best we can do," we might say, "given the realities." Still, many sense, as did Tolstoy, that to actually do something serious would require us to confront much deeper problems than we are commonly willing to.

"What then must we do?" is not shouted in the streets, but it is a question that more and more Americans—young and old, liberal, radical, and conservative—are quietly beginning to ask themselves in much more penetrating ways.

So let us begin. My starting point is the obvious fact that despite its great wealth the United States today faces enormous difficulties, with no easily discernible political answers that even begin to offer strategic handholds on a truly democratic future. Elections occur, and major fiscal debates ensue, but many of the most pressing problems facing ordinary citizens are only marginally affected (and in many cases in ways that increase burdens, not reduce them). The issue is not simply that our situation is worrisome, however; it is that there are growing reasons to believe that in fact we face systemic problems, not simply political problems.

Systemic problems in the fundamental, not the superficial, sense. In the pages ahead I will suggest that our nation's truly critical problems are built into the very structure of the economic and political system; they are not something passing in the night that will go away even when we elect forward-looking leaders and actively pressure them to move in a different direction. I won't load you down with statistics at this point. (I'll provide many more details in due course.) A couple of obvious reminders, however: Not only has the economy been stagnating for a long time, but for the average person—and the average family—things have been bad for a *very* long time.

Real wages for 80 percent of American workers, for instance, have not gone up more than a trivial amount for at least three decades.[2] At the same time, income for the top 1 percent has jumped from roughly 10 percent of all income to roughly 20 percent.[3] Put another way, *virtually all the gains of the entire economic system have gone to a tiny, tiny group at the top for at least three decades.*

Worth pausing to think about that one. What is going on when virtually all the gains in the entire economic system go to the top? I'm not interested here in criticizing those at the top (we can deal with that later). The question is: What is going on with the system when this kind of thing happens—*and continues to happen in an ongoing way, year by year, decade by decade over time*?

Another reminder: Almost fifty million Americans live in officially defined poverty. The rate is higher, not lower, than in the late 1960s—another disturbing trend marker. Moreover, if we used the measuring standard common throughout the advanced world (which considers the poverty level to be half the median income level), the number would be just under seventy million, and the rate almost 23 percent.[4]

This is to say nothing of steady increases in global warming and an unemployment rate that, if properly measured, is stuck in the range of roughly 15 percent.[5]

At the most superficial level, Washington—as the saying goes—is broken. Give or take an occasional gain in selected areas, the political system is simply incapable of dealing with the deeper challenges. It focuses on deficits, not answers. Long trends that don't change are a clear signal that it's not simply the "modern" period of partisan bickering and congressional stalemate that is causing the problems. The trends were moving steadily downward long before the Tea Party and the recent partisan foolishness, long before the *Citizens United* Supreme Court decision allowed corporations to put big money directly into politics, and long before many events that have been heralded as tipping points of one kind or another.

Nor are people stupid. More and more have a sense that something different is going on—both with the economy and, more fundamentally, with democracy itself. A few more bits of information just as reminders, again, of something we are all beginning to sense: A mid-2011 poll found that roughly 80 percent of Americans believe their congressional representatives to be "more interested in serving the needs of special interests groups" than "the people they represent."[6] Another poll found that almost four out of five believe a few rich people and corporations have much too much power.[7] And only 37 percent—not much more than a third of the population—have confidence in the most solemn and august of American institutions, the Supreme Court.[8]

I'm going to dig much, much deeper into all this, of course. But for now let's leave it at this: When critical long, long trends do not improve—*when they steadily get worse, year in and year out*—it is clear that we face deeply rooted systemic problems, not simply political problems in the usual sense of the term. Moreover, as those polls suggest, people increasingly understand that something is really wrong.

The question is: How do we deal with a systemic crisis—*something built in to the way the political-economic world works*—rather than a simple political crisis or economic crisis?

How do we really confront *that question* squarely?

The traditional (very general) answer has been to "organize a movement" to build political power and pressure leaders to act, and I certainly agree that this is necessary. But urging this in general terms is hardly a *strategy*, much less, if taken seriously, an answer to the question of how serious trend-shifting change can be achieved. Rather, it is a general call to arms with little more in deeper strategic understanding than a recognition that we had better begin, somehow, to act, or we are in trouble. (But not, for most people, more than that.)

No, a serious answer demands both a call to arms and a clear strategy. This book does not claim to answer every question. It will, however, urge an explicit strategy—one that I hope is sufficiently well developed that at least a beginning answer to the question "What then must we do?" will be on the table—one that I hope may be improved by ongoing debate and dialogue as we go forward.

It will also suggest that our emerging historical context is both radically different from that of the Great Depression and New Deal era and different, too, from the postwar boom era of progressive change. Which means that it may now be possible to develop very different organizing and system-changing strategies than many have thought seriously about in recent years.

For this reason, I am going to put off for just a bit some traditional questions of political tactics, organizing, and even vague rhetorical calls for "revolution." We'll get back to them after we have dealt with the system-related issues and the question of what the unusual nature of the emerging historical context might make possible.

Finally, by the way, as a historian and political economist, it is obvious to me that difficult historical times do not always or even commonly persist forever. In my judgment "we shall overcome" is not simply a slogan but in fact the likely, though not inevitable, outcome of the long struggle ahead.

It is possible, quite simply, that we may lay the groundwork for a truly American form of community-sustaining and wealth-democratizing transformative change—and thereby also the reconstitution of genuine democracy, step by step, from the ground up.

PART I

THE SYSTEM PROBLEM

How to Detect a System Problem Without Really Trying

People toss around the phrase *It's the system* pretty loosely in everyday language. Usually they mean that things are sort of set up, by either design or accident, to run the way they run—and that the game is pretty well rigged so that those at the top (and their organizations) control the action. You can't really buck the system: Too much power, too much red tape, too much bureaucracy—they'll wear you down.

And so on.

That's not a bad way to start thinking about the *big* system that defines the overarching contours of our national life—namely, the large corporate-dominated economic system and the heavily constrained political system that set the terms of reference for almost everything else.

I want to push a bit deeper, however. Here's the essential point: A system problem—as opposed to your usual garden-variety political problem—is one that isn't going to go away through politics as usual. It will require somehow changing the way things are rigged deeper down in the machinery of institutions, corporations, bureaucracy, and all the other elements of the system that produce the outcomes we experience.

A system problem is difficult. It runs deep.

Everyone knows we have problems in the United States: unemployment, poverty, environmental decay, global warming—to say nothing of whole cities like Detroit, Cleveland, St. Louis, and many others that have essentially been thrown away. If you are black or brown, your prospects are far worse. And wars keep happening, with little positive outcome and lots of dead American kids (to say nothing of dead Iraqis, Afghanis, and others). Civil liberties decay, day by day, year by year.

So much is obvious. Moreover, this wealthiest of all wealthy nations has been steadily falling behind many other nations of the world. Consider just a few wake-up-call facts from a long and dreary list: The United States now ranks lowest or close to lowest among advanced "affluent" nations in connection with inequality (21st out of 21), poverty (21st out of 21), life expectancy (21st out of 21), infant mortality (21st out of 21), mental health (18th out of 20), obesity (18th out of 18), public spending on social programs as a percentage of GDP (19th out of 21), maternity leave (21st out of 21), paid annual leave (20th out of 20), the "material well-being of children" (19th out of 21), and overall environmental performance (21st out of 21).

Add in low scores for student performance in math (17th out of 21), one of the highest school dropout rates (14th out of 16), the second-highest per capita carbon dioxide emissions (2nd out of 21), and the third-highest ecological footprint (3rd out of 20).

Also for the record: We have the worst score on the UN's gender inequality index (21st out of 21), one of the highest rates of failing to ratify international agreements, the highest military spending as a portion of GDP (1st out of 21), and among the lowest spending on international development and humanitarian assistance as a percentage of GDP.[1]

Such facts are pretty hefty elbow nudges in the direction I'd like you to think about, but they aren't (yet) much more than that. Everyone knows that if you don't like the way things are turning out, the thing to do is to "get involved"—elect a congressman, or senator, or president. We've all been told (and maybe even told others!) that things aren't going to change unless we all roll up our sleeves and get into the game.

I don't have any problem whatsoever with that kind of advice—nor, as I mentioned in the introduction, with advice suggesting that we need to build a political movement. The problem is not with what is being said, but with what is not being said.

What is usually being said is this (in only slightly oversimplified language): We know that the economic system is dominated by large and powerful corporate institutions—and we know that the political system is dominated by money and lobbying, and also, in practice, by large corporate institutions.

The fundamental judgment, however, is that it is possible (without altering "the above") to organize enough political power so that "the above" can be made responsive to the concerns of the vast majority of people in these United States.

Usually the way politics does this trick, it is hoped, is that enough power can be put together to tax "the above" and then spend for good things like schools, roads, bridges, and maybe even health care. Also, politics, it is hoped, can put together enough power to regulate "the above" to achieve health, a clean environment, safety, and other outcomes of importance to the people.

Now, it's surely possible that this can be done sometimes. Moreover, almost certainly something like this (give or take some difficult questions we will shortly come to) has worked (sort of) in the past.

But there is a really interesting and challenging—and also profoundly important—matter I'd like you to ponder. Things seem to have changed. It no longer seems that "the system" can be managed in the old way. It is possible, of course, that this means that maybe it can't be managed at all. Alternatively, clearly some way other than the above formula must be found to get us out of the box we are in.

The best way to ponder this matter *at the outset* is to take a look at some of the long, long trends documenting the outcomes flowing from the traditional assumptions and traditional political theory of change. Then we can consider what they tell us about whether the underlying system is being managed or if it is managing us.

Note carefully: Here and in what follows, I am not saying that traditional politics never works, or has never worked in the past. That is a different question. Nor am I suggesting (yet) what might be done about the way the world seems to be proceeding. (More on that later, too.)

What I'm asking you to ponder with me is the simple fact that the system (the way underlying institutional power is currently arranged) seems now to be producing outcomes, year in and year out, that do not much respond to the old theory of politics. Something deeper is going on.

For instance:

- As noted in the introduction, the share of income taken by the top 1 percent of Americans has gone from 10 percent to roughly 20 percent over the last three decades. (The top 1 percent now has more income than just about the entire bottom 180 million Americans taken together.)[2, 3]
- At the same time, self-evidently, the share of the rest of society— the bottom 99 percent—has dropped by a corresponding amount, roughly 10 percent of all income.
- During the last several decades top marginal tax rates for the top bracket have been slashed by more than 50 percent—from 91 percent in 1950 to 70 percent in 1980 to 35 percent in 2011, with

modest and mostly temporary upticks during the Johnson, Bush (I), Clinton, and, recently, Obama eras.[4, 5]

- For more than forty years there has been virtually no change in the percentage of Americans in poverty. If anything there is evidence of a worsening trend—from a historic low of 11.1 percent in 1973 to 15 percent in 2011. (The percentages for African Americans and Hispanics are almost double the national average: 27.6 and 25.3 percent, respectively, in 2011.)[6]

- Again, as noted in the introduction, for almost forty years there has been only a minuscule, token change in weekly earnings for most Americans—approximately one-tenth of 1 percent per year for roughly 80 percent of all wage and salary workers. Private production and nonsupervisory workers made an average of $18.74 per hour in 1973 (in 2011 dollars); by 2011—*thirty-eight years later*—this had edged up only to $19.47.[7]

- Corporate taxes have steadily declined: from 32.1 percent of federal revenues in 1952 to 15.5 percent of such revenues in 1972 to 10.2 percent in 2000 to 7.9 percent in 2011.[8]

- Corporate taxes as a share of GDP declined from a modest 6.1 percent in 1952 to 2.1 percent in 2000 to a mere 1.2 percent in 2011.[9]

- US output of CO_2 and other global-warming greenhouse gas emissions has risen steadily—by 10.5 percent over the last twenty years.[10] CO_2 emissions alone are up 30 percent over their 1970 levels.[11]

- The proportion of the population in federal and state prisons and jails in the United States has gone from 93 (per 100,000) to 500 over the last forty years. When prisoners held in local jails are included, the 2010 rate totaled 743—a figure far higher than that of any other European country (Russia included) and more than eight times higher than the average for Western European counterparts.[12] (This, by the way, is a very concrete test of the degree to which "systems" do or do not deprive people of liberty.)

- The amount of money spent to sell candidates in presidential elections has gone from around $92 million (1980) to $1.1 billion (2008) in the last three decades. (It reached around $2 billion in 2012.)[13]

By the way: I assume you noticed that the above trends involve some of the most important American values—including equality, liberty, and ecological sustainability. But they also involve democracy itself, as we currently know it, and force us to ask whether our democracy in its current form can achieve outcomes in accord with such basic American values.

(Also by the way: Note that I haven't as yet even mentioned the fiscal crisis, congressional deadlocks, or "the economy" and its stagnating, painful failings. We'll come back to all of this, big-time, in due course.)

CHAPTER TWO

But Hasn't What We Normally Call Politics Done What Needs to Be Done in the Past?

I'm not trying to be a contrarian. Just trying to stare some pretty nasty realities in the face.

Indeed, if it's already obvious to you that we face a systemic problem that traditional strategies clearly don't deal with very well—and if you want to get on with how we might nonetheless proceed with building a positive different way forward—it's fine with me if you jump over to part 2.

On the other hand, if you stick around, I'm going to ask you to dig more deeply into what ordinary politics can and can't do (and how perhaps to clarify this for folks we work with and talk to and maybe even hope to convince). And if projects, locally or nationally, are your thing, I'm going to ask you to think about what I call "projectism," and what it can and can't do, as well.

Again, to be clear about it: I think projects and organizing and demonstrations and related efforts are important. However, down deep most people sense—rightly, in my view—that those big trends aren't going to budge much in the most powerful corporate capitalist system in the world unless we come up with something a lot more serious and sophisticated than what most people have been talking about so far.

I'm also not saying that nothing useful can be done through traditional political efforts. The 2009 Lilly Ledbetter Fair Pay Act, which makes it harder for employers to pay women less than men for equal work, is a clear example of forward movement—and there are many more in many areas. Nonetheless—and the point is always to keep your eye on the overarching reality—those powerful downward-moving systemic trends continue.

Also, even some of the useful things that get done are inadvertent reminders of the big picture of decay. For instance, in 2007 many people got excited about having passed legislation to raise the minimum wage in three stages from $5.15 to $7.25 an hour. Again, great so far as it went. However, the larger, longer-term negative trend pretty much continued nonetheless: *The minimum wage adjusted for inflation was more than $2 higher in 1968.**

The great environmentalist, the late Donella Meadows, once titled an article "Things Getting Worse at a Slower Rate." However, that was before they started getting worse faster again.[1] Clearly, when great victories don't even get us to where we were more than forty years ago, we need to pay close attention. We are being reminded that something more profound, something systemic, now has to be confronted and dealt with in ways different from what most people have been talking about if we want to start getting serious about moving the trends, positively, in the direction of a decent and democratic future.

(And by the way, think again a bit about most of the projects, and organizing, and demonstrations, and even bits and pieces of civil disobedience—all of which are important—and ask yourself whether they look to be making a serious dent in the systemically generated trends producing global warming.)

Sometimes, exceptions prove the rule. In the next chapters I'll take up some major modern policy achievements that seem to challenge the judgment that what we call traditional politics no longer has much capacity to alter the negative trends, that either something deeper and systemic must be changed or the trends will continue.

I'll suggest that even the most promising modern exceptions to the rule, in fact, *are* exceptions in that only very, very special and likely nonrepeatable circumstances explain them. Also, on close examination they tend to document other aspects of profoundly disturbing systemic power relationships—even when they seem to move in a more positive direction.

---

* The increase to $7.25 was completed by 2010. Had the 1968 $1.60 minimum wage kept up with inflation it would have been an estimated $10 in 2010 dollars—that is, $2.75 higher than what the much-heralded law requires. See: Oregon State University, "Minimum Wage History," OSU, November 9, 2011, accessed August 28, 2012, http://oregonstate .edu/instruct/anth484/minwage.html. Inflation calculated using MeasuringWorth.com: Lawrence H. Officer and Samuel H. Williamson, "Annual Inflation Rates in the United States, 1775–2011, and United Kingdom, 1265–2010," MeasuringWorth, 2011, accessed October 25, 2012, http://www.measuringworth.com/inflation; Office of Communications, "Changes in Basic Minimum Wages in Non-Farm Employment Under State Law: Selected Years 1968 to 2012," US Department of Labor, December 2011, accessed August 28, 2012, www.dol.gov/whd/state/stateMinWageHis.htm.

For the moment, however, let's probe a bit more deeply into the problem of systemic change in general.

The traditional theory of change (and of democracy) many Americans have been working with is that politics in the usual sense (augmented by projects, movement building, and so on) can, in fact, achieve major trend shifts in outcomes that uphold important values.

Actually, however, on examination, when you study things a bit closer, there have always been some rather large systemic flies in this ointment, especially as it applies to modern experience (the experience most of us have in mind when we think about these things).

The first theoretical fly has to do with whether what we mean by "politics" in the usual sense of that term is what, in fact, has produced some of the most important modern outcomes—or whether something else really did the job.

For a start, many progressives hark back to the great days of the New Deal to recall how politics demonstrably can impact the underlying system, can achieve great results, can alter profoundly important trends. After all, many of the most important things we take for granted—like Social Security, labor laws permitting union organization, banking reforms (including deposit insurance and Glass-Steagall banking legislation, for example), agricultural programs, and many, many more specific legislative achievements—were, in fact, enacted because politics brought together an alliance (the New Deal coalition) capable of dealing with the underlying systemic power relationships. No question about it—except one that is pretty obvious: Would any of the above have been possible in normal times? *Or was what happened in large part the result above all of the Depression crisis creating a highly unusual opportunity allowing for unusual changes that normal politics could not achieve on its own?*

No way to answer that question definitively, of course. But for openers, it's useful to recall that in "normal times"—the preceding decade of the 1920s—Franklin Delano Roosevelt was campaigning as a budget-balancing fiscal conservative, and nobody in their right mind would have believed that anything like what became the New Deal agenda was feasible.

Another way to get at the underlying point—namely, that a highly unusual context (rather than politics in the usual sense) allowed for or produced changes not otherwise possible—is this: What do you think might have happened if a Democratic president had by chance been in office in 1929 when the Great Depression hit, and if he, instead of Herbert Hoover, paid the political price for the crisis? How likely is it that a hard-charging conservative challenger would have responded by putting forward the kind of program that Roosevelt actually did put forward in response to the collapse?

You only have to look to Europe to understand how differently things could have gone. There, the hard-charging conservative challengers who responded to severe economic distress put forward authoritarian regimes—and made them stick—in more than one country.[2] (And even highly respected Americans like George F. Kennan, an important figure who was to play a major role in Cold War strategy, thought that some kind of authoritarian regime might be the answer in this country.[3])

No, I am not trying to rewrite all this history. My point is a very simple one: Many progressives look to the New Deal era for a precedent suggesting that "politics" in the usual sense of what we mean by the word can, in fact, alter the big trends. Yet on examination everyone knows that this is not what happened. This argument, by the way, is not really very controversial, though the point is painful. Everyone knows that the achievements of that era were very, very much dependent on highly unusual circumstances.[4]

Why bother with all this? Why focus on this particular fly in the ointment—or the argument that politics in the usual meaning of that term (plus organizing, movement building, projects, demonstrations, civil disobedience, et cetera) may not have the capacity to achieve trend-changing outcomes?

I'm not at all interested in pouring cold water on progressive hopes. Quite the contrary. I'm trying to put something else on the table in clear terms— namely, that if we are to get anywhere in the future, we had better think twice about one of the most important precedents many people rely on when they hold (implicitly or explicitly) that politics (again as we usually understand that term) can alter the profoundly powerful trends emanating from much deeper systemic processes.

If it takes the collapse of a massive worldwide depression to do the trick— along with the good luck from a progressive point of view that a conservative happened to be in office to take the blame when everything fell apart—then either these circumstances must prevail in the future, or the long, painful trends outlined in the previous chapter are likely to continue.

Note carefully in the above the words *if it takes the collapse*—especially the word *if.*

There have obviously been other modern periods of great progressive achievement that were able to alter painful underlying systemically produced trends. The question, again, is whether the most important of these also depended upon highly unusual circumstances—or whether or not they offer hope that systemic trends can be reversed through normal political processes.

We'll come back to these questions, and also to the question of whether we should expect another collapse or maybe something different in the future—matters that are not quite so easy to chew on as many on the left, right, and center sometimes suggest.

Before we move on, it's probably useful also to mention something obvious. Even though the New Deal passed a considerable amount of progressive legislation, it did not, in fact, solve by far the most important problem of the Depression era. Unemployment still plagued 17.2 percent of the civilian labor force and 23.8 percent of the non-farm workforce in 1939.[5]

World War II solved that problem, which leads us to other flies in the ointment.

CHAPTER THREE

Flies Number Two and Three in the Traditional Theory of Politics

The most important period other than the Great Depression that most people hark back to in holding that systemic trends can be altered by ordinary politics (in the usual sense of that term) is obviously the modern postwar era, and especially the 1960s (and to a degree, the early 1970s).

For those of you who care about the environment, also time to listen up!

I don't particularly like pointing out flies in ointments, but there are two big ones here that also make past precedents a bit dicey if we are looking for arguments about whether the long trends we looked at in chapter 1 can be altered by traditional approaches.

And whether, accordingly, we might need to begin to develop different (system-changing) strategies.

And, further, how this might be done.

Which brings us to big fly number two: The postwar era in general, and the "postwar boom" in particular, were extremely unusual in a way that is pretty much the polar opposite of the special conditions of the Depression. The years 1945–70 define the most powerful economic boom in modern history—a time when the economy grew at an annual rate of 3.05 percent per year and median family income came close to almost doubling (from $27,000 to $48,300 in inflation-adjusted 2011 dollars).[1]

Again the thing to note about this unusual moment in history is how truly exceptional were the circumstances that produced it—the most important of which was a massive, global, industrial-scale war and its aftermath, a war that was not fought on American soil (something very different from what happened to many other nations at this point in twentieth-century history).

Federal military spending skyrocketed to 37.8 percent of the economy in 1944 (and 37.5 percent in 1945), producing a massive economic stimulus six and a half times that of the recent Obama effort relative to the size of the economy.[2]

World War II not only ended the Depression and put everyone back to work; it also produced wartime savings for millions of workers, and this in turn helped fuel the boom when the savings were turned into new postwar consumer purchases. Moreover, the high demand for unskilled workers during the war made labor union organizing much easier; National War Labor Board regulations also helped raise wages and reduce inequality. The war also gave rise to a temporary postwar politics that allowed for enactment of special programs for returning veterans, further fueling the boom. One of the most significant was the GI Bill, which paid for college educations or training programs for 7.8 million World War II veterans.[3]

Most important of all was that World War II radically impacted the industrial capacity of America's most important competitors and potential competitors—including, but not limited to, Germany, Japan, Great Britain, France, and Italy.

Not only did the US economy benefit from Marshall Plan and other spending to help rebuild these nations (as funds were used to purchase American goods, which were shipped overseas on American merchant ships), but for a substantial (boom) period the United States had very few major global competitors—*until they came back.*

Bottom line: The first essential condition in which the most important trend-shifting programs of this era were enacted was a massive and highly unusual economic boom that both created something approaching full employment and was accompanied, not incidentally, by a flow of significant fiscal revenues.

Among the big programs enacted were a large housing program and Social Security expansion under Truman, the Interstate Highway System under Eisenhower, and above all Medicare and Medicaid, the War on Poverty, and education programs under Johnson. The minimum wage was increased repeatedly. In addition, civil rights legislation moved onto center stage. That milestone followed a different dynamic, but also in part depended for its timing on the fact that black Americans had fought in the war—and also that wartime industry had disrupted the South, sending a huge migration north.[4] We'll come back to this shortly.

Some of our most important environmental legislation—including the Clean Air and Clean Water Acts—was also part and parcel of the boom era. (Economic booms are good for environmental legislation: They tend to reduce the fear of job loss that often comes with regulation. Unfortunately, the same fear, as now, conversely, keeps those negative trends moving right along in the wrong direction when the economy falters and decays. One recent analysis shows that just four of the main environmental laws were passed when annual unemployment was greater than 7 percent, and none when unemployment was over 7.5 percent.[5])

So, again, a very, very unusual context. If the New Deal was in large part made possible by a massive global depression (and luck that a Republican was in office at the moment of political danger), the postwar achievements were in significant part made possible by the ongoing impact of a massive (and highly unusual, global-scale) war and its extraordinary aftermath.

Also, the economy was further boosted by big, big military spending—during the Cold War, the Korean War, and the Vietnam War especially—from the early 1950s through the early 1970s. Such spending hit 13.2 percent of GDP in 1952 during the Korean War (and 14.2 percent in 1953); it peaked at 9.4 percent in 1968 during the Vietnam War; it's less than 5 percent now—even with the large commitments in Afghanistan and Iraq.[6]

All very, very unusual when viewed in a longer-term historical perspective.

But all this is still only fly number two.

That we learn very little from either the New Deal or the big postwar and Great Society boom-era programs about what politics in the traditional sense can do about deep system-related trends in non-special times is even clearer when we look at fly number three.

This is the simple fact that a capacity to alter big trends in virtually all advanced nations has almost always depended in significant part on the strength not simply of politics in general, and not only of movements in general, but also on the existence of powerful *institutions*—above all, labor unions.

Indeed, in all of the postwar boom programs, labor played a major, major role—especially with regard to the Great Society programs. Labor historian Nelson Lichtenstein observes that by the end of World War II, the AFL and CIO had both "built political machines that gave labor a distinctive, well-defined political profile at both the national and local levels. The unions invented the political action committee in the 1940s: during the 1944 election the CIO-PAC proved the backbone of the Roosevelt Reelection effort in the urban, industrial North . . . Unionism boosted turnout and Democratic Party loyalty for fully a third of the electorate."[7]

The new power of labor organizations, in turn, was critical in the political effort that produced passage of the Medicare and Medicaid legislation, the true powerhouse funding programs of the era. Studies by Yale public policy expert Theodore Marmor and others reveal a legislative battle over the two major Johnson-era achievements dominated, on the one hand, by labor and labor-based organizations and, on the other, by the American Medical Association.

When Medicare was first proposed, the American Association of Retired Persons (AARP) was not yet a large organization and at the time was far less supportive of government insurance. A new organization launched by the AFL-CIO—the National Council of Senior Citizens—became critical in the push for Medicare. Largely made up of union retirees, it held "giant rallies, organiz[ed] major letter-writing campaigns, [and] vigorously picketed opponents." In the 1964 election cycle, the AFL-CIO spent a then extraordinary $1-million-plus (over $7 million in 2011 dollars) on contributions and political education efforts in support of its successful Medicare/Medicaid campaign.[8]

Labor was also central to environmental successes. The UAW hosted an important early conference on water quality issues and subsequently, in 1965, added a Conservation and Resource Development Department to work with environmental groups. Among other issues, the union fought for the banning of DDT and even advocated tougher automobile emission standards. And although they often fought with environmentalists, in general labor unions were essential to the election of many of the liberals who voted for environmental legislation. Senator Gaylord Nelson, the founder of Earth Day, for example, had initially worked as a labor lawyer and always relied on unions for political support.[*9]

The first truly big difficulty to get your mind around here (for our own time in history) is that the institution of the labor union has declined radically, and is likely to continue to decline. This in turn means—critically—that any serious future politics will have to find some other way—*if it can!*—to do what labor once did.

The second difficulty for anyone who hopes to build a serious future politics and may be thinking about a genuine rebuilding of labor is that there is pretty strong evidence that union building itself was in significant part impacted by the two big crises we have been discussing.

---

* By the way, the important 1960s and especially early-1970s environment laws (the latter passed when Nixon was in office) occurred at a time, note carefully, when the Republican Party was entirely a northern party, and the central problem it faced was how to attract white suburban voters. After adoption of its "Southern Strategy," a very different, more conservative, and implicitly race-related politics became the norm.

Labor union membership stood at roughly 11 percent in 1929. The Depression made possible passage of the Wagner Act and section 7(a) of the National Industrial Recovery Act, which guaranteed labor organizing and collective bargaining rights. Union membership more than doubled—to 28.6 percent in 1939. The openings for labor made possible by World War II (especially in defense-related industries) brought union membership to a record high of 35.4 percent in 1945.[10]

Scholars now debate the many diverse reasons for what happened thereafter, but for our purposes the critical point is that it has been pretty much downhill ever since—and labor's power in politics (though clearly still very important) is not likely to come back in trend-reversing ways:[11] Overall union membership declined to 11.8 percent in 2011 (and a mere 6.9 percent in the private sector.)[12] Not only are we now back down to roughly the 1929 level but—aided and abetted by corporate and other conservative attacks—the trend is going in the wrong direction.

So . . .

Massive crisis, on the one hand, and massive global war and its aftermath, on the other: two overarching history-shaping elements at the heart of a once powerful, trend-altering progressive politics. Also, the political impact of once powerful labor unions, whose strength was in significant part related to the two big crises—and is now declining rapidly.

It should not be surprising, accordingly, that an important recent study by historians Nick Salvatore and Jefferson Cowie sees the progressive gains of the middle third of the twentieth century, quite simply, as largely an aberration. "Absent major national shocks, the capacity for fundamental political change is limited in the American context. Our founding mythos of individualism has . . . become so intimately intertwined with the very essence of the nation itself that its limitations become most difficult to perceive."[13]

Former labor secretary Robert Reich has also concluded (in some writings) that "the period extending from 1933 to 1965—the New Deal and the Great Society—was an historical aberration . . . animated by the unique crises of the Great Depression and World War II, and the social cohesion that flowed from them for another generation. Ronald Reagan merely picked up where Calvin Coolidge and Herbert Hoover left off."[14]

However we come to terms with these judgments, another way of underscoring the critical challenge is simply to note that if we hope to deal with the systemic issues, we had better think much more deeply about what it will take—and "what then we must do"—if we want to get beyond occasional token protests and the election of people who posture as the long, long trends continue to decay.

I know this is pretty dreary stuff—especially for a book that in the end (as you will see) offers a reasonably hopeful sense of the future, and a strategy aimed at possibly getting there. (Moreover, except in passing I haven't even discussed race, and how racism was used to suppress votes in the South and to divide potential progressive constituencies, including labor, in the North.)

Unfortunately, however, I don't think we are going to get anywhere without getting some myths out of the way. To put it simply: On the basis of the evidence (so far) it appears unlikely that strategies hoping simply to revive politics in the traditional ways—even intensified by movement building, and especially given the decline of labor—are going to get us very far in addressing some of the profoundly depressing system-produced trends we are facing.

The trends are likely to continue—give or take a minor uptick gain—unless we come up with something different.

CHAPTER FOUR

The Fading Power
of Traditional Politics

Just a couple more things before we can really get going—and to wrap up this question of whether or not change along traditional lines (I mean trend change, of course) is likely on our current path.

Isn't the fact that Obama health care legislation passed evidence, after all, that if you really work at traditional politics it will all work out in the end?

Well, maybe.

This is another case where digging a bit deeper into how things really worked in the era we are coming out of helps clarify our own challenge—the era, that is, most people have in mind when they remember the future.

Americans have talked about universal health care for a long, long time—way back, indeed, to the time of Theodore Roosevelt. If you look closely at the historical and institutional foundations that created the preconditions of the Obama health care legislation, however, what you find is a tale most people simply don't know much about—a tale that puts recent events in a somewhat different perspective.

First, the very idea that there should be any serious kind of health insurance for Americans (beyond tiny elites) simply did not have much reality until World War II—and it was (again) the war that gave it reality. With wartime labor scarce, wage-price controls were enacted to keep bidding wars in check. Corporations, unable to offer more pay, tried to compete with benefits instead. The modern idea of widespread employer-provided health insurance developed as a strategy to attract wartime workers, and continued in many industries after the war, especially during the boom era.[1]

Although it is possible (perhaps even likely) that a serious demand for health care would have occurred sometime in American history, the widespread general idea that health insurance should be provided to large numbers, in fact, was—and is—a creation of the World War II moment in history. Second, as we have noted, one of the key constituencies that built upon this new health insurance idea and helped lead the fight for the first modern public extensions of the concept—Medicare and Medicaid—was obviously organized labor. And again, the strength of organized labor in the postwar period is inseparable from the two major system-shaping events of the twentieth century: the Great Depression and World War II.

Third, the other important constituency that helped establish Medicare and Medicaid was and is obviously the elderly. And in many ways the elderly as a political constituency (rather than an age class) was largely brought into being by Social Security and the events of the Depression.

Fourth, the context in which Medicare and Medicaid became possible was also—as we have seen—the special context of the postwar boom, and the financial flows it produced.

Fifth, it is upon the institutional structures, as well as the political-economic constituencies established by these processes, that further extensions were added—especially support for HMOs during the Nixon era, COBRA legislation during the Reagan administration, the State Children's Health Insurance Program (SCHIP) in the Clinton years, and also the massive Bush-era drug program (Medicare Part D).

And sixth, it is upon this long-developing political-economic scaffolding of institutions and constituencies—ultimately explainable only by reference to the Depression, the New Deal, World War II, and the postwar boom—that Obama legislation even became imaginable.

You can't just say "Obamacare passed, and therefore all we need to do is get organized and get to work." (We *do* need to do that; but as the above suggests, that is only part of the story, looking back—and especially looking forward, as we ask what it will take to achieve large-order trend-changing politics in other areas.)[2]

So, again it may in theory have been possible to get to this point in some other way, but what in fact got us here was very, very dependent on a long series of highly unusual prior changes, the most important of which were anchored in those odd mid-twentieth-century global crises called the Great Depression and the massive global Second World War.

Bottom line again: I am certainly not advocating a return of either of the above. Just trying to clarify that our theories about the power of traditional politics in this particular corporate system often ignore some very important things as people grasp for hope—or perhaps wishful thought—that traditional strategies might somehow alter those big trends and that we really don't have to deal directly with the system that is generating the trends.

What about civil rights, feminism, gay rights? Don't the transformations on these fronts tell us the system is capable of changing course by reacting to traditional politics and movements?

Yes and no.

There have clearly been political successes in these areas, extremely important successes—and, thankfully, we are indeed on the way to one day genuinely achieving a society of individual respect and equality. Moreover, the kind of political activism that most people associate with progressive causes—demonstrations, movement building, civil disobedience, but also electioneering, canvassing, and all of the traditional political models—has been effective for these causes.

But there are a few obvious points (and one not so obvious that we'll come to at the end) to consider here.

One: What this has all been about is *getting into the existing system.*

Not changing it.

The battle for equality on all these fronts has largely been about rights, and about fulfilling the enduring elements of the individualist American culture.

(I in no way mean to denigrate the drive to full equality. My concern is simply to keep the critical questions in focus and to remind you of those big, big decaying trends that continue on their way even as more and more people find that personal discrimination is slowly—all too slowly—declining.)

Professor Michael Kazin underscores the obvious point in his recent book on the left in American politics: "Radicals in the U.S. [he might well have added "progressives in general"] have seldom mounted a serious challenge to those who held power in either the government or the economy. But they have done far better at helping to transform the moral culture, the 'common sense' of society—how Americans understand what is just and what is unjust in the conduct of public affairs. And that is no small thing."[3]

Two: World War II obviously also played a role here, helping accelerate things a great deal, producing some (not all) of the conditions that permitted successful activists and activism. Many women, for instance, were drawn deeply into the industrial workforce—and then sent back to suburban homemaking, an experience that they and their daughters found world-shaking. Black Americans were drawn north, out of the cotton fields, into a different economic and ultimately social and political world, and many entered the military. The postwar world was never the same—for them and for their sons and daughters.

At the same time we rarely consider fully the implications of the simple truth that it was not until the two-thirds point of the twentieth century (!) that black Americans were able to vote in most parts of the South—in a "democracy" that looked the other way while terrorist groups like the Ku Klux Klan enforced the old order, in a vast region of the nation home to 30 percent of the entire population, with violence and murder.[4]

Three: There has also been backsliding in several areas, especially as the decaying social and economic trends have continued their powerful impact. Schools, for instance, are now as or more segregated than before civil rights legislation spurred serious desegregation in the late 1960s and early 1970s.[5] And as the black professional middle class has left the city, the remaining neighborhoods have become less, not more, stable. Correspondingly, poverty trends for black Americans have reversed in recent years: The rate has increased steadily from its historic low of 22.5 percent in 2000 to 27.6 percent in 2011.[6]

Four: The modern achievements of the gay rights movement, and the equality of marriage effort, are clearly also on a trajectory to achieve full acceptance in American society—and again, with great difficulty and much pain. And also with not much impact, one way or another, on the larger economic and social trends that define the system problem in its larger dimensions. Indeed, even as the major trends are getting worse.

Martin Luther King Jr. confronted the depth of the systemic challenge in the mid-1960s and again shortly before his death in 1968. The fight to end discrimination was one thing; challenging the economic system was another. Speaking to his staff, one member recalled, King "asked us to turn off the tape recorder . . . He talked about what he called democratic socialism, and he said, 'I can't say this publicly, and if you say I said it I'm not gonna admit to it . . .'. . . and he talked about the fact that he didn't believe that capitalism as it was constructed could meet the needs of poor people, and that what we might need to look at was a kind of socialism, but a democratic form of socialism."[*][7]

Let us leave aside the word *socialism* for the moment. The challenge, King declared shortly before he was assassinated, was structural and systemic,

---

[*] King evidently was of two minds about whether it was right to think these thoughts but not speak them publicly. In a 1965 speech to the Negro American Labor Council, he reportedly stated: "Call it democracy, or call it democratic socialism, but there must be a better distribution of wealth within this country for all God's children." See: May 1965 speech to the Negro American Labor Council, quoted in Thomas F. Jackson, *From Civil Rights to Human Rights: Martin Luther King, Jr., and the Struggle for Economic Justice*, (Philadelphia, PA: University of Pennsylvania Press, 2007), p. 230.

not simply political in the traditional sense: "We are dealing with issues that cannot be solved without the nation . . . undergoing a radical redistribution of economic power."[8]

King's final judgment stands as instructive evidence of his understanding of the nature of systemic challenge—and also as a reminder that given the failures of both traditional socialism and corporate capitalism, it is time to get serious about clarifying not only the question of strategy, but what, in fact, the meaning of changing the system in a truly democratic direction might one day entail.

PART II

SYSTEMS OLD AND NEW: EVOLUTIONARY RECONSTRUCTION

CHAPTER FIVE

A Note About Systems and History and Prehistory

—— *And Also About Just Plain Useful Change* ——

O ur question, of course, is still "What then must we do?"
If the long and painful trends are likely to continue, if they are deeply rooted in the way the underlying corporate-dominated system is designed, and if the old ways of hoping the trends might be altered are pretty much illusions—what then?

Yes, lots of folks are doing very creative things; lots of wonderful organizing, great local projects, and important experiments with self-organizing and open-source theory are under way. Some are testing out civil disobedience. Exciting green projects, in particular, are exploding around the country. All part and parcel of getting serious about real movement building. All important, all part of where we need to go.

But if the box we are in is truly systemic, will this, in fact, get us where we need to go? What do we really need to do to change the largest, most powerful system in the world? How, really, do we proceed?

Moreover, except briefly, we haven't even begun to discuss the ecological crisis, to say nothing of climate change, and the nation's—indeed the world's— addiction to economic "growth."

Now the hard work begins!

Margaret Thatcher, the famous conservative British prime minister, coined the term *TINA* to popularize her belief that "There Is No Alternative" to one or another variety of corporate capitalism (especially one with a very thin veneer of public programs).

Truth be told, most Americans in their heart of hearts almost certainly think she was right and cannot really imagine any genuine alternative.

25

(Or they have simply given up on "systems." There are some pretty serious anarchists out there these days.)

But of course, if we face a systemic crisis—*if the system is the problem (and if the old balancing mechanisms are rapidly disappearing)*—then either an alternative to corporate capitalism (to say nothing of state socialism, or whatever name we give the other old system) must be found, or we are obviously in deep trouble.

Accordingly, and simply to begin to dig just a bit more seriously into the problem, here's a brief review of some of the major historical systems and how they have been structured.

For the most part political-economic systems are largely defined by the way property is owned and controlled (particularly productive economic property). *It tends to produce political as well as economic power.*

Thus, all too briefly:

- Feudalism was a political-economic system structured above all around who controlled productive land—namely the lords, church, and king, not the peasants.
- Nineteenth-century free-enterprise capitalism was largely structured around small- and medium-scale competitive entrepreneurial capitalist ownership.
- State socialism in the Soviet Union and Eastern Europe was structured around state ownership of productive wealth.
- Corporate capitalism has so far come in three broad flavors:
  1. Fairly pure corporate domination of the kind that emerged in the late nineteenth century in this country—and to which the trends may now be pointing again unless a different path forward is developed (the end point of which could be a corporate state).
  2. "Managed corporate capitalism" balanced by labor of the kind common in many European nations (with union strength, as in Sweden, sometimes more than double our own) and, to a much lesser degree, the system mainly operating in the United States circa 1945–80.
  3. Fascism—corporate capitalism managed by authoritarian rule of the kind that existed in Germany, Italy, and Spain during the 1930s and 1940s and (in different form) among some Latin American dictatorships until recently.

- Socialism with Chinese characteristics has so far been an odd mix of corporate ownership plus state ownership, with authoritarian rule.

Once again, a reminder and a basic point to keep in mind about the above: The most recent estimate is that a mere 400 *individuals* in the United States now own more wealth than the bottom 180 million Americans taken together—a degree of wealth concentration that is accurately, not rhetorically, properly designated medieval.[1]

Since political power in large part seems to go along, one way or another, with economic power, this particular number (along with the corporations that such wealth concentration also controls) is obviously something to keep your eye on.

The first system question to struggle with—if you don't happen to like any of the above—is whether there might be an alternative, even in theory.

The second question is whether there might be a path from here to there even if we knew where "there" was.

Both questions, in turn, lead to two additional questions.

Are there any ways to begin to conceive of a different system that might truly democratize the ownership of wealth in some way that points in the direction of a democratic system in general? (Especially since in different systems political power seems inevitably related, directly or indirectly, to a greater or lesser degree, to wealth?)

And are there any processes at work that might begin to move us in a new direction, even over long periods of time?

Those are the (first) big questions, and we're going to take them in steps. So for the moment—and to be quite clear—here are the issues we'll be chewing on in part 2:

How do we *begin* to get a different sense of what a different, better next system might entail?

And how do we *begin* to get a sense of a different strategy to get from here to there? (And yes, in due course we will come back to struggle not only with the ultimate system questions, but also with halfway houses, systemic hybrids, political fallback positions, and the like—not to mention how new institutional sources of power might be developed.)

All in due course.

CHAPTER SIX

An Initial Way to Think About System Change

L et me begin by telling you a tale my father once told me about his first day at college—and then a real-life story about history, and prehistory, and changing the system (maybe).

My father was an engineer. He entered the University of Wisconsin at age sixteen in 1924, and he loved to recall his first professor of engineering—a gruff, mustachioed, white-haired, detail-demanding Germanic hard-liner (at least so he stands in my childhood memory).

The very first day, across the entire front of the 1924 classroom (this, of course, was pre-PowerPoint), our professor had unscrolled a huge picture of a giant locomotive—the kind we no longer know about or see, the kind with dozens of wheels, smoke pouring out the smokestack, and massive power bursting forth on all sides.

The task for the entering freshman class? "We will redesign this entire locomotive!"

How to proceed? "We begin today with one bolt."

Yes, I'm suggesting we start by breaking down the system problem—both in general, and in connection with the "how do we get from here to there" question. We will, of course, have to assemble the bolts in due course, but I find it helps to start with very concrete realities.

Accordingly, on to that story I mentioned at the outset about history and prehistory (and maybe changing the system).

Many years ago—in 1977—a very large steel mill was closed down on one very unhappy September day in the city of Youngstown, Ohio. Five thousand workers lost their jobs, their livelihoods, and their futures when Youngstown Sheet and Tube went down.

Five thousand on one day was a very big deal, nationally, in 1977. It made the front page of newspapers and was the top story on the evening news—the reason being: This had not happened very often in the United States of America up to that point. (Now, tragically, it is hardly news, since it happens all the time. That is another feature of the systemic crisis.)

The steelworkers back in 1977 called it Black Monday, and I remember all too well how, as the reality sank in, we heard reports of men who could no longer support their families going out into the garage and putting a pistol to their heads.

That was not the only response, however.

One young steelworker named Gerald Dickey somehow got to thinking that there was no reason the steelworkers themselves couldn't run this facility, and he began to urge and organize and push and shove to get some interest in his outrageous idea.

Just to give you an idea of what *outrageous* meant in Youngstown: Dickey was taken aside by one of the town's leading businessmen and advised in a very fatherly manner, "If you're interested in steel mills, let me suggest a couple stocks you might buy . . ." But of course Dickey and others had a some-what different idea, and they (along with many others) began to get serious.

First, they got a number of their activist friends who worked at the mill together. Second, they found that a group of Youngstown religious lead-ers were also upset because if the huge mill went down, a good part of the economy and livelihood of the community would go down. Third, the steelworkers and a new ecumenical coalition headed by a Catholic and an Episcopal bishop began to demand that the mill be put back to work under some form of worker or worker–community ownership. Fourth, they found a sympathetic ear in one Washington bureaucrat (an assistant secretary of housing and urban affairs named Bob Embry)—and suddenly they had enough money to finance a really professional plan for how to put the old mill back into operation with the latest modern technology.

(I was called in to help oversee the development of the plan, and to help advise on other matters. All this now seems like only yesterday. Especially because, as we shall see, lots more folks are doing this kind of thing now.)

Long story short: The young steelworkers and the ecumenical coalition were very sophisticated about what they were taking on. They knew their only chance against the big steel companies (all of which were less than enthusiastic about the idea of workers owning mills, to say the least!) was to build a popular political base around the state and, to the extent feasible, around the nation. This meant capitalizing on the bold tale of workers taking on the big guys, and drawing in the press, and also mobilizing the national religious community.

(By the way, they also had to take on the national union leadership: The United Steelworkers in 1977 also had absolutely no interest in the idea of workers owning a mill—and indeed thought of the young steelworkers in Youngstown as upstart troublemakers who might also perhaps one day cause problems for the established national union leadership.)

A major victory occurred: The Carter administration studied their plan and agreed to allocate at least $100 million in loan guarantees to put it into operation.

You will not be surprised to learn, however, that though they won the first major battles, the Youngstown steelworkers and the ecumenical coalition lost the war. Somehow, oddly (!), just after the midterm elections of 1978 were over and the national politicians no longer had to worry about a backlash, the Carter administration's interest faded away, and the $100 million never quite got allocated.

(And somehow, oddly, the major steel corporations and the steelworkers union, it was rumored, were somehow, maybe involved—though, of course, no one could prove anything.)[1]

Why, you might ask, are we starting off this chapter with a total fiasco, a major loss, and a profound tragedy (we do not know how many workers went out to the garage as the stark realities became increasingly clear)?

The answer is: The story did not end there. And if you are interested in systemic change, rather than token politics, the next steps are perhaps of greater significance. They are also instructive—particularly about what it takes and how maybe to think about change in a different way.

Neither the young steelworkers nor the ecumenical coalition were naive. They knew they were up against some of the most powerful corporate (and at the time union) players in the country. They were fully aware that they might well lose the battle. They also knew, however, that they were on to a very important idea, one whose time—they hoped—would one day come no matter what.

Why should workers *not* own the companies in which they work? they kept asking. Why can't this become an idea to put into everyday practice—now or in the future? Accordingly, as part and parcel of their strategy they made it their business to help educate the public and the press and the politicians in the state and around the country about what they were trying to do both locally and, in a much more fundamental sense, as a larger national strategy and vision.

Once again, long story short: The Youngstown story did not, in fact, die when the Carter administration turned its back on the workers in 1978. Instead, the inspiring example of the workers and the ecumenical coalition—*plus the very sophisticated educational and political work they did to spread the word*—had ongoing impact.

There are now many, many worker-owned businesses in the state of Ohio, and the support system for building them is one of the best in the nation. There is also a very energetic Ohio Employee Ownership Center at Kent State University that provides assistance to workers and others who want to establish such firms. (The center was put together by a Kent State professor, the late John Logue, who was directly and personally inspired by the Youngstown effort.) And the simple idea that workers can and should own their own factories or stores or other businesses is an idea that is now almost conventional in many parts of Ohio, not only among workers but also among businessmen, many of whom (aided by certain tax benefits) now sell their successful businesses to their former employees when they retire.

That last paragraph compresses roughly thirty years into five sentences. So obviously, there's lots more to the tale. I'm sure you get the general point (or points), however. Except that, in fact, things start to get even more interesting if we go down the track just a bit farther.

It is not simply that the idea of worker ownership is now pretty much commonplace in various parts of the state. Something else has happened: The concept has gotten much more sophisticated as time has gone on, and as people have thought about things, and worked on them in different ways. Innovation has also occurred.

And as a result of work done in the last several years there now exists in Cleveland a group of very sophisticated worker-owned companies, linked together with a community-building nonprofit corporation and a revolving fund designed to help create more and more such linked, community-building cooperative businesses as time goes on. Furthermore, part of the new design involves getting big hospitals and universities in the area (like Cleveland Clinic, Case Western Reserve University, and University Hospitals) to agree to purchase some part of their needs from the worker-owned companies.

The goal now is not simply worker ownership, but worker ownership linked to a community-building strategy—and supported in part by larger institutions that not only have broad interests in the community but also are dependent in part on public programs supported by the workers' and the community's tax dollars, such as Medicare, Medicaid, and educational funds. Put another way, the process that can be traced to the Youngstown effort—*including its seeming failure*—has also led to innovation, and further development, and greater sophistication.

As time has passed, new priorities and another set of alliances have begun to develop. Now, all of the linked worker-owned companies are very, very green by design. For instance, the Evergreen Cooperative Laundry operates out of a LEED Gold-certified building and uses (and has to heat) around one-third the amount of water that other commercial laundries use and heat. Evergreen Energy Solutions is poised to install twice as much solar capacity in the coming period than currently exists in the entire state of Ohio. And Green City Growers Cooperative—a three-and-a-quarter-acre hydroponic greenhouse (the largest in any American city)—currently produces some three million heads of lettuce a year along with hundreds of thousands of pounds of herbs.(Two new cooperative businesses are scheduled to come online each year as the building processes continue.)

By the way, local businessmen have been helpful in all this. The overall effort builds consumers, helps the local economy, and supports the tax base, and thereby all local businesses as well. Many also feel good about doing something for the community. And the politics of this seems to work, too: The mayor as of this writing, Frank Jackson, looks very, very good in the press.

Just for the hell of it, I suggest you go back one chapter to the introduction to this part for a moment to think about the following: To the extent that systems revolve in significant part around who owns productive wealth, a system based on the institution of workers owning factories and other businesses is more likely to represent the interests of the workers than the interests of the tiny group of four hundred or so who now own so much of the wealth in the United States.

I offer this obvious point for rumination, but quickly also add that any serious approach to system-changing ideas needs to be very thoughtful about structural and ownership relationships. As noted, at one point the Youngstown effort focused also on a joint "Community–Worker Partnership"—following the idea that the interests of the whole community, not just the steelworkers at one particular plant, were at stake. And the Cleveland effort—along, as we shall see, with many others—offers further ways to think about this broader idea, about many different ways to democratize ownership, and about the logical community building and other relationships involved in systemic design.*

---

* See the afterword for further discussion of these questions.

The tale does not end in Ohio, though. Let me take you just one or two more steps along the trajectory of this story. Many other workers' groups and many other cities around the nation have picked up on—*and been inspired by*—the line of development represented (all too briefly) in the above tale. Efforts like that in Cleveland are now being developed in Atlanta, Pittsburgh, Washington DC, Amarillo (Texas), and many other cities.

Nor is that all. United Steelworkers, whose national leadership once opposed the Youngstown effort, has also evolved. The union has recently announced a major strategy to help build "union co-op" worker-owned companies around the nation. Efforts are under way, in particular, in Pittsburgh and Cincinnati.[2] There are also signs that other unions are beginning to realize they might gain additional leverage by exploring new strategies. The Service Employees International Union is launching a worker-owned and unionized laundry project in Pittsburgh and is involved in a groundbreaking partnership with New York City's Cooperative Home Care Associates, an effort that provides home services for the elderly, chronically ill, and people living with disabilities, and is the largest worker cooperative in the United States.[3] And the United Food and Commercial Workers Union and Homeland Acquisition Corporation, an Oklahoma- and Texas-based grocery chain, have joined together to transform the company into a 100 percent employee-owned business.[4]

Also, lots of people are suddenly talking about the Mondragon Corporation, a spectacular eighty-three-thousand-person grouping of worker-owned cooperatives in Spain's Basque region that is teaching the world how to move this idea into high gear and large scale. The first Mondragon cooperative dates from 1956, and the overall effort has evolved over the years into a federation of more than one hundred cooperatives—all based on the one-worker, one-vote principle. The modern steelworkers' effort is a joint project undertaken with Mondragon; and the Cleveland co-ops have drawn on many of the Mondragon principles, particularly in connection with revolving loan funds to help incubate new co-ops.[5]

Again, some of the nation's business schools are now offering courses on worker ownership and other democratized business structures that they never offered before.

And by the way (speaking as something of an old-timer who has been concerned with this kind of thing for longer than I care to mention), there are lots and lots of ordinary people who are now beginning to get very serious about changing ownership, and about this as an idea whose time has come—or might come if we get serious.

It's important to note, too, that support for worker ownership doesn't necessarily always sway left or right. Take a guess at who said this, as long ago as 1987: "I can't help but believe that in the future we will see in the United States and throughout the western world an increasing trend toward the next logical step, employee ownership. It is a path that befits a free people." If Ronald Reagan came to mind, you are right.[6]

So, some things to think about as we go forward.

First and most important: If you want to play the system-changing game, don't look only to short-term, quickie answers. Yes, answers are important in the here and now, very important. But if the system is the problem, the truth is that there will not be satisfactory answers in the here and now for lots of people.

That is one of the (painful) ways you know the problem is systemic.

Which means that either you build forward no matter what, or you lose. Period.

Second, it is by no means obvious that a longer developmental path is inevitably blocked if you are very serious and roll up your sleeves.

Third (and this is really worth your time and thought): Ohio has for more than three decades been experiencing the kind of economic pain other parts of the nation are now just beginning to experience. In Ohio and now elsewhere it is in large part precisely because none of the traditional solutions offers answers to the problems and the pain that people are forced to develop new ways. It's either that or continue to experience the pain.

Fourth, and critically: Note carefully that we are talking here about developing *institutions*, not just trying to change policy. And the institutions we are talking about are directly concerned with the critical system question of who owns (and how to democratize) productive wealth.

If you think I am telling you this story—and underlining the above logic—because there is a possibility that *ongoing stalemate, stagnation, and economic pain* may continue in other parts of the nation, forcing choices and potentially incubating new processes (maybe even, bolt by bolt, system-changing *strategies*), you are right.

But of course, that is by no means inevitable.

Nor is the tale told so far the only process to think about.

To be continued . . .

CHAPTER SEVEN

Quiet Democratization Everywhere

That long thirty-five-year process I sketched in the previous chapter is not your typical reform. Change did not come about through the traditional strategies, such as trying to regulate or tax or incentivize existing corporate or other institutions. Nor did it emerge from revolution. Instead it came from building institutions, workplaces, and cultures concerned with democratizing wealth—a process that, just to put a label on it for the moment, we'll call "evolutionary reconstruction." (We'll take up other strategies in due course.)

Worker-owned companies are not, in fact, the only forms of democratized ownership developing under the radar (or more broadly) in the United States. Indeed, there are many, many strategies the media simply doesn't much cover. Moreover, as the social and economic pain of the new era we appear to be entering intensifies, most are developing in numbers, scale, sophistication, and reach.

For a start, more than 130 million Americans—40 percent of the population—are members of one or another form of cooperative, a traditional organizational form that now includes agricultural co-ops dating back to the 1930s, electrical co-ops prevalent in many rural areas, insurance co-ops, food co-ops, retail co-ops (such as the outdoor recreational company REI and the hardware purchasing cooperative ACE), health care co-ops, artist co-ops, credit unions, and many, many more. New efforts keep appearing in different areas of the economy.

A number of co-ops are high-tech and innovative, like the Isthmus Engineering and Manufacturing Company in Madison, Wisconsin, which has been a cooperative for more than thirty years and specializes in "precision" robotic assembly machinery, custom machining, large-scale integrated assemblies, and custom packaging robots.[1] In the same city, a worker-owned cab company—Union Cab—has long provided transportation services, with over two hundred worker-owners and $7 million in annual revenues.[2] In Kentucky, the Louisville Biodiesel Cooperative recycles used cooking oil into a low-polluting, nontoxic source of fuel for local school buses and small family farms.[3]

In North Carolina, the Sandhills Farm to Table Cooperative brings together farmers, consumers, and workers in a food production and distribution system that delivers locally grown food to 1,250 households at the same time that it helps support and stabilize the local economy.[4] The Edmonds Community Solar Cooperative in Washington State partners with the city government to build renewable power capacity.[5] More than eighteen hundred farmer-owners who practice sustainable agriculture across thirty-three states and four Canadian provinces market and distribute their products through the Organic Valley co-op.[6]

In western Massachusetts, the Alliance to Develop Power has created an $80 million "community economy" of housing co-ops and other cooperatively controlled businesses.[7] And in Austin, Texas, thousands of beer drinkers own the Black Star Co-op pub and microbrewery.[8]

I could go on . . .

By far the largest number of co-ops are credit unions—essentially democratized, one-person, one-vote banks. More than ninety-five million Americans are involved; total assets are approximately $1 trillion. Activists have also begun to get interested in this particular cooperative form: "Move your money" efforts shifted hundreds of millions, if not billions, of dollars away from Wall Street and large banks and into credit unions and smaller banks in 2011 and 2012.[9]

Credit unions also lie at the heart of a new and potentially explosive movement to break down the traditional barriers to funding nontraditional business models. As one-person, one-vote institutions, credit unions are obviously subject to the will of the members. However, in many cases democratic processes have faded as staff and officers have established de facto control over the years. Efforts are under way, though, to turn the often somewhat traditional credit unions into more innovative investors—and potential sources of capital for other forms of democratized investment. In early 2012 organizers in Burlington, Vermont, for instance, mounted a successful campaign to elect a new activist member to the Vermont Federal Credit Union Board. (At this writing plans are being laid in Burlington for ongoing and upcoming elections of more board members).[10]

There are also thousands of "social enterprises" that use democratized ownership to make money and use both the money and the enterprise itself to achieve a broader social purpose. One of the most impressive is Pioneer Human Services (PHS), in Seattle, Washington, an organization that provides employment, job training, counseling, education, and housing to recovering alcoholics and drug addicts. PHS was established some fifty years ago as a nonprofit corporation dependent upon donations and grants. Its $67 million annual budget is now in significant part funded by revenues from businesses it created as part of its overall strategy.

Among other things, PHS runs a full-service precision sheet metal fabrication and machining shop, produces thousands of aerospace parts for Boeing, and through its catering services prepares and distributes more than fifteen hundred meals a day to hospitals, care centers, and nonprofit and government facilities. PHS's social enterprises employ nearly a thousand theoretically impaired and unemployable people.[11]

At the other end of the continent Greyston Bakery in Yonkers, New York, was founded by a Buddhist teacher to employ his students, but the organization's mission quickly expanded to provide jobs for neighboring inner-city residents. Greyston now inhabits a twenty-three-thousand-square-foot facility and operates several additional businesses and services, including a day care center, a housing development that provides shelter for low-income individuals and people with HIV/AIDS, community gardens used by two thousand adults and children, counseling and support services, and a technology education center.[12]

Another direction in social enterprise development is illustrated by Southwest Key Programs in the heavily Latino East Austin section of Austin, Texas. Presently the fourth largest Hispanic nonprofit in the country, Southwest Key Programs has an annual budget of over $74 million and a staff of more than thirteen hundred employees. Following a path similar to that of Pioneer Human Services, it decided to expand into business development both to support its projects and to offer work to trainees. Start-ups include Café del Sol and Southwest Key Maintenance & Janitorial.[13]

By far the most common social enterprise is the traditional community development corporation, or CDC. Nearly five thousand have long been in operation in almost every US city of significant size.[14] For the most part CDCs have served as low-income housing developers and incubators for small businesses. Early on in the fifty-year history of the movement, however, a different, larger vision was in play—one that is still present in some of the more advanced CDC efforts, and one that suggests additional possibilities for the future.

New Community Corporation (NCC) in Newark, New Jersey, is a large-scale neighborhood nonprofit that employs roughly thirteen hundred neighborhood residents, manages two thousand housing units, has $500 million in assets, and has an approximately $200 million operating budget. Though modest in the total picture, proceeds from NCC businesses—including a shopping center anchored by a major supermarket—help support day care and after-school programs, a nursing home, and four medical day care centers for seniors. NCC also runs the School of Practical Nursing and Gateway to Work programs, both designed to train young residents for future careers.[15]

Another large-scale effort, Bethel New Life in Chicago, is a faith-based community development organization serving residents of the West Garfield neighborhood of Chicago since 1979. In Oakland, California, the Unity Council, started in 1964 by Hispanic community organizers, has spearheaded the Fruitvale Village project, an ambitious ten-acre urban revitalization project anchored by a mass transit station that has created affordable housing and ground-level retail, including a micro-enterprise incubator.[16]

Still another form of democratized ownership involves growing numbers of "land trusts"—essentially nonprofit corporations that own housing and other property in ways that prevent gentrification and turn development profits into support of low- and moderate-income housing. One of the best known is the Champlain Housing Trust in Burlington, Vermont, which traces its modest beginnings to the early 1980s and now provides accommodation for more than two thousand households.[17]

Like other democratized forms of ownership, today's land trusts are also the benefactors of early experiments that planted innovative seeds—the heart of any long-term evolutionary reconstruction process. Some of the first serious modern efforts, for instance, were begun in the 1960s and 1970s in western Massachusetts (by Robert Swann) and in southwest Georgia (by Charles and Shirley Sherrod). All three were deeply involved in the civil rights movement and saw cooperative land ownership both as an answer to systemic problems and, in the case of the Sherrods, as a way to help poor black farmers forced off the land by mechanization and political retaliation for their civil rights activities.[18] At the time the early trusts were conventionally seen as interesting utopian experiments signifying hard work and idealism, but essentially not going anywhere serious.

However . . .

Hundreds of such efforts now exist, and new land trusts are now being established on an expanding, ongoing basis in diverse contexts and cities all over the country. (By 2012, 255 community land trusts were operating in forty-five states and the District of Columbia.) The reason? By emphasizing social as well as financial outcomes, democratizing ownership solves problems that can't easily be solved in other ways—especially gentrification pressures.

Two of the most recent have been established in cities as different as Chicago, Illinois, and Irvine, California. The first is a city-run project designed to incubate the trust until it is financially self-sufficient, when it will be spun off as a separate organization. In the second, the city of Irvine has plans under way to create five thousand units of land trust housing—a number that represents 50 percent of its goal of almost ten thousand units of affordable housing.[19]

Again, I could go on and on.* But I think you get the idea, and perhaps a sense, too, of the evolving process, and how innovations are occurring right and left as experience grows over time and—given the failures of traditional policies and the deepening pain—how the necessity and possibility of taking things into one's own hands becomes increasingly understood. A few additional important recent developments, however, illustrate the diversity of the evolutionary process.

One of the obstacles to ordinary businesses factoring social benefit into their operating plans has been the design of corporations themselves. Since a traditional corporation is required by law to make decisions that financially benefit its stockholders, officers who devote significant resources to social purposes can be sued by stockholders for not paying attention to their primary business responsibilities.

For companies that want to pursue what has often been called the triple bottom line (emphasizing people and planet in addition to profit), the traditional legal structure thus poses challenges—a reality that led private-equity expert Andrew Kassoy to join with two others to found B Lab and invent the B Corporation, a corporate structure that facilitates the use of business profits for social purposes. In a B Corp (also known as a benefit corporation) people who invest know from the outset that the goal is both to make profits and to use some part of them for social purposes.† Laws permitting companies to charter themselves as B Corporations have been enacted in twelve states—California, Hawaii, Illinois, Louisiana, Maryland, Massachusetts, New Jersey, New York, Pennsylvania, South Carolina, Vermont, and Virginia.

---

* This website keeps track of the flow in many, many areas: www.community-wealth.org.

† Also, a traditional non-B-Corp company must legally accept the highest price offered in buyout situations, even if the board of directors believes a buyer offering a lower price is likely to do a better job of maintaining the corporation's social values. This was the complaint of Ben & Jerry's owners, who would have preferred to sell their company to a competing, more socially minded bidder than Unilever, but legally had to sell to the highest bidder—a development that helped lead to the B Corp movement. One of the most innovative B Corps is King Arthur Flour, a highly successful Vermont-based 100 percent employee-owned company that is quite explicit in stating that "making money in itself

In Illinois, Louisiana, Maine, Michigan, North Carolina, Rhode Island, Utah, Vermont, and Wyoming a related low-profit limited liability corporate form—the so-called L3C—is a cross between a nonprofit organization and a for-profit corporation that also promotes development of socially oriented business. In Louisiana, former lieutenant governor Mitch Landrieu (currently New Orleans mayor) founded the Louisiana Office of Social Entrepreneurship in 2007 to promote citizen involvement in locally owned social enterprise.[20]

Associated with these various directions is a movement among significant numbers of businesspeople to undertake what many now term "impact investing" with the explicit goal of achieving important social, environmental, or equity goals. Among the leading efforts are Social Capital Markets (SOCAP) and the Global Impact Investing Network (GIIN).

A very different direction in ongoing innovation is suggested by Market Creek Plaza in San Diego. At the center of the project is a $23.5 million commercial and cultural complex, anchored by a shopping center. Neighborhood residents have become direct individual owners (and are personally accumulating assets) by purchasing shares in the shopping center through an unusual limited initial public offering legally restricted to community members. A total of 415 investors representing six hundred residents and other nonprofit and for-profit organizations purchased shares at the outset, raising $500,000 in the process, and collectively establishing ownership of 20 percent of the equity in the project.

A new neighborhood foundation owns another 20 percent of the shopping center, thereby also providing a funding stream for future community wealth-building efforts. (The Jacobs Foundation, which launched the effort and currently retains 60 percent ownership, intends to exit by 2018, with ownership thereafter evenly split among community residents and the neighborhood foundation it created.[21])

Look around, and you'll likely see signs of quiet democratization and evolutionary reconstruction where, perhaps, you least expect it in your own community.

---

is not our highest priority." Another is Patagonia, the Ventura, California–based outdoor apparel and sporting-equipment retailer that prides itself on the utility, simplicity, and sustainability of its products. See: B Lab, "King Arthur Flour Company," Certified B Corporation, 2012, accessed December 7, 2012, www.bcorporation.net/community/directory /kingarthurflour; B Lab, "Patagonia, Inc.," Certified B Corporation, 2012, accessed December 7, 2012, www.bcorporation.net/community/directory/patagonia.

CHAPTER EIGHT

Worker Ownership Redux

By the way, and finally (for the moment), there are also many, many worker-owned companies structured in ways different from traditional co-ops—indeed, around eleven thousand of them, involving 10.3 million people, in virtually every sector, some very large and sophisticated.[1] Technically, these companies are called ESOPs (employee stock ownership plans), and in fact three million more individuals are involved in worker-owned companies of this kind than are members of unions in the private sector.[2]

Here are some examples from different sectors.

The Appleton company is a large paper products manufacturer based in Appleton, Wisconsin. Formed in 1907, it employs around two thousand people and has been 100 percent employee-owned since 2001. In 2010 net sales were around $850 million. Appleton become employee-owned when the company was put up for sale by Arjo Wiggins Appleton, the multinational corporation that owned it—and the employees decided they had just as much right to buy it as anyone else.[3]

W. L. Gore—the maker of Gore-Tex apparel—has been owned since 1974 by (currently more than ninety-five hundred) worker-owners in thirty countries across the world and has annual revenues of around $3 billion. It regularly ranks on Fortune's Best Companies to Work For list.[4]

Although a majority of ESOP firms are small or medium in size, typically with one hundred to five hundred employees, some are a good deal larger. For instance, Hy-Vee, a midwestern supermarket chain with fifty-six thousand employees, 235 retail stores, and $7.6 billion in sales, is employee-owned through a profit-sharing program and is forty-eighth on Forbes's list of the largest American private companies.[5] Lifetouch, a company specializing in school pictures, has twenty-six thousand employee-owners working in all fifty states and over $1 billion in annual revenues.[6]

The growth of ESOPs is a very American tale. It involves a corporate law-yer and banker named Louis Kelso who became convinced that some way to democratize ownership was important—and put his skills to work figuring out how to do it. It also involves the late senator Russell Long, the son of the radical 1930s populist governor and senator from Louisiana, Huey Long. (Long Junior happened to be chairman of the Senate Finance Committee, and he and Kelso worked out very significant tax incentives for businesses that sell their companies to employees.[7])

Historically, some folks—and some unions as well—haven't always liked ESOPs, and for a couple of reasons. First, there have been some very highly publicized "bad apple" tales. This has created suspicion about all the apples even though the vast majority of ESOPs have a solid record of performance. Second, most ESOPs have not been set up to encourage democratic control. They have been structured so that a trust votes the shares owned by the work-ers; in these cases the employees still partake in the profits, but they don't necessarily have a say in how the company is run. This framework arose in part because the original legislation reflected the concerns of bankers financ-ing ESOPs, as well as some tactical fights in Congress—and this fact, too, has raised legitimate questions.

The bottom line is that in general most ESOPs work best in small- and medium-sized companies. Also, importantly, there has been a great deal of forward movement—and the possibility of much more forward movement—in connection with the democratic control issue.[8]

Critically, research done in that interesting and pain-driven state of Ohio suggests that there has been a clear trend toward ever-greater control by worker-owners as time has gone on, and as workers in specific firms accu-mulate more stock, year by year, and ownership thus moves from minority to majority status. Also, giving ESOP workers the right to vote their stock—permitted but not required by the original ESOP legislation—has been much more common in Ohio than elsewhere, jumping from 14 to 42 percent in a seven-year period. And majority-owned ESOPs have doubled, from 15 to 30 percent of ESOPs in the state. A wide range of informal mechanisms to facili-tate greater employee consultation have been growing outside Ohio as well.[9]

Second, legislation was proposed in 2001 that would make ESOPs much more democratic by making those operating as one-person, one-vote businesses eligible for additional federal tax benefits. Here is another tale involving unexpected mavericks: The primary sponsor of this legislation, Representative Dana Rohrabacher (R-CA), is one of the most conservative members of Congress; the legislation's co-sponsors included prominent liberal Democrats Marcy Kaptur and former representative Dennis Kucinich of Ohio as well as fellow conservative Ron Paul of Texas.[10] More recent bipartisan legislation expresses continuing support for ESOP efforts in general.[11]

Third, and far more important than any of the above: Repeated studies show that worker-owned firms tend to be more profitable, more competitive, and more efficient—especially when adequate training has been done in self-management—than comparable firms.[12] In other words (big surprise!), the more workers own, and the more they experience their ownership, the more productive they are over time—and that also means more competitive (and likely to grow for this reason alone).[13]

There has also been a good deal of practical developmental work done on the participation front. Here, for instance, are two of many examples: New Belgium Brewing Company, a Fort Collins, Colorado–based brewery that is now 100 percent owned by its employees, has focused on a high-involvement culture in its triple-bottom-line operations. This includes a commitment to employee participation in decision making throughout all levels of the business. New Belgium also operates on the principle of open-book management whereby all employee-owners are encouraged to review any and all of the company's financial documents and to provide feedback.[14]

Carris Reels, a Proctor, Vermont–based reel and spool manufacturer, has been 100 percent owned by its 450 employees since 2008. The company has a corporate steering committee that exists as a shared management body comprising one-third corporate representatives, one-third management representatives, and one-third elected employee representatives—all of whom share equal authority. At this writing the company is in the process of designing procedures by which employee-owners will directly select a majority of ESOP trustees and board members.[15]

Finally—and importantly—a number of unions have also quietly been coming around and have begun to see opportunities here, just as they have begun to urge union co-ops and other democratized ownership efforts. Here, for instance, are several instances in which important unions have found ways to take advantage of the ESOP form in very different parts of the country:

Litecontrol, founded in 1936, is an architectural lighting design, development, and manufacturing company operating two plants and employing nearly two hundred workers in Hanson and Plympton, Massachusetts.[16] In 1999 an ESOP was established, and since 2007 the company has been 100 percent employee-owned. More than 60 percent of the workforce is union-ized through the International Brotherhood of Electrical Workers (IBEW).[17]

Maryland Brush Company was established in 1851 and is now a leading manufacturer and supplier of industrial brushes worldwide. A subsidiary of Pittsburgh Plate & Glass from 1901 to 1989, it was spun off and incorporated as an ESOP in 1990 that is currently 100 percent owned by its employees. Because of the involvement of the United Steelworkers union in the sale, the union and management each received three seats on the board of directors, with a seventh person selected by mutual agreement of the parties.[18]

Recology is a San Francisco–based recycling company 100 percent employee-owned by its twenty-one hundred employees, 80 percent of whom are unionized through the International Brotherhood of Teamsters (IBT) Local 350. Founded in 1986, Recology is "the largest employee owned com-pany in the solid waste industry." It collects recyclable waste from twenty-one hundred area restaurants and also provides waste management services for more than 670,000 residential and ninety-five thousand commercial customers in four states.[19] Annual revenues have increased by 7 to 8 percent a year over the past five years (and now stand at over half a billion dollars).[20]

Other unions that have experimented in positive ways with ESOPs include the United Food and Commercial Workers (UFCW), the International Asso-ciation of Machinists and Aerospace Workers (IAM), and the International Union of Electronic, Electrical, Salaried, Machine and Furniture Workers.[21]

My hunch: Some of the unions that have not liked ESOPS for one or another reason in the past may begin to turn them to the workers' advantage, restructuring the voting and other powers, using the tax advantages to good purpose, and, of course, unionizing them, as a number are already doing. This is, after all, a huge, huge area of potential worker involvement—and could be of strategic importance in the future, given the difficulties facing the labor movement. That, however, is only a hunch; some of the unions are pretty divided on this question.

Here's another subtle nudge about the general trajectory of change involved in all of these examples. Look back at the last three chapters, and you will see, again, a certain diverse but nonetheless powerful process of evolution-ary change over time. A process that suggests quite significant institution-building possibilities at work. And also one that suggests how powerful the change could be if it were more fully embraced, and embraced with specific political-economic intent.

Especially as the economy continues to deteriorate, offering few alternatives other than innovating and taking things into one's own hands, community by community.

I also remind you that we are not here interested only in nice projects, or neat little efforts. The name of the game is systemic change. So the question is not simply whether what we are looking at is interesting or novel, it is whether the ideas and strategies and principles—including, above all, democratizing wealth in very down-home American ways—might offer handholds and building blocks over the long haul for something more important.

There is also this: Most ESOPs are created when owners retire and do not have an heir who wants to run the business. It is to their great (tax) advantage then to sell to the employees.

And we are now also entering the era of the (massive) retirement of the baby boom, a time when such companies will be either largely absorbed by big corporations or possibly (actively) taken over as part of a new direction in democratized worker ownership.

To be continued (again) . . .

CHAPTER NINE

Cultural and Ideological Hegemony, Utopia—and Us

A ntonio Gramsci was a famous Italian Marxist revolutionary who got particularly interested in the problem of cultural and ideological "hegemony," by which he meant (among other things) that certain critical ideas, favorable to the dominant (capitalist) class, were often so deeply ingrained in social and economic processes that it was hard for most people (especially "the working class") to penetrate the idea fog, and even to think about a new direction—to say nothing of contemplating whether another system was (is?) possible.

Gramsci's line of thought emphasized a long, hard ongoing effort to break down the dominant ideology and develop a new direction, one that begins to build something of an overarching yet commonsense idea of a new way forward—something obviously important especially in a country where corporations are "persons" and can spend as much as they like pumping up the dominant ideology and marginalizing other ideas (to say nothing of polluting the political process).

In fact, however, the deepest form of ideological hegemony is the kind reflected in Margaret Thatcher's TINA idea—the notion, powerfully held and embraced by assumption (taken in with your mother's milk, as it were), that quite simply *There Is No Alternative to corporate capitalism. Period.*

So, a challenge: I've been telling the tale of Youngstown, the Cleveland model, worker-owned companies, social enterprises, and others primarily (or so it seems) to suggest that if you roll up your sleeves it may well be possible to do something different—something embodying principles that, in accord perhaps with a different longer-term vision, emphasize the democratization of wealth.

I've also been suggesting the possibility of a certain longer-term evolutionary institution-building and institution-shifting strategy—one not for the faint of heart or for the short-term, instant-gratification folks among us.

I now want to push just a bit harder: In a very profound sense, the struggle is also about changing the dominant ideological patterns—about cracking through the dominant cultural and ideological hegemony.

This means grasping fully and firmly that part of the job is to create a new sense of what might one day be possible. *But not simply in the abstract*. If democratizing the ownership of wealth is one (only one . . . *so far*) of the key principles of a serious approach to systemic change, then we need to grasp that point explicitly, and affirm it, and find ways to illuminate its importance to one and all.

So . . .

All this stuff about Youngstown, co-ops, Cleveland models, and ESOPs (and the movement beyond old-form ESOPs) is also important—perhaps even more important—in what might be called the ideological sphere. Not simply at the level of challenging the dominant ideology but, importantly, in beginning to specify some (just *some*!) of the elements of a different and very down-home American idea of what a different way forward might be.

Not to be too academic, but it's worth mentioning that we are also talking about the sociology of knowledge and scholars like Karl Mannheim, an important mid-twentieth-century Hungarian who did most of his work in Germany and Britain. Mannheim held that the dominant ideology legitimated and helped defend the dominant class and dominant system. What he called "utopia," on the other hand, represented a set of ideas posing a fundamental challenge to the dominant ideas. In Mannheim's world utopia was not, as we often think of it, a state that can never be reached; it was the emerging new direction.

From this broader perspective new forms of ownership are important not only on their own, but also in that they begin to offer handholds on a new longer-term vision, a set of ideas about democratization that—if they were to become widespread, embraced, evolved, refined, and widely understood—form the basis, potentially, of bringing people together, both to challenge the dominant hegemonic ideology and to build a democratized economic basis for a new vision and new system.

Whoa! That is pushing all this a bit farther than most of us have as yet thought we might go.

Yes.

My goal is to suggest not only that you begin to think with me about evolutionary paths building forward—*get out there and help create an actual co-op or worker-owned firm or many other things yet to be discussed*—but also, if you are going to play this game, that you start getting self-conscious about the fact that you (we) are also working to alter the way folks think about what is possible.

The current corporate-dominated hegemonic ideology that prevents us from acting together in new ways, quite simply, needs to be replaced.

And who is going to do that work other than us?

Over time, slow but sure.

PART III

"CHECKERBOARD": EMERGENT MUNICIPAL AND STATE POSSIBILITIES

CHAPTER TEN

How the Conservatives Buried Adam Smith

And What It Might Mean for Us

What about government?
How does it relate to what we've been talking about (and might begin to talk much more about—especially, first, at the local community level)? Might it have a significant role to play in advancing the democratizing direction we have been discussing?

A good place to begin to explore the question is with a brief word about old Adam Smith, the father of modern free-market economics, and about his (former) conservative allies.

It used to be—long, long ago—that (some) genuine conservatives genuinely believed in the free market. Here, for instance, is conservative Nobel Prize winner Milton Friedman: "The only way that has ever been discovered to have a lot of people cooperate together voluntarily is through the free market."[1] And here are the views of another Nobel-winning conservative economist, Friedrich Hayek: "I regard the preservation . . . of the system of free markets and the private ownership of the means of production, as an essential condition of the very survival of mankind."[2]

Now, if the free market really worked in the wonderful way Freidman and Hayek imagined, propelled entirely by elective individual behavior, I would take them seriously, even though there are lots of reasons to believe that this idea is wildly utopian—not in Mannheim's sense, but in the real-world sense. But it does not. Friedman, Hayek, and countless others describe the economy in ways that simply ignore the vast role of government in virtually all so-called free-market experience.

Indeed—and here's the thing to note about our own time in history, especially at the local level we've been talking about (but also, as we shall see, at the state and national level)—it's been a long, long, long time since anybody really acted as if they believed any of the old free-market shibboleths in the real world.

Especially most conservatives.

The truth is, business uses government all the time, irrespective of free-market theory—and, again, particularly at the local level where the action has gotten really intense in the last few decades. When progressives and conservatives cross fire over free-market issues, the battle is often construed to be over how much influence government should have in the marketplace, with most conservatives pushing the notion that government involvement disrupts the natural flow of a free market. That may be handy framing to ward off unwanted regulations, but even free-market evangelists know the market commonly stands on government legs.

Consider, for example, the vast amounts of government (taxpayer) money used to bribe big corporations to invest in cities. Lots and lots of examples of this now conventional process can be found in almost every metropolis. Moreover, it is now estimated that big companies often extract public subsidies of between $100,000 and $200,000 *per promised job brought to a city*.[3]

The practice, however dubious to begin with, is also ripe for abuse. A classic example (but really only an illustration of general practice) involved the Marriott Corporation, a company that between 1997 and 1999 threatened to move its four-thousand-employee headquarters facility from Bethesda, Maryland, to suburban Virginia. In exchange for an agreement to stay, Marriott got state and local officials to provide multiple subsidies worth between $49 million and $74 million (the precise amount depending on the company's future growth). Subsequently an investigation by the *Baltimore Sun* found that Marriott had never planned to leave. Indeed, it had informed the state of Virginia it wasn't moving a month before Maryland made its offer. The threat had simply been a tactic to extract more money from the state and county leaders as executives played one group off against another.[4]

Ask your conservative friends who urge such programs to square *that* with Adam Smith, the free market, and all the traditional posturing. (Then ask their business friends if they will disdain from accepting the big public bucks in connection with business strategies *they* might be contemplating.)

By the way, in the real world businesses that extract large subsidies from municipalities and states often move on, leaving them high and dry as they look for another place willing to play the same game. In 2004, for example, North Carolina amassed a package of benefits valued at around $242 million to encourage Dell to build a $100 million computer assembly plant to employ fifteen hundred people. Dell also collected an additional $37.2 million in local economic development subsidy dollars from Forsyth County and Winston-Salem.[5] The overall cost to the taxpayer amounted to more than $200,000 per job, but in October 2009 Dell announced that it would be closing its four-year-old facility and would instead outsource most of the nine hundred jobs to plants in Mexico.[6]

The absurdity, waste, and ideological dishonesty involved in such now conventional processes—and now conventional conservative blather about "free markets"—is one thing. Quite another (and much more important) is how profoundly things have changed in the direction of explicit government economic planning at the local level (we'll explore national later), all largely at the behest of businessmen and free-market conservatives. And this in turn suggests some new possibilities for democratization as well.

In city after city government officials now routinely use tax incentives, tax abatements, loan guarantees, loans, special zoning, public–private joint ventures, and many other economic "tools" as a way to encourage business development. They have done so precisely because the free market operating on its own often simply results in local economic dislocation and decay.

Recent trends take us far beyond garden-variety tax deals and other routine strategies that disregard free-market theory. A big trend in many cities these days involves explicit public investment in specific businesses ("socialism," if you like). Two respected urban policy experts, Susan Clarke and the late Gary Gaile, have underscored the speed with which this strategy became conventional once it got under way.

They found that in 1989 a mere 5.4 percent of the cities surveyed (population over one hundred thousand) were engaged in venture capital investing; by 1996 there was a sixfold increase to 33.2 percent doing direct venture capital investing. Even more impressive was the trend in connection with equity investing: In 1989, 20.4 percent of cities surveyed were making direct municipal equity investments in local businesses; by 1996 a majority—56.3 percent—were doing so as part of their routine development strategy.[7]

Another leading local economic development expert, Peter Eisinger, describes what municipalities now do on a routine basis as the new "entrepreneurial state." A common strategy involves establishing a local economic development corporation to channel municipal investments to specific businesses. In addition such corporations issue revenue bonds, own and maintain industrial parks, employ revolving loan funds to make below-market loans to businesses, use tax increment financing to subsidize business development, and provide tax abatements to encourage business formation in targeted sectors.[8]

I could list many more techniques that are now commonplace. We also could spend a long, long time deciding when this is in the public interest and when not, but let's pass on that for the moment. (There is a huge literature.) From the larger perspective we have been exploring there is a much more interesting thing to note.

Namely, once we recognize that government is now inevitably involved in many, many economic development issues, a very different question becomes obvious: Couldn't such involvement help support the developing movement toward democratized businesses as well? Indeed, why not make this a priority? Virtually all of the things that are now routinely done for business in general can in fact also be done for co-ops, social enterprises, and nonprofit land development efforts. Indeed, in the most interesting developing efforts, that is precisely what is already happening, every day, more and more, in the real world.

Again, let's take a look at Cleveland. The Department of Housing and Urban Development (HUD) section 108 and BEDI (Brownfields Economic Development Initiative) funds helped clear land for the greenhouse; Department of Treasury New Markets Tax Credits helped support the laundry; Ohio Solar Renewable Energy Certificates have played a role in the solar co-op's installation work; City of Cleveland NSP (Neighborhood Stabilization Program) grants and Department of Commerce EDA (Economic Development Administration) working capital loans helped the overall effort.[9, 10]

And in San Diego's Market Creek Plaza, government support came from such programs as the federal New Markets Tax Credits; tax reimbursements from the Southeastern Economic Development Corporation; and a low-interest loan through Clearinghouse CDFI with help from the California Southern Small Business Development Corporation. Further work will draw upon additional public funds—including $1.35 million in a brownfields remediation award, which in turn will give the project priority status with eleven state agencies, putting it at the front of the line with each for additional funding.[11]

Federal strategies to support economic development and related efforts obviously come in many forms.[12] Two, however, may serve to further illustrate what is now conventional practice.

The Community Economic Development (CED) program of the US Department of Health and Human Services funds a wide range of projects.

In Tampa, Florida, a community development corporation was able to use federal funds to make a $759,000 equity investment in the 22nd Street Retail Center, which will bring healthy food to a neighborhood that, lacking grocery stores with fresh food, has been a food desert.[13]

A very different form of now conventional public policy involves the very large-order tax benefits—roughly $2 billion per year—given to business-people who sell at least 30 percent of their company to their workers in ESOP efforts.[14]

I am less interested here in hypocrisy—how businesspeople and conservatives continually spout rhetoric about how and why the "free market" must, *really must*, keep government away from business. The big point is not about the hunger of conservative businesspeople for subsidies. It is that government now routinely uses taxpayer money and other programs to achieve economic goals.

And this historical reality opens up many interesting new questions and possibilities for supporting the various efforts we have been examining in the previous chapters. In parts 5 and 6 we'll take a deeper dive into all this, exploring why such public efforts are important to any thoughtful developmental approach to larger-order change.

Most significant at this point is simply this: If you're going to get serious about systemic change—not just "projects"—you're ultimately going to have to consider what government does, and how it can be used to further the vision and model you affirm. If you don't, somebody else will (all the while denying or obfuscating what they are doing).

Which also means that we need to begin to think in specific, practical, and serious terms about adding, to our longer-term democratization strategy, both policy and politics that support specific institutional development efforts.

(And yes, the question over time is whether this can move beyond developing models to real scale. And yes, that depends on pain levels, the nature of the emerging context, and whether a common direction is embraced. And yes, we will get deeper into all this, too, especially in part 6.)

One more local thing before we move on—something pretty obvious, but worth a reminder. In a number of cities, folks have gotten pretty hip to the reality that government itself also must be (and should be!) *directly* involved in any serious new longer-term strategic approach, especially now, given that the environment·is a central concern. Not only are they already helping democratized economic efforts, but they are using municipal powers that suggest new and truly impressive additional directions—directions that are feasible as part and parcel of any larger community institution-building and democratizing strategy, and *feasible now*.

Famously, municipal efforts in Portland, Oregon, have paved the way through the city's Bureau of Planning and Sustainability (BPS). For one thing, the BPS is helping implement a major climate action plan to reduce the city's carbon emissions by 80 percent from 1990 levels by 2050. Other initiatives include Clean Energy Works Portland (a nonprofit designed to help finance energy improvements in six thousand homes by 2013), transit-oriented development (including developments around the city's new and expanded tram system), solar energy (aiming to install at least ten megawatts of solar capacity in the city), waste reduction and recycling programs (designed to increase recycling to 75 percent), new "ecodistricts" (such as the Rose Quarter), neighborhood greenways (where bicycles are given priority over automobiles), the River Plan (to promote industrial development while at the same time reducing environmental destruction), and city government sustainability programs (designed to save the city $4 million a year in energy costs).[15]

The out-of-the-box Portland tale in the Pacific Northwest, however, is by no means the only one.

In Kansas City, Missouri, the municipal "Green Impact Zone" has brought together public and private resources to transform a decaying neighborhood into a sustainable urban community. The effort includes school improvements, weatherization, job training and placement programs, business development (initially targeted at improving energy efficiency), renewable energy and water conservation programs, installation of a smart grid by Kansas City Power and Light, and new programs to develop housing on abandoned lots, remove dangerous buildings, enforce code violations, and ensure rental property maintenance.[16]

In Austin, Texas, another green municipal development initiative is working to build a regional economy that emphasizes green business leadership, clean technology, new jobs, and expanding opportunity.[17] The city supports local companies that "green" their operations (offering awards, free online and print advertising, networking opportunities, and the like).[18] It also includes an effort slated to make the city's operations completely carbon-neutral by 2020, including reducing greenhouse gas emissions by switching to renewable energy, replacing inefficient lighting, and replacing vehicle fleets, plus (among other things) conservation programs covering water, air quality, waste reduction and recycling, and green gardening.[19, 20]

In Oberlin, Ohio, the city and Oberlin College have embarked on the ambitious "Oberlin Project" aimed at radically transforming the city economically, socially, and environmentally. The project includes development of a thirteen-acre "Green Arts District" of new and renovated environmentally advanced buildings; creation of environmentally sustainable, democratically owned businesses in the energy, food, and agriculture sectors; transition of both the city and college to renewable energy delivered by locally owned and operated sources; creation of a twenty-thousand-acre "greenbelt" to provide locally grown food to the city and to increase employment and study opportunities; formation of an educational partnership among Oberlin College, Oberlin public schools, and community colleges and vocational schools to foster a curriculum based on sustainability; and an effort, finally, to replicate the project on different scales in cities and regions across the country.[21]

Many, many more tales like these are available to draw upon for those who want to get serious about using government in new ways—first to boost democratizing efforts, but also to mobilize the entire panoply of municipal and other policies in a new direction.[22]

So, onward! Perhaps even offering condolences to old Adam, if you like—and even thanks, too, to his many conservative followers who have been all too happy to face and use (and teach us how to use!) the real world of public policy in everyday practice, all the while marvelously unable to resist denying that use at every possible turn of the political debate.

CHAPTER ELEVEN

Everyday Socialism, All the Time, American-Style

O ne more obvious step, for the moment, in connection with real-world democratization (and maybe also about what can be done if you want to start getting serious).

I assume you are aware that socialism—real socialism, not the fuzzy kind conservatives try to pin on Barack Obama—is as common as grass (well, maybe not *that* common, but still very common indeed) in the United States.

I'm not talking about the public programs that come to many minds when socialism is discussed in an American context. These programs often help people in need and do many other useful things, but they don't attempt to change the underlying systemic design and the political power it confers on corporate actors.

I'm talking about the (efficient) government ownership of businesses, some set up in the past and still working very nicely, thank you, and many new efforts now also flourishing big-time.

For a start: It's often forgotten—or simply not known—that there are more than two thousand publicly owned electric utilities now operating, day by day, week by week, throughout the United States (many in the conservative South). Indeed, 25 percent of US electricity is supplied by locally owned public utilities and co-ops.[1]

Moreover, most of these now conventional "socialist" operations have a demonstrated capacity to provide electricity at lower cost to the consumer, not to mention cheaper and more accessible broadband. (Nationally, on average, customers of private utilities pay 14 percent more than customers of public utilities.)[2]

One obvious reason: Public utilities and co-ops simply don't pay the same exorbitant executive salaries common in the private sector. They get pretty much the same work done for far less. General managers of the largest class of publicly owned power companies earned an average salary of roughly

$260,000 in 2011. Average compensation for CEOs of large investor-owned utilities was $6 million—almost twenty-five times as much.[3]

Also, of course, public utilities and co-op producers don't have to pay private shareholders any dividends. And they return a portion of their revenues to the city or county to help supplement local budgets, easing the pressure on taxpayers. A recent study found an average transfer of 5.2 percent of revenues to municipalities—compared with average tax payments by private-investor-owned utilities of 3.9 percent.[4]

In smaller communities revenues from public utilities are often a crucial component of city budgets. In Ashland, Oregon, for instance, fully 30 percent of the general fund that pays for such services as police, fire, and street maintenance comes from public utility profits; only 16 percent comes from property taxes.[5] Similarly, the century-old public utility in Norwich, Connecticut, is a major contributor to the city, with more than 10 percent of its total billings—more than 5 percent of the city's total annual budget—going to the municipal general fund.[6]

A number of public utilities also play a powerful role in building a green economy. In California the Sacramento Municipal Utility District (SMUD)— one of the ten largest public utilities in the United States—now supplies more than 24 percent of its retail energy sales from renewable sources; it expects to reach a goal of 37 percent renewable energy by 2020. SMUD is also on target to slash CO_2 emissions to just 10 percent of 1990 levels by 2050.[7]

Another leader, Austin Energy in Texas, runs the most successful utility-sponsored green energy marketing program in the country.[8] Approximately 15 to 17 percent of its power currently comes from renewable sources—primarily wind, with landfill methane gas a distant second. The utility expects to reach 30 to 35 percent renewable energy by 2020. It also has a twenty-year agreement to purchase power from a large wood-fired power plant in East Texas, and it expects to achieve a CO_2 reduction goal of 20 percent below 2005 levels by 2020.[9]

A number of cities are now also regularly involved in the public land development business—increasingly in situations where public policies, such as those involving mass transit, create huge land value increases and other benefits that would otherwise simply go to private developers.

Boston was one of the first to realize this possibility. In 1970 the city embarked on a joint venture with the Rouse Company to develop historic eighteenth-century Faneuil Hall Marketplace (a six-and-a-half-acre downtown retail complex with forty-nine shops, eighteen restaurants and pubs, twenty-five eateries, and forty-four carts). Boston kept the property under municipal ownership and negotiated a lease agreement in which the city got a portion of the development's profits in lieu of property taxes. By the mid-1980s Boston was collecting some $2.5 million per year from the marketplace, and by 2008 this had increased to several million a year.[10] One expert estimate is that the approach allowed the city to take in "40 percent more [revenue] than it would have collected through conventional property tax channels."[11]

Some of the most interesting examples of what might be called "development socialism" occur when a city develops and leases land it owns in and around entrances to publicly funded mass transportation subways and light rail systems. Land values go up dramatically at such locations, and cities used to simply let developers grab the publicly created opportunities—and then try to tax back whatever they could. Now many cities routinely maintain public ownership of the land, directly capturing the increased values the public investment creates.

In Miami, Florida Miami-Dade Transit is involved in the ownership of multiple large transit-linked joint development ventures. Dadeland South Station, for instance, includes multiple office buildings, a luxury hotel, and ground-level retail space. Dadeland North Station comprises more than 370,000 square feet of retail space, a large residential rental building, and a luxury apartment building. Taken together the projects generate annual revenues of around $1.3 million for Miami-Dade County.[12]

The San Francisco Bay Area Rapid Transit (BART) has eighteen transit-oriented development projects under way (and numerous others in various stages of development).[13] In the nation's capital, the Washington Metropolitan Area Transit Authority has established more than fifty revenue-generating joint development projects.[14] The Valley Transportation Authority of Santa Clara County, California, has designed its Transit-Oriented Development Program to encourage mixed-use development within two thousand feet of transit stops. Not only does its Almaden Lake Village Project return revenues to the city, but 20 percent of the 250 residential units are offered at below-market cost to low-income households.[15]

I mentioned at the outset that many utilities now help create broadband services. This is another area where public enterprise has become increasingly common, both via utility-based strategies and through other independent municipal efforts. More than 130 cities have built citywide public Internet networks. Hundreds have partial networks (connecting schools, businesses, and government buildings), and hundreds more are actively planning the construction of such networks.[16]

Many others have made Internet provision a priority and are investing in telecommunications, including cable television, high-speed Internet services, local and long-distance telephone service, fiber leasing, and wireless data transmission. Indeed, by 2007 over seven hundred public power companies—or more than a third of them—were offering some form of advanced telecommunication services.[17]

OptiNet, the broadband division of the city-owned utility in Bristol, Virginia (BVU), was the first utility in the nation to provide voice, video, and broadband over a fiber-to-the-user network. By early 2012 OptiNet had achieved approximately 70 percent market penetration in its primary service area (city limits of Bristol, Virginia) and had reached 53 percent of total homes and businesses in more recent expansion (counties surrounding Bristol served by BVU).[18] In 2010 and 2012 OptiNet increased Internet speeds without raising prices and now provides connections that can be faster than those of many large cable companies.[19]

Chattanooga, Tennessee, offers the fastest citywide fiber network in the country (up to 1 Gbps) for prices that are often eight to ten times cheaper than in neighboring locales served by Comcast and AT&T.[20] As a result, several companies have relocated their operations and jobs to Chattanooga. The city's network was also influential in convincing Amazon to expand its massive distribution center in the city.[21]

Here, for the record, are a few more illustrations of conventional "socialism" in action.

Many cities are involved in hotel construction and ownership—and making profits on these efforts. City-owned hotels can be found in communities as different as Austin, Houston, Chicago, Omaha, Overland Park (Kansas), Sacramento, Marietta (Georgia), Oceanside (California), Myrtle Beach (South Carolina), Denver, Phoenix, and Vancouver, Washington (near Portland, Oregon).

To take just one example from a seemingly conservative area: In May 2008, the Dallas City Council, led by mayor Tom Leppert, voted by an 11–2 margin to pursue construction and operation of a publicly owned convention center hotel.[22] A charter amendment that would have stopped the effort was defeated in a public referendum,[23] and in November 2011 the city celebrated the grand opening of its convention-oriented city-owned $500 million, 1.2-million-square-foot, twenty-three-story, 1,001-room hotel.*[24]

---

* Omni Dallas Hotel. (Many modern hotels are owned by public or private investors but are commonly managed and operated for the investor-owners by hotel chains.)

Cities are also involved in one or another form of hospital ownership, with a recent survey (2010) finding that roughly one-fifth of hospitals in the United States are publicly owned.[25] One of the most interesting is Denver Health. Once an insolvent city agency ($39 million in debt in 1992), Denver Health is now a competitive health care system structured as an innovative blend of democratized ownership and direct municipal accountability.[26] As a quasi-governmental agency it now has relative autonomy over decisions, yet it is subject to the state's open-meetings law (allowing for public involvement) and has a board that is appointed by the city's mayor.[27]

Denver Health operates a highly efficient system that includes eight primary care centers and thirteen school-based clinics. An award-winning leader in its field, and consistently profitable for more than two decades, it employs roughly fifty-six hundred Denver-area residents and treats more than a third of Denver's population, including a full 37 percent of the city's children. About 65 percent of the patients are ethnic minorities, and more than 40 percent are uninsured.[28]

One of the most interesting developments—now to be found in nearly seven hundred local projects—involves green operations that capture methane and turn it into fuel to produce electricity (and make money for the city).[29] Here for instance is how Riverview, Michigan, does it—using a formula to be found in one form or another in many other cities.

Riverview teamed up with Detroit Edison (the local public utility) and a private corporation, Landfill Energy Systems, to develop a landfill gas-to-energy project on its 178-acre landfill. The project captures 4.3 million cubic feet of landfill gas per day and in turn uses it to provide electricity for over five thousand homes—in the process generating more than $150,000 a year in royalty income to help fund needed public services. The carbon emissions impact is also significant: The utility estimates the conversion operation removes the equivalent of the emissions produced by almost fifty thousand passenger vehicles each year.[30]

A variation on the same theme is a wastewater-to-energy facility at California's Point Loma Treatment Plant, which serves a 450-square-mile area near San Diego. The methane produced through the treatment process there generates electricity for process pumps, lights, and computers. Since 2000, San Diego has saved around $3 million annually in energy costs through the operations of the facility.[31]

You didn't know about such things?

Most people don't, and the decaying American press isn't much help. Also, "the other side" doesn't have any interest at all in letting you know what can be done. Indeed, *what is being done all the time* in the way of large-scale democratization throughout the country, even (if you like) "socialism," American-style.

(That is one of the best reasons, by the way, to get serious about digging deeply. There are lots more practical precedents out there to build on if somebody does the work of finding out about—and refining and adapting— things that work for current and future use *and, above all, moving the process beyond partial experiments to ever greater publicly benefitting democratization over time*.)

We've just looked at the tip of the iceberg here. Many interesting things are also happening at the state level.

In California, CalPERS (the state pension fund, now in operation for eighty years) oversees $237 billion in investments. Even factoring in the negative effects of the financial crisis and recession, the market value of its portfolio has risen 52 percent in the past ten years.[32] Not only is CalPERS one of the largest investors in the state of California, it has taken a lead in directing a share of its investments to community-building efforts in the state (rather than handing over all state pension asset investments to Wall Street and other financial advisers and investment firms).[33] (We're not talking small potatoes here: Such state investments totaled $23.5 billion as of September 2012.[34])

In Alabama the public pension system—Retirement Systems of Alabama (RSA)—invests in numerous local Alabama industries, in many cases also helping create worker-owned firms. Investments range from aerospace to tourism development and include, among others, Navistar International—a firm that paid its engine manufacturing plant employees to work in the community rather than lay them off when the recession caused a drop in production.[35]

In Alaska, the Alaska Permanent Fund invests oil revenues on behalf of citizens of the state. Earnings provide annual dividends to state residents as a matter of legal "right." In 2011, a low payout year, each individual state resident received dividends of $1,174 (almost $6,000 for a couple with three children). In 2008 each resident received $2,069 (over $10,000 for a family of five).[36]

Roughly two-fifths of the states (38 percent) also actively provide aid to worker-owned companies.[37] Several directly support ESOPs (and/or worker cooperatives) with initiatives ranging from the linked deposit/investment programs in Indiana to education, technical assistance, and training programs in many states. Two states—Vermont and Ohio—support employee ownership centers that in turn leverage public funds to offer a variety of services to ESOPs and worker cooperatives.

By the way, almost half the states—twenty-three—in "capitalist" America also directly invest public funds in promising start-up companies.[38] In Maryland, to take just one example, the Enterprise Investment Fund regularly invests in start-ups in exchange for equity and a guarantee from the firm that it will continue to operate in the state for at least five years. The fund has performed exceptionally well: Between 1994 and 2011 the state made total returns of $62.5 million on its investments.[39] Successful ventures range from high-tech fluorescence and luminescence companies like Plasmonix to Advanced BioNutrition Corp., a Columbia-based company that extracts fatty acids from algae for use as nutritional ingredients in aquaculture (fish farming) and domestic animal feeds.[40]

You get the idea: If you start getting serious about democratizing the ownership of wealth, there are many, many examples to build upon—and then extend. Most provide profits to cities and states that badly need revenues—and in turn, this obvious boon to taxpayers suggests some potentially interesting political possibilities for the future.

More to chew on in this regard shortly.

I can't resist one last illustration, just for the record, from that rock-ribbed bastion of Adam Smith–spouting conservatism—the great state of Texas.

The Texas Permanent School Fund was established more than 150 years ago with $2 million from the state's general fund. In 1876 roughly half of all the land (and associated mineral rights) in the state still in the public domain was added to the fund, and beginning in 1953 coastal "submerged lands" were also added after being relinquished by the federal government. The state-owned fund currently (2011) owns 626,000 acres of surface land and 12 million acres of mineral land and submerged land.

Every year a distribution is made from the profits of the publicly owned ("socialized") fund to defray education costs for every county in the state—roughly $2 billion in the last two years. The fund also guarantees bonds for local school districts, enabling them to pay significantly lower interest rates on their debt.[41]

If Texas can find ways to do things like this, I suspect your state can explore quite different possibilities as well (with a little help from its friends).

CHAPTER TWELVE

Checkerboard Strategies, and Beyond

In all of these efforts, experiments, and partial experiments the trick is again to move forward, building upon and extending ever more advanced forms as new opportunities arise.

Writing about the various strategies, a line from T. S. Eliot comes to mind: "I gotta use words when I talk to you. But if you understand or if you don't, that's nothing to me and nothing to you . . ."[1]

Except it *is something to me* and I hope something to you. Without words, especially words that clearly distinguish one strategy from another, nothing serious can be communicated. It may be useful, accordingly, at this point to revisit and clarify a few specific terms:

We talked initially about building up various forms of democratized ownership through what I called evolutionary reconstruction. This process (and strategy) involves the pain-driven local, community-based building of new democratized institutional forms, step by step, along with support for them, in ways that slowly but steadily change the nature and culture of how wealth is owned and (to a degree) how political power might be altered over time.

How far the process (or strategy) of evolutionary reconstruction might develop, I suggested, would likely depend on a few factors: the degree to which problems continue to deepen and pain continues to force a choice between innovation and decay; whether or not folks come to terms with the choice this state of affairs presents and explicitly embrace the institution-building concept; and whether those who do embrace it make it part of a new strategic politics over time.

I'm going to introduce the term *checkerboard strategies* at this point because it's time to clarify another distinct strategic idea related to some painful realities emerging in many parts of the country, but also to some important new opportunities.

Anyone who is paying attention knows there are a lot of cities and states in trouble so severe that there is little chance for an early solution (even an evolutionary reconstructive one). In such places the power game is heavily rigged against almost any change at this particular moment. These are cities and states where programs are being cut, assets are being sold off, unions are being attacked, and progressive forces are weak or on the defensive. Where, quite simply, it is likely that the pain and decay will continue for a long, long time.

The state of Arizona, for instance, has eliminated health services for thousands of children, closed down Department of Motor Vehicle locations all over the state, and even sold off (and leased back) the state capitol building—trying subsequently to buy it back from the private owners at a large loss.[2] Florida has hiked public university tuition by 32 percent, cut $1 billion from state worker pensions, and eliminated thousands of state jobs—all the while preserving high-end corporate tax cuts and incentives that will cost the state an estimated $2.5 billion over three years.[3] Similarly, the state of California has enacted cuts to public education, higher education, public safety, and many other programs.[4] State parks have seen a 20 percent reduction in funding, and state officials have begun privatizing operations in the parks.[5] Three California cities have been forced to declare bankruptcy—including Stockton, the largest US city ever to go bankrupt—and more are expected.[6] San Diego and San Jose have voted to cut retirement benefits for public workers.[7]

No choice at this point except simply to face realities of this kind where they occur and not give up the ship. The difficult challenge we face requires a clear understanding that the overall fight is going to be long and hard, and much of it in many cities and states will be largely defensive. Where situations are dire, the work ahead will be about holding the line as best we can, even as new explorations in a new direction are tried—again as best we can.

On the other hand—and this is the important point—if hold-the-line efforts are all we see, there can clearly be no way forward. *And often that is, in fact, all some people see. They are so focused on what cannot be done, they ignore other possibilities.*

This is where a checkerboard strategy comes in. The term is simply meant to suggest that the game of politics out there is not monolithic. It actually involves lots of different squares on the board—some of which are blocked, but others of which (as we saw in the last few chapters) may be open for doing something interesting. *It also suggests there may be a longer-term strategic option on the board.*

We have, in fact, reviewed some very, very interesting things going on in some cities and states occupying different squares on the board. Like, for instance, city support of democratized ownership, land development, power generation, and Internet delivery; new energy strategies; even publicly owned hotels and health care facilities. Also some things that could be turned to advantage and expanded over time—if there were a will to do so (and a lot of hard work)—like methane-capture efforts, city investing strategies, state venture capital investing, pension and retirement fund investing, land and mineral revenues for public benefit, and so on. Moreover, in the next sections we are going to review several other major possibilities, particularly at the state level. Enough said.

The second reason for nudging a new term like *checkerboard* into the game is strategic. Here the argument to think about is this: There is every reason to build up and steadily, step by step, *expand* the squares on the checkerboard that are currently open to expansion—first, to do what needs doing, but also to demonstrate to the other squares what makes sense as they flounder and fail on their current path over time.

And also, slowly, to surround the others with positive examples of an alternative way forward as they falter.

I won't bore you by going on, again, on how all this depends, too, on the degree to which the emerging historical context drives people to think about new things as the pain level increases.

I do want to suggest, however, that monolithic thinking about *what cannot be done* needs to be questioned.

As it *is* questioned, it's important to have a compass—a possible way forward—and also to have a way to talk about that way forward that's not clouded in notions of the past. That's why it's helpful to break down (and name) quite distinct avenues of long-term evolving strategy—so far, evolutionary reconstruction and checkerboard strategies.

You might even begin to think about these as part of a long-term pincer movement to move in on the opposition from more than one direction.

We'll obviously need to grapple with some traditional strategic notions, and terms, as well; we haven't yet even begun to discuss the deeper possibilities of politics and movement building.

By the way, and not to be too crude about it: There is a difference between dismissive pessimism and careful judgments about the difficulties we face. Also, simply to note the obvious: All of us have a vested interest in pessimism. We don't have to do anything if nothing can be done!

So—and partly to suggest that you (yes, *you*) might also get into the game to explore, invent, and refine further strategic possibilities—here's something interesting to consider that is beginning to emerge in certain cities.

By now it is obvious that the fiscal crisis increasingly pits local taxpayers against two specific groups in any city: local public employees (and retirees), on the one hand, and low-income groups needing services, on the other. As the economy continues to decay and tax revenues decline, something has got to give.

The reaction of most unions, on the one hand, and activist groups concerned about the poor on the other, has so far been almost entirely defensive: "Don't cut wages, don't cut benefits, don't cut retirement programs—and don't cut housing, welfare, and social programs."

Defensively attempting to hold the line to the degree possible is obviously necessary. It also obviously keeps the initiative firmly in the hands of those making ever-increasing cutback demands and is ultimately a very weak posture. Nor does it add anything positive to the mix.

Some have also urged (even enacted) higher taxation on corporations and the wealthy in a number of scattered states on the checkerboard—including California, Connecticut, Delaware, Hawaii, Illinois, Iowa, Maryland, Montana, New Jersey, New York, North Carolina, and Oregon.[8] Great whenever possible, but tax-raising strategies have also often been self-limiting, and they tend to help groups trying to bolster the status quo drum up taxpayer anger to support their side.

On the other hand, in certain checkerboard cities another strategic option appears to be opening up—and the question is how it might be tested, refined, and then put forward as a serious approach in these and other cities, or ultimately in a number of squares on the board (maybe even, ultimately, in an encircling move).

As noted, traditional progressive strategy has always tried to focus taxation at the very top to the extent feasible—as a matter both of equity and of good politics (keeping the middle class out of the line of fire and out of the political embrace of the opposition). Let's keep this in the package. Nothing wrong with it except that it is obviously inadequate—as the ongoing budget, program, salary, and benefit cutting so painfully reminds us.

The longer-term strategic way out of the box, logically, is clearly an approach that rebuilds the local economy (and the local tax base) in ways that are efficient, effective, stable, redistributive, and ongoing. It also should involve capturing greater revenues and profits for municipal use. Which means a different form of development—and a specific plan for how to do it over time so as to secure funds for public-sector employees, teachers, and retirees, and also to secure services for those who need them.

There is a potentially interesting alliance here that can even include local small businesses interested in getting the economy going, and some taxpayers interested in finding new resources to reduce the pressure they face. Not to mention some interesting groups that might act together—including public-sector and teachers' unions, along with activists who have fought (and rightly continue to fight) the good fight in many areas along traditional lines.

By now the specific ingredients to add to the mix in such a strategy should be self-evident (and also demonstrably practical). They include:

- The use of city, school, hospital, university, and other purchasing power to help stabilize jobs in a manner that both is anchored and democratized in terms of ownership and also benefits (and improves the economy of) low-income neighborhoods and local small- and medium-sized businesses. Precedents include the kinds of things now happening or being explored in Cleveland, Pittsburgh, Atlanta, Washington DC, and many other cities—and especially the use of public and quasi-public (nonprofit hospital and university) contracts to add leverage to the effort.
- The use of public and quasi-public land trusts (both for housing and also for commercial development) to capture development profits for community use and to prevent gentrification—as is happening in Irvine, California; Sarasota County, Florida; North Camden, New Jersey; Austin, Texas; Las Vegas, Nevada; Highland Park, Illinois; Delray Beach, Florida; Chaska, Minnesota; Chicago, Illinois; Flagstaff, Arizona; and many other places.[9]
- An all-out attack on the absurdly wasteful and costly giveaways that corporations often extract from local governments. As we've seen, such giveaways are commonly used to entice corporations to move into the economy, but all too often the firms quickly leave or threaten to leave unless new or renewed subsidies are provided.
- The use of community benefit strategies—and community organizing, backed also by labor unions—not just to achieve

traditional development but also, where possible, to move new efforts forward that democratize the economy (thereby also helping stabilize the tax base that supports public services).

- The exploration of further ways for cities to make money and thereby offset costs and taxpayer burdens. Examples of this approach can be seen in many land ownership efforts; the nearly seven hundred projects in cities and counties that capture methane from garbage, turning it into jobs, revenue, and electricity; public ownership; and other new ownership ideas and practices now emerging in many cities.

In some locales, additional strategies can be added to the overall effort, including:

- Taking over and municipalizing electric utilities to improve services, reduce costs (in line with the experience of the roughly two thousand existing public utilities), and secure added revenues for the city. Check out the recent hard-fought struggle to municipalize the electricity in Boulder, Colorado, and successful efforts over the last decade in a number of cities.*
- Improving the local economy through the development of local municipalized Internet and cable services.
- Expanding "participatory lease" arrangements that make money for the city through ownership of other forms of property and in ways other than taxation. (In such efforts developers pay the public landlord a yearly agreed rent and an additional amount pegged to project performance, based on criteria like private profits or gross income.)

These and other elements of a coherent plan simply draw on existing, practical options now emerging in various squares on the board. What has yet to be done is for someone—and some city—to put together the pieces and put forward a fully developed *strategic plan*.

---

* Over the past decade sixteen new public utilities have been formed, in cities as diverse as Hermiston, Oregon; Jefferson County, Washington; Lubbock, Texas; and Winter Park, Florida. See: American Public Power Association, *Straight Answers to False Charges Against Public Power* (Washington, DC: APPA, 2012), p. 34, accessed November 14, 2012, www.publicpower.org/files/PDFs/StraightAnswersMore.pdf.

Such a plan would (1) suggest a coherent economic way forward that (2) also increases the tax base, thereby (3) offsetting some taxpayer pressures (and weakening and dividing the opposing coalition), and at the same time (4) permitting the organization of an effective political alliance involving public service workers, teachers, hospital workers, and janitors and other blue-collar workers—and community groups and local activists—plus small-business groups that benefit from a revival of local economic health.

Obviously, not easy to do. And, at least right away, not likely for many squares on the board.

On the other hand, times are getting worse (and are probably likely to get still worse) and at some point one or another square will light up. As always, it will take some specific person who decides that he or she, personally, will grab the reins and set the wheels in motion to flip the switch (possibly even you, dear reader . . .).

Part IV

HOT SPOTS: BANKING, HEALTH CARE, AND CRISIS TRANSFORMATIONS

CHAPTER THIRTEEN

Banking

A bit ago I suggested that there might be another "distinction"—another strategic possibility different from evolutionary reconstruction or checkerboard strategies, a strategic possibility that might also lead in the direction of the democratization of wealth and even, one day, perhaps systemic change.

We'll come back to give it a name in due course. First, though, it will be useful to stand way back from neighborhoods, cities, and even unusual state possibilities and take a look at the large-order logic of some things happening at the level of the national system.

You may have noticed that the big banks almost collapsed the entire US economy from 2008 to 2010. Indeed, during the heart of the crisis the possibility of total breakdown was very real—*all too real*. Current estimates are that at least $2.6 trillion of GDP was lost, $19.2 trillion in household net worth disappeared, and nearly nine million jobs were lost from the time the Great Recession began in December 2007 to its lowest point in mid-2009.[1]

Not a small problem.

Indeed, as George W. Bush famously put it at one point in the crisis: "This sucker could go down."[2] (And might well have, had nothing been done.)

The thing is this: Most economists—left, right, and center—who know anything about this kind of thing are united in the judgment that more crises are going to happen as time goes on (and probably again and again).

Nouriel Roubini, who had famously predicted the recent crisis, put it this way: "Nothing has changed fundamentally . . . chances are we're going to have a couple of financial crises over the next ten years."[3] Former IMF chief economist and MIT professor Simon Johnson explained: The only question is whether a new crisis might come in "three years or seven years."[4] And more than one Wall Street insider (to say the least!) agrees with the blunt conclusion of Mark Mobius, chairman of Templeton Asset Management: "There is definitely going to be another financial crisis around the corner because we haven't solved any of the things that caused the previous crisis."[5]

Nor are such people alone. Two well-known and highly respected Harvard scholars, Kenneth Rogoff and Carmen Reinhart, published a huge book in 2009 looking back on the regular, repeated occurrence of major financial crises over the years. Their tongue-in-cheek title *This Time Is Different* was an elbow nudge to all those who in the past had predicted things would be fine and have been proven wrong again and again.[6]

In fact, matters are even worse. It's no longer just the United States that doesn't seem able to manage these things; Europe is now facing similar dangers, even worse, perhaps—and is equally capable of slipping into crisis and slamming the US economy, hard. Very hard.

By the way, notice that most of these judgments were offered *despite the fact* that in 2010 the United States enacted the Dodd-Frank Wall Street Reform and Consumer Protection Act, aimed at regulating the financial system so that another collapse would not happen.

The fact is, no one who knows anything about the way Washington works believes you can really regulate the truly big financial institutions. Indeed, since the crisis—*and since enactment of the new legislation*—many of the giant financial corporations have increased, not decreased, in size. Prior to the crisis (in 2006) the top six banks had assets equal to roughly 55 percent of the US GDP.[7] As of June 2012 the figure was up to roughly 60.1 percent.[8]

Big banks like JPMorgan Chase, Bank of America, Wells Fargo, Citigroup, and Goldman Sachs are simply too powerful to be systematically regulated. For one thing, the amount of money they spend on lobbying and politics is stupendous. The year Dodd-Frank was passed, the FIRE sector (finance, insurance, and real estate) spent more than $475 million on lobbying. This was followed up the next year, 2011, with just under $480 million.[9] That's almost a billion dollars' worth of high-priced lobbyists who do nothing but try to write loopholes into the law—and this is for only two years.

Senator Dick Durbin is blunt: "The banks . . . are still the most powerful lobby on Capitol Hill. And they frankly own the place."[10]

(Also, by the way, often the regulators are people making modest government salaries facing lawyers making more than a million a year—and also implicitly suggesting to them, very gently of course, that with all their government experience they might well think about moving over to the banking side of the table at some point: "Not trying to influence you by offering the possibility someday of a big job, of course; just saying . . .")

To repeat: Very, very few people who know anything about the way Washington really works, in truth, believe you can effectively regulate the really big banks.

So the question is this: What happens when the next big crisis explodes and we again have to face to the impossibility of regulating banks that are too big to fail—banks that, when they topple, can bring down the entire system?

The current nostrum—partially provided for in the Dodd-Frank legislation under certain circumstances, and promoted generally by a wide array of commentators and politicians—is: "Well, let's break them up into smaller banks!"*

Yet we only have to look as far as the history of banking, on the one hand, and of antitrust law, on the other, to see that even when break-them-up efforts occur (which is rarely), the big fish tend to find a way to eat the little fish, and in due course we're back where we started.

Take a look, for instance, at how fast bank concentration developed in recent years. The average size of US banks increased fivefold (measured in inflation-adjusted total assets) between 1984 and 2008, and the number of banks, correspondingly, dropped by more than 50 percent—from over fourteen thousand to barely seven thousand.[11] In 1984, for instance, forty-two different banks held 25 percent of all US deposits.[12] By 2012 one-tenth that number—the top four (Bank of America, JPMorgan Chase, Wells Fargo, and Citigroup)—held far more: 36.6 percent of all US deposits.[13]

The power of big fish in general to regroup is hardly restricted to banking. When Standard Oil was broken up in 1911, the immediate effect was to replace a national monopoly with a number of regional monopolies controlled by many of the same Wall Street interests.[14] Ultimately, the regional monopolies

---

* One element of Dodd-Frank—resolution authority—technically allows the government to "wind down" failing banks without resorting to 2008-style bailouts. However, most experts are highly skeptical that this could work with large, international megabanks. During "the debate over the Dodd-Frank financial regulation . . . ," Simon Johnson observes, "Senator Ted Kaufman, Democrat of Delaware, emphasized repeatedly on the Senate floor that the proposed 'resolution authority' (the power to shut banks) was an illusion . . . At the time, Senator Kaufman's objections were dismissed by 'experts' from both the official sector and the private sector. Now these same people (or their close colleagues) are falling over themselves to argue that resolution cannot work for the country's giant bank holding companies." See: Simon Johnson, "The Myth of Resolution Authority," *New York Times*, March 31, 2011, accessed November 14, 2012, http://economix.blogs.nytimes.com/2011/03/31/the-myth-of-resolution-authority.

regrouped: In 1999 Exxon (formerly Standard Oil Company of New Jersey) and Mobil (formerly Standard Oil Company of New York) reconvened in one of the largest mergers in US history.[15] In 1961 Kyso (formerly Standard Oil of Kentucky) was purchased by Chevron (formerly Standard Oil of California);[16] and in the 1960s and 1970s Sohio (formerly Standard Oil of Ohio) was bought by British Petroleum (BP), which then, in 1998, merged with Amoco (formerly Standard Oil of Indiana).[17]

The tale of AT&T is similar. As the result of an antitrust settlement with the government, on January 1, 1984, AT&T spun off its local operations so as to create seven so-called Baby Bells. But the Baby Bells quickly began to merge and regroup. By 2006 four of the Baby Bells were reunited with their parent company AT&T, and two others (Bell Atlantic and NYNEX) merged to form Verizon.[18]

So the hope that you can make a banking breakup stick (even if it were to be achieved) flies in the face of some pretty daunting experience. Also, note carefully a major political fact: The time when traditional reformers had enough power to make tough banking regulation really work was the time when progressive politics still had the powerful institutional backing of strong labor unions.

But as we have seen, that time is long ago and far away.

Let me offer just one more reminder about political power and a further sign of the times (and of the changes within the progressive movement and the Democratic Party). It was President Bill Clinton, not simply the conservative Republicans, who led the fight to deregulate the banks. Passage of the Gramm-Leach-Bliley Act of 1999 repealed the New Deal–era Glass-Steagall legislation that had prohibited commercial banks from engaging in speculative investing activities (the very thing that would nearly bring us down almost a decade later). Additionally, the Commodity Futures Modernization Act, also signed by Clinton in 2000, famously exempted derivatives from federal regulation. This is to say nothing, of course, of ongoing moves to weaken the new Dodd-Frank regulatory legislation.[19]

Interestingly, the conservative founders of the Chicago School of Economics understood better than most liberals and progressives the general logic at work in situations involving really large and powerful corporate institutions. Even as the latter kept urging regulation or breakups, leading economists like Henry C. Simons cut to the heart of the matter.

For one thing, Simons and his colleagues were clear about the economics involved. "Few of our gigantic corporations," he wrote, "can be defended on the ground that their present size is necessary to reasonably full exploitation of production economies."[20]

For another, they knew that the big fish could easily manipulate the regulators. Chicago School conservative and Nobel laureate George Stigler, for instance, demonstrated how regulation was commonly "designed and operated primarily for" the benefit of the industries involved. Numerous conservatives, including Simons, concluded that antitrust break-them-up efforts could also easily be managed by large corporate players—a view conservative Nobel laureate Milton Friedman also came to a few years later.[21]

Simons—Friedman's revered teacher, and one of the most important leaders—did not shrink from the obvious conclusion: "Every industry should be either effectively competitive or socialized."[22] If other remedies were unworkable, "the state should face the necessity of actually taking over, owning, and managing directly" all "industries in which it is impossible to maintain effectively competitive conditions."[23]

At the height of the Depression, eight major Chicago School conservative economists (including Simons and Frank H. Knight) also put forward a "Chicago Plan" that called for outright public ownership of Federal Reserve Banks, the nationalization of money creation, and the transformation of private banks into highly restricted savings-and-loan-like institutions.[24]

The thing about a powerful logic of the kind the old conservatives so clearly understood is that it has a way of simply not going away. Quite likely we shall go through a number of rounds of crisis, partial crisis, attempts at regulation—maybe even some break-up-the-big-banks efforts.

Almost certainly, however, the underlying institutional power, and the logic it generates, will continue, with three all-but-certain results.

First, at some point we will really "get" that the Chicago argument is correct. Like it or not, regulation doesn't work in these situations. The big guys will capture the regulators.

Second, at some point we will really "get" that breaking up the banks also doesn't work. The slightly slimmed-down big guys will fatten up quickly by eating up the little fish, and we will be back at square one.

Which—third—logically means that if we want to stop the crises, at some point there is only one thing left: Take them over; turn them into public utilities.

Have I forgotten to mention that big banks that rip off the public and crash the economy and then pay themselves big bonuses tend to make people angry? Let's drop the logic for a moment: It's a simple fact that anger at the big banks is already huge.

That anger intensified when several banks nearly tumbled in 2008 after engaging in risky behavior at the height of deregulation. But it grew hotter than ever when taxpayers, many of whom were facing joblessness or foreclosure, were asked to bail them out to the tune of up to $700 billion through the Troubled Asset Relief Program, better known as TARP. (And hotter still when they began rewarding themselves with big bonuses.) In his 2010 State of the Union address President Obama acknowledged that the bank bailout was "about as popular as a root canal," and at a meeting with CEOs of thirteen of the nation's biggest banks, he cut off complaints over efforts to curb bonuses and salaries with the reminder that "my administration is the only thing between you and the pitchforks."[25]

Another insider, Douglas Elliott of the Brookings Institution, coolly observed: "Truthfully, you would find considerable support for hanging a number of bankers . . . to satisfy the public's anger." And the former business and economics editor of *The Atlantic* thought Congress should be able to "cheerfully defenestrate" investment bankers. (*Merriam-Webster Dictionary*: "defenestrate: to throw out the window.")[26]

Which, suggests, again, that the convergence of bank-created crises and public pain and anger—together with the truth of the Chicago School logic—points to only one logical outcome: like it or not, some form of public takeover.

If this sounds unlikely to you at the moment, consider the following:

- There is already lots and lots of public and cooperative banking going on in these United States. Unknown to most Americans, there have been a large number of small- and medium-sized public banking institutions operating for a long, long time. They have financed small businesses, renewable energy, co-ops, housing, infrastructure, and other specifically targeted areas. As we have seen, there are also just under seventy-two hundred community-based credit unions with more than $1 trillion in total assets.[27] Further precedents for public banking range from Small Business Administration loans to the US Export-Import Bank to the activities of the US-dominated World Bank. In fact, the federal government already operates around 140 banks and quasi-banks that provide loans and loan guarantees for an extraordinary range of domestic and international economic activities.[28]

- We've long been told, and often believed, that the free-market operation of big banks benefits us all. But a number of people increasingly recognize that the emperor has no clothes—and they are beginning to state the obvious, even though the press doesn't often cover it.[29] Here's the chief economist of Citicorp no less (just before he got his job): "Is the reality . . . that large private firms make enormous private profits when the going is good and get bailed out and taken into temporary public ownership when the going gets bad, with the tax payer taking the risk and the losses? If so, then why not keep these activities in permanent public ownership?"[30]

So, for those of you who understand that we face a systemic crisis, not simply a political crisis, there are two things to do. The first should be self-evident from the above: Begin to be as up-front in your discussion, advocacy, and analysis as the old conservatives and the chief economist of Citicorp. It's time simply to tell the truth. The really big banks need to be taken over before they really crash the system—the sooner the better.

The second would be to familiarize yourself with—and build up some public understanding of—how public banking works. For starters, you might look at the Bank of North Dakota, a state-owned public bank operating successfully, and with broad political backing, for nearly one hundred years. In the past ten years alone it has contributed more than $300 million in revenues to the state (approximately $1,200 for every North Dakota family), all the while strengthening and supporting the local private banking sector.[31]

There are some things to learn, too, from related initiatives, including One PacificCoast Bank, a B Corp that serves low-income communities; the Bremer Bank, a Minnesota, North Dakota, and Wisconsin–based bank that is co-owned by its employees and a nonprofit charitable trust and specializes in helping local farms and businesses; and Southern Bancorp, a for-profit bank with unusual restrictions on ownership that serves low-income communities in Arkansas and Mississippi.[32]

And if you want to do something now, just roll up your sleeves and see what you can do in your own state both to make something happen, building on these and other developing precedents, and to help educate the public about new possibilities. You won't be alone: At this writing some twenty different states have had legislation introduced to establish state-owned banks like that of North Dakota.[33]

Some cities are also showing the way, as in San Francisco, where local legislators have proposed a city bank, and Portland, Oregon, where the mayor has embarked on a project to transfer considerable amounts of city funds into local banks and credit unions.[34] Kansas City also unanimously approved responsible banking legislation that directs the city manager to do business only with banks that "are responsible to [the] community's needs and do not engage in predatory lending."[35]

Similar legislation was approved by the Pittsburgh City Council in April 2012 (after having previously been passed and vetoed by the mayor in December 2011), and activists in New York City and Hennepin County, Minnesota, have also proposed such legislation.[36] Philadelphia and Cleveland have had versions of the law in place since the 1990s.[37]

And yes, it may take longer than we might hope for the point to sink in nationally, but the buildup of experience, state by state, community by community—as in the prehistory of the New Deal—is also ultimately likely to help put a truly refined model in place nationally.

Especially as the pain of the emerging era continues to deepen.

CHAPTER FOURTEEN

Health Care

A reminder: To get serious about systemic change is to get serious about decades, not weeks or months, of work. It also requires getting serious about large-order processes, not simply elections and policies.

It's not that short time frames and everyday politics are unimportant. The point is first to get a handle on deeper and longer and larger dynamic processes (and *possible* dynamic processes) so that we can come back to elections, policies, and short-term results with new perspective and hopefully a more powerful strategy.

All of which is important to bear in mind as we consider an issue potentially even more challenging than banking: health care.

As almost everyone knows, cost is the epicenter of the health care debate. The American health care system is one of the most expensive in the world. The United States spends just under 18 percent of its entire economy on health care each year, and the number could easily reach 20 percent.[1]

Many other advanced societies spend roughly half as much, as a percent of their economies, as we do to cover their health care needs. South Korea spends 7.1 percent; Ireland, Iceland, Italy, Norway, and Japan spend 9.2 percent, 9.3 percent, 9.3 percent, 9.4 percent, and 9.5 percent, respectively; the United Kingdom, Sweden, and Spain spend 9.6 percent; Canada and Switzerland spend 11.4 percent; and France and Germany spend 11.6 percent. The United States' closest advanced competitor in costs is the Netherlands at just 12 percent—still a third less than our 18 percent of GDP.[2]

You would expect that all of our spending would yield spectacular results. But, as is less well known, the United States has some of the worst health outcome statistics in the advanced world.

Here are just a few of many, many examples:[3]

- The United States ranks thirty-first out of thirty-four OECD countries in infant mortality at 6.1 deaths per thousand live births—ahead of only Chile, Turkey, and Mexico, and far behind the 2.2 and 2.3 rates found in Iceland, Finland, and Japan.[4]

- The US ranks twenty-seventh out of thirty-four OECD countries in life expectancy at 78.7 years—ahead of only Poland, Estonia, Mexico, Slovakia, Turkey, the Czech Republic, and Hungary, and far behind the 83-year life expectancy of Japan and the approximately 82 years of Switzerland, Spain, and Italy.[5]
- The US ranks dead last out of thirty-four OECD countries in connection with obesity, with around one-third of the population obese, twice the OECD average.[6]

The basic reason both for the extraordinary waste and our low outcome record is that, unlike most other countries, the United States has a health care system that is dominated by insurance companies, hospital chains (increasingly concentrated and near monopolies in many markets), big drug companies, and, to a much lesser extent, private fee-for-service doctors. (The doctors have fallen a bit lower on the food chain in recent years as the insurance companies and hospitals have become more and more powerful.)

Everybody gets a profit when somebody gets sick in this system.

The obvious answer is something that functions pretty much like Medicare, the popular and effective government-run program that currently insures people sixty-five and older as well as some with disabilities and certain medical conditions. The concept isn't very complicated. A national single-payer system—"Medicare for all"—would, like Medicare, have just one insurer—the government, not a company that is out to make a profit.

The job of a private insurance company, unlike such a public insurer, is to add a profit margin to everything it can, and to avoid paying bills to the degree possible. So, first, add approximately 20 percent for administrative expenses, marketing, and profits (the latter ran around 8.65 percent in 2011) onto everything.[7] Second, try to keep really sick people off the rolls, or move them onto some other insurance company's rolls. This all also involves additional expense: lots of paperwork, lots of paper pushers, and lots of people trying to make absolutely certain that when you get sick, you (or your doctor or lab or other provider) isn't trying to squeeze a few extra dollars out of the company.

In a single-payer system like Medicare, you can knock off a good part of the 20 percent. There's no point in trying to get you onto some other company's rolls, either, as there is no other company. And it's agreed at the outset that the health care costs are going to be paid. Accordingly, there's no need for a huge army of clerks: Most single-payer systems are far, far less costly to administer. On average the United States currently spends roughly three times as much nationwide on administration costs per person as does Canada—a figure that, if it didn't include public along with private expenditures, would likely be even higher.[8] And Medicare typically registers administrative costs around 80 to 90 percent lower than private "Medicare Advantage" plans.[9]

So, if you want to save a trillion dollars or so, minimally, a single-payer system is the way to go.[10]

I urge you to read that sentence again. *A trillion dollars a year is the equivalent of roughly a third of all federal expenditures and half of all federal revenues.*[11]

If we could find a way both to cut these costs and to pick up some of the benefits for better use, lots of schools, bridges, roads, and jobs might be paid for—even some tax breaks, perhaps.

But of course, we can't pick up these benefits. At least not for the moment.

The Obama administration bowed to what it judged to be politically the only option available and passed legislation (referred to now by both critics and supporters as Obamacare) that kept the insurance companies and the drug companies in the game in exchange for their agreement not to fight the legislation. What *they* got was a promise of tens of millions of new customers who had to join the system, or face penalties.*[12]

So the system continues. More people are now covered, in the early phases of Obamacare, and more people will continue to be covered as the plan rolls out. But the costs keep rising, and the insurance company bureaucracies keep squeezing, and the system as a whole keeps falling farther and farther behind what everyone knows can be done better and cheaper by looking at the experience of other countries.

On the other hand, consider a new law of economics once stated by Herbert Stein, chairman of the Council of Economic Advisers under Presidents Nixon and Ford: "If something cannot go on forever, it will stop."[13]

Which probably offers a pretty accurate forecast for American-style health care. Right now we are beginning to enter what is all but certain to be a period of major reconsideration of the whole mess.

---

* The insurance companies welched on the deal when Congress changed some of the terms, making the penalties insufficiently powerful, the companies thought, to get them all the new customers they wanted. Adam Smith again be damned! As Lawrence Jacobs and Theda Skocpol write: "*Too little* government was what moved insurers into open revolt." See: Lawrence R. Jacobs and Theda Skocpol, *Health Care Reform and American Politics: What Everyone Needs to Know* (New York, NY: Oxford University Press, 2010), p. 73.

The signs are many. As costs keep rising, things are clearly going to get a lot worse for a lot of people. The insurance companies are already scrambling to protect profits. Some are pressing state regulators to permit so-called stop-loss insurance plans that get around consumer protection requirements. Others are seeking to avoid regulations requiring that 80 to 85 percent of premiums go to patient care. Premium raising and high-deductible plans that shift more of costs to families are also ongoing priorities.[14]

Absent real reform—and given the growing fiscal crisis—the government will also clearly be driving hard to reduce costs. The Republicans have made it clear they will do their best to cut back Obamacare and "reform" Medicare and its counterpart for low-income Americans, Medicaid. And the Obama administration and some Democrats in Congress have also signaled their willingness to reduce funding for Medicare as part of debt and deficit negotiations.[15] Many fear that so-called reform will mean less coverage for those who depend on these programs.

In addition, many businesses are trying to make as many people as possible into part-time workers so they don't have to pay for insurance—which, in turn, means that more people who are sick, injured, or in pain are simply not getting treated.

There are also a lot of people out there (at least thirty million) who aren't even in the system—and probably won't be, at least not for a long time. Some will be in great pain, some will be dying. Some will be tossed out of hospitals onto the streets or made into what insiders call "hot potato" patients whom hospitals try to dump in one another's laps.[16]

We may well witness more tales of pain and tragedy like that of Carol Ann Reyes. In 2006 surveillance cameras outside the Union Rescue Mission in Los Angeles recorded a taxi dropping the sixty-three-year-old Reyes off, leaving her to wander around in a confused state in her hospital gown before a shelter volunteer came to her aid.[17] There is also the more recent case of James Verone, who at age fifty-nine attempted to rob a bank in Gastonia, North Carolina—but only, he made clear, for one dollar. The reason: Unemployed and in pain, he saw no way other than going to jail to get health care for a growth on his chest, difficulties with his feet, and back problems.[18]

Perhaps the most important reason our broken health care system is not likely to continue indefinitely is that American corporations are competing with companies abroad that are not paying health care costs for their employees. Why? Because they operate in countries with public health care systems. Some of these companies are already chafing at the bit. "If the global economy were a 100-yard dash," a March 2009 Business Roundtable report declared, "the US would start 23 yards behind its closest competitors because of health care that costs too much and delivers too little."[19] As the pressures increase, the demand for change is likely to increase.

Indeed, as far back as the early 1990s the united front of businesses ideologically opposed to universal health care did, in fact, begin to crack under the pressure of rising costs. Though little noticed at the time, a number of leading companies—including American Airlines, Safeway, Westinghouse, Archer Daniels Midland, and the Big Three automakers—provided support for Clinton's attempt to establish universal health care, even financing limited advertising campaigns and writing letters to Congress.[20]

Finally, and not surprisingly, public distrust of the insurance companies is high—indeed, very high. A 2011 Harris poll found just 8 percent of Americans believed that health insurance companies were "generally honest and trustworthy." Pharmaceutical companies likewise scored a mere 8 percent.[21]

All in all, the prospect is for more costs and more pain, for a substantial period.

But we can also expect a buildup of anger and a demand for a real answer, somehow, some way.

As the costs increase and the burdens intensify, most likely the breakthroughs will come first at the state level. And, indeed, at this writing more than fifteen states have seen legislation introduced pointing toward some form of a single-payer public system.[22]

In 2011 Vermont approved legislation that would ultimately allow state residents to move into a publicly funded insurance pool. Universal coverage would begin in 2017 if a federal waiver is approved (and possibly as early as 2014).[23] In California a universal "Medicare for all" bill failed in the Senate by just two votes in 2012. (Similar legislation was, in fact, approved by both the House and the Senate but was vetoed by then-governor Schwarzenegger in 2006 and 2008.)[24] Since 2009 Connecticut has been struggling politically over legislation to build a system of affordable health care for virtually all residents—one that in the future is reasonably likely to include a nonprofit public insurance program.[25] And of course Massachusetts was an early innovator, passing a health reform law in 2006 that focused on achieving near-universal health care coverage (however, it did little to control costs).[26]

So again, state by state by state—checkerboard fashion—we are likely to go on, until (maybe) we experience a jolt and jump at the right moment that takes the scattered pain-driven change to the national level (again, as in the prehistory of the New Deal).

Maybe, too, we'll have the help of some of the corporations in competition with others worldwide.

Time, too, to remember the Chicago School argument about trying to regulate big corporations. Yes, of course, in theory you might try to regulate the big insurance players in the current system the way, say, the Swiss do (whereby private insurance companies are required to offer, and cannot profit from, basic health insurance plans to all residents regardless of age or preexisting conditions—but can make money from supplemental plans).[27] The trouble is that in practice, and given the historic weakness of our reform capacities compared with Switzerland and many other nations, American companies can play the regulatory game better than you can—which takes us back by another route, Chicago-style, to having to turn them into a publicly owned enterprise if you want to solve the problem.

Also, have I forgotten to mention this? It is not only big corporations (not to mention struggling workers and the jobless) whose interests are now at odds with the health insurance companies. The hospitals, the drug companies, the medical equipment manufacturers, the doctors, and many others have needs and priorities that may not dovetail with those of the insurers. If (when) the crunch deepens the pain, we are also likely to see defections from some of these groups.

Over the coming decade (or decades), not the coming election—over time, as the pain develops, and the anger increases—we shall see.[28]

By the way, in effect a single-payer system like Medicare is one that involves another form of democratized ownership. The government in essence runs a public insurance company—in fact, a de facto public utility.

Most of the folks concerned with health care—like most folks working with co-ops, worker-owned companies, municipal businesses, state-owned investments, and the like—rarely look over the top of their own silo to see what's going on elsewhere. *They* may be "democratizing the economy," but they are by no means clear that, or how, anyone else is.

On the other hand, if you think democratizing the economy in general (piece by piece) may be important as a matter of a comprehensive overall political-economic strategy, but you haven't been thinking about health care, you might start to do so as well; 20 percent of the GDP is a very hefty chunk of any economic system.

CHAPTER FIFTEEN

Beyond Countervailing Power

A while ago I promised I'd come back at you with a way to talk about the specific kind of political-economic processes we've been reviewing in the last two chapters. It's hard to find an elegant word or phrase for what is happening and appears likely to continue to happen in connection with banking and health care by virtue of internal dynamic changes going on in each sector (plus potential political action at key points in time). For the moment, though, let's acknowledge that the banking crisis is big, crashing, and explosive and that the developing health care crisis is excruciating and inexorable. And then let's talk about where we can go from here with what we'll call both these processes: "crisis transformations." As we've seen, there are a number of possibilities that appear likely to arise out of the current havoc—*if* we develop a strategy aimed at both solving problems in the most effective way and also democratizing the economy, step by step over time.

This is also probably a good time to mention something about the theory of power that many once embraced (and is dying), and the emergence of what is beginning to look like a new theory of power—potentially an important one, to the degree we can move it forward over time.

In the old days, when things were still working (sort of) for the old progressive theory, many folks implicitly and explicitly operated on a quite clearly defined set of assumptions about the relationships among institutions, politics, and power. The commonly held view was that it was possible to balance the power of institutions (like mega corporations) by exerting political or other pressure on them.

This mode of thought was best explained (at least for our purposes) during the postwar-boom era by the great liberal economist, the late John Kenneth Galbraith. In what he called the theory of "countervailing power," Galbraith suggested that the advantages enjoyed by corporations in the free market were offset by other institutional powers. And, he noted, labor unions were by far the most important "countervailing" power functioning to balance the power of the corporation.

Beginning in 1952 at the height of union power, and continuing thereafter (for a while . . .), Galbraith held that "the operation of countervailing power is to be seen with the greatest clarity in the labor market where it is also most fully developed" (1956).[1] "Union power is the natural answer to the power of the corporation" (1979).[2] "The symmetry between the sources of power and the countervailing response has a certain classic clarity in the field of labor relations. But it is also evident in many other areas" (1983).[3]

The power of labor is important not only on the shop floor, of course, but also in politics. And in any event, the famous liberal economist lost faith in his theory as time went on, and as labor's capacity dwindled. One problem was that once blue-collar workers made it into the middle class, he held, they turned their back on others. In 1980 he wrote: "I would no longer argue as to the inevitability of countervailing power."[4]

And as the big trends continued to move in the wrong direction, by 1984 his belief in his theory of progressive power was all but exhausted:

> It was the unarticulated assumption of American liberals . . . that the newly affluent—blue-collar workers . . . [would] have political attitudes different from those of the older rich . . . The liberals were wrong.
>
> One effect of affluence is a continuing conservative trend in politics, and . . . those who dismiss the pro-affluent movements of these past years as a temporary departure from some socially concerned norm are quite wrong.[5]

So if Galbraith's traditional theory of countervailing power no longer holds, what does?

Look carefully and you'll see that a new theory of power, and how to balance it, is suggested by the emerging developments we have been reviewing—one that might be called an institutional "displacement" theory of (evolutionary) political power and strategy.

As, for instance, when, slowly and step by step, institutions like insurance companies are backed out of states like Vermont—and also, step by step, backed out of powering the underlying politics in those states, and maybe, eventually, in the nation. Or when slowly, step by step—or quickly, as in the context of a collapse—some of the banks get nudged to the side *institutionally and politically*.

Major corporations also find themselves slowly displaced (to the extent feasible), and their bargaining power reduced, when alternative forms of local economic development are available to the mayor.

Not simply displaced in general, but also displaced in a very specific political sense. Every time one source of institutional power is removed from one side of the table, one source of potential institutional power is added to the other side of the table.

Obviously important.

The question is, how far might this power shift be developed—and in what specific circumstances—as we go forward in the difficult years ahead?

I don't want to make too much of all this at this point. (We will return to it.) Just want to get you thinking about these things with me.

I also want to get you thinking about one other thing—namely, the quiet, slow, but also perhaps steady potential emergence of a real politics, one informed by a new possibility, and one that builds power, ideas, culture, institutions, and organization over time, starting at the very bottom and working up.

If you look closely at the community-building, wealth-democratizing (evolutionary reconstructive) strategies, the (checkerboard) city and state strategies, the (crisis transformations) strategies—and even the idea of displacement in general—you will notice something different that takes us beyond the idea of institutional development and wealth democratization, critical as these are.

Something, too, that takes us beyond ideological development and may also begin to penetrate (to recall Gramsci and Mannheim) the dominant hegemonic cultural and idea system with a new possibility, in this case, the democratization of the economy, step by step in everyday life and culture.

That "something different" involves political power in another very specific and concrete sense of that term: Slowly building an alternative basis of the economy in local communities and states through democratization strategies (co-ops, worker-owned firms, land trusts, city-owned businesses, and maybe public utilities and other public businesses at various levels) *also creates new constituencies, building from the bottom up, who are allied to and benefit from these efforts.*

It also begins to help change local experience in the direction of a community-sustaining vision, one that is informed both by democratization ideas and by new ecological thinking.

* * * * *

For the above strategic notions to move beyond fragments, preliminary steps, interesting possibilities, or a couple of exciting and dramatic forms of change here and there would require a few other things (to say the least!). Among the most obvious:

- A substantial developmental period in which each of the processes—evolutionary reconstruction, checkerboard strategies, crisis transformations, and displacement—went forward, step by step, over time.
- An era of history that continually forced people to realize that the old ways don't work anymore—and that the pain will continue until a new way is found.
- People with clear ideas in their heads about what is to be done (in other words, an agreed-upon *strategy*).
- A lot of allies built up over time.
- A lot of patience developed the hard way (yes, once again, step by step over time—because there are no alternatives).
- And some luck.

'Nuff said for the moment. (More later, especially in part 6.)

CHAPTER SIXTEEN

Bigger Possibilities and Precedents

For Something, One Day,
Possibly Even More Interesting

O h, by the way, did you happen to notice that the US government nation-alized a very large auto company during the big crisis (GM), and also one of the world's largest insurance companies (AIG), and it could easily have done the same with some of the big banks (since it gave $45 billion to Bank of America and Citigroup, $25 billion to JPMorgan Chase and Wells Fargo, and $10 billion to Goldman Sachs)?[1]

Also, interestingly, in the case of GM (as well as the slightly different Chrys-ler takeover), the new auto companies were established as temporary joint ventures in a structure that included partial ownership by a union-related entity (a voluntary employee beneficiary association, or VEBA). Although the latter was initially established by the auto companies and the United Auto Workers to finance retiree health benefits, its use in connection with the new structures now also suggests one approach to a joint public–worker ownership concept that might well be developed in new directions in future situations of this kind.[2]

Now, what are we to make of all that?

It is not, as many believe, impossible to imagine taking over and making into public enterprises some of the largest corporations in the nation.

We just did it.

Before giving them back, once they began making a profit again.

We are likely to be in the same situation again, particularly if the world we are entering is increasingly unstable rather than a sweet return to the best of all possible growth paths that some hope for. And particularly to rescue companies, like the auto and insurance giants, that are "systemically" important—which is to say, have the power to bring down truly critical sectors of the entire economy.

But must we do it the same way, or can we take it a step farther?

In the future, big crisis transformations might very well (*perhaps almost certainly will*) include larger forms of potential democratization. Which is another way of saying that crises in corporations that are too big to fail might also be handled strategically, and potentially used as turning points to transform faltering but important corporations into democratized institutions.

Before we explore this possibility further, let me say that I am not big on nationalization, particularly in a very large nation like our own. I see far more promise in regionalized public enterprise for most large firms when democratization is appropriate. Nonetheless, it's important at this point to take up a phony argument and a myth related to both.

It is commonly claimed that all forms of publicly owned enterprise must be inefficient. The fact is, the modern literature on this subject no longer rubber-stamps this once traditional hoary conservative argument. For one thing, prior to Margaret Thatcher's famous gutting of the British public sector, productivity growth in British nationalized mining, utility, transportation, and communication companies consistently outpaced that of similar privately owned industries in the United States.[3]

For another, it all depends on how you measure things.

For instance, how in the world can anyone claim that the American health care system, dominated as it is by private insurance companies, private hospitals, private drug companies, and so on, is *more efficient* than European systems that produce better results at far, far lower cost? Not just minor improvements, but better results obtained through a system that if we were to follow (even in part) might save us something of the order of $1 trillion per year.

Again, it may (or may not?) be that American megabanks are more efficient in the ways they manage accounts and charge customers for services.[4] What it means to be efficient when competing with banks in other countries for high-risk (and huge-consequence) speculative investments, though, is by no means obvious. What is obvious, however, is that it is absurd to call the US banking system "efficient" if we neglect to notice that the way it's run brought the entire US economy close to collapse—at an overall cost, again, of trillions of dollars.

There is something wrong—something truly nutty!—about calling these systems efficient without even considering such costs.

Most serious modern discussions of the public enterprise alternative, in fact, now take into account more comprehensive measures of efficiency, and even when there may be accounting or innovation inefficiencies within some public firms the overall efficiencies are commonly more than acceptable.[5] A recent *Harvard International Review* report observed simply that in the modern era many public enterprises can be "efficient, even in comparison to their private counterparts."[6]

Also, while most Americans are pretty much in the dark about all of this, public enterprise is extremely common around the world, and it is growing. Here—simply by way of indicating what is possible and now conventional—is a very partial rundown.

Publicly owned corporations worldwide produce roughly 75 percent of all oil.[7] High-speed rail systems are run by the government in France, Spain, Belgium, Germany, Italy, the Netherlands, China, and South Korea.[8] Public ownership of significant or controlling shares of airlines is also common: France holds 15.9 percent of Air France–KLM; Sweden, Denmark, and Norway hold a 50 percent stake in SAS; Israel, 34.6 percent of El Al; Singapore, 55.9 percent of Singapore Airlines (ranked as one of the world's best).[9] EADS (the European Aeronautics Defense and Space Company)—producer of Airbus and other major planes and helicopters—is partly owned by the French and Spanish governments (as well as the city of Hamburg, Germany).[10]

More than two hundred public and semi-public banks, along with another eighty-one related public funding agencies (including national and regional development agencies, municipal credit agencies, and export credit agencies), control a fifth of all bank assets in the European Union.[11] Japan Post Bank is the world's biggest public bank and one of that nation's largest employers.[12]

Much better and faster Internet service than our own is provided in many countries where public corporations exist side by side with private companies. (Public telecommunications companies are conventional in most parts of the world, including in Austria, Japan, Sweden, France, Germany, Switzerland, and Norway.)[13]

Brazil, an economic powerhouse, has more than one hundred state-owned or state-controlled enterprises, including major banks, utilities, and a large oil company, Petrobras, renowned for its deep-water exploration achievements.[14]

Again, I could go on.

In an article surveying such developments, *Economist* author Adrian Wooldridge concludes that state enterprises have become more productive largely "thanks to a mixture of judicious pruning and relentless restructuring." But whatever the reasons, there is little doubt about the trend.[15]

So in the future—given the developing possibility of a long evolutionary buildup of practical experience and learning with various forms of democratization at the local and state level—it may well be that we will find it useful to do what most other nations in the world do in connection with larger enterprise in certain key sectors. Especially when the big banks, insurance companies, and auto companies go down again, or other systemically important firms flounder.

Part V

NARROW-MINDED EFFICIENCY, PUBLIC ENTERPRISE, AND ALL THAT

CHAPTER SEVENTEEN

Public Enterprise
Redux I

And Just a Bit More on the
Use and Misuse of "Efficiency Talk"

Public enterprise, nationalization, regionalization . . .
     Even though all this is clearly speculative, it is important to ponder what role such possibilities might or might not ultimately play in the next American system. Talk about needing a new paradigm, about changing the system, abounds. But so far we have no clear and explicit vision of where we want to go and no commonly accepted strategy. Correct that: At least some change makers have a shared *vision* (or, you could say, shared *values*). But the critical next step—a *systemic design that might achieve and sustain that vision*—remains to be taken. To change the system in keeping with those values—even over long periods of time—it's necessary to think much more clearly about how key institutions might ultimately be organized to support them.

     Which brings us back, again, to the question: If you don't like corporate capitalism and you don't like state socialism, what do you want?

Let's take another step.
     Efficiency is, in fact, the bugaboo that has stopped most discussion of democratizing public options for much of the last half century. But the fact is, most American economists are extremely narrow-minded about what they mean by efficiency—especially when they talk about public versus private efforts.
     I am not trying to insult my brothers and sisters in the profession; I mean *narrow*-minded in a very specific sense: When most economists talk enterprise efficiency, they look narrowly at whether one company is more or less efficient than another at doing the same kind of thing. So, as we have

seen, they might ask if a private bank does its job more or less efficiently than a public one. Working with a narrow set of data (comparing internal efficiencies and often ignoring external factors like the public subsidies they might depend on, their environmental impact, or the economic risk they pose), many conclude that private enterprise as a rule is more efficient than public. Yet such an approach, as we just also saw, inherently neglects the huge additional costs to the economy that may come with the current casino-style banking system *and its inherent political as well as economic power relationships and practices*. The same goes for the current health care system.

So, to repeat: Even if a private bank were to be temporarily more efficient in its (internal) investing, lending, administrative, and other capacities, if this meant that it could also generate a massive economic crisis costing trillions of dollars, obliterating tens of millions of jobs, and injuring scores of millions of people, then its (narrowly defined) internal efficiency would be a pittance against its large-order-related external inefficacies.

And if so, then a boring publicly owned bank—even if marginally less efficient internally (which, as we have noted, is by no means necessarily the case)—would be preferable (and far more efficient) if it were able to avoid the reckless gambling and speculation that put the entire system at risk.

And even if a public health care system had slightly longer delays for some nonemergency procedures for some individuals (which also, by the way, is not necessarily the case), its minor inefficiencies would pale against its major overall efficiencies if it saved the society a trillion dollars a year—and simultaneously produced much better overall outcome results across the board (which as we have seen is common in many other systems).

You get the idea.

I'm underscoring the central issue here precisely because I find it difficult to understand why most of the economics profession doesn't discuss such obvious points. But the fact is, much of the profession simply doesn't.[1]

It's worth going down this path just a little farther—again simply to try to get our heads around a few key concepts that we will come back to and because, as we shall see, it also brings us smack up against the question of whether we can solve some of our really critical problems without having (minimally) to consider alternatives to a free-market-at-all-costs system.

Let's look at another truly major example of the kind of thing we need to think much more clearly about: We've seen that private corporations often find it efficient to move from one city to another (often because they can get some mayor to pay more than the last mayor). This may be efficient from the narrow point of view of the company, but again it may well be very inefficient from the point of view of the economy.

Here's the problem.

Consider all those factory jobs that once existed in Cleveland, Ohio: At its peak Cleveland had over nine hundred thousand residents. It now has less than four hundred thousand, since thousands and thousands of jobs have moved away.[2] Some losses were due to overall national unemployment, some to foreign trade. To make life simple, let's assume that only half of the lost jobs moved to other cities.

Note carefully, first, that in Cleveland we end up literally throwing away the housing, schoolrooms, hospital rooms, transportation facilities, stores, barbershops, and other businesses that were once needed to house, educate, and service the approximately 250,000 people whose jobs moved to other cities. Moreover, wherever these people went when the companies moved, the same quantity of houses, schoolrooms, hospital rooms, transportation facilities, stores, barbershops, and businesses now somehow had to be built anew to provide for their basic needs.

There is obviously a huge, huge cost to the economy of literally throwing away cities when corporations decide to move jobs elsewhere. Also a huge carbon cost in having to rebuild all these things someplace else. Furthermore, the instability makes it hard to do local sustainability planning, particularly of high-density housing and mass transit, both of which are important to reducing greenhouse gases and carbon emissions.

I don't need to go on. Take a trip to Detroit when you've got nothing else to do: It lost more than a million people in the last six decades.[3] It looks like a bombed-out World War II city. (And someplace else—indeed many someplace elses—somebody has paid the costs of rebuilding everything that was once in Detroit for the people who were forced to move.)*

---

* I probably should also at least mention a related issue: Private corporations sometimes work explicitly to destroy important options. As Bradford Snell, a former Senate Judiciary Committee staff attorney, has demonstrated, General Motors was instrumental in working to rip up existing (efficient) trolley car systems in many cities—the main reason being that they wanted to sell these same cities their buses. According to Snell, "GM admitted, in court documents, that by the mid-1950s, its agents had canvassed more than 1,000 electric railways and that, of these, they had motorized 90 percent, more than 900 systems." One of the front companies GM used in this operation, called National City Lines, was actually a partnership of GM, Firestone, and Standard Oil of California. In April 1949 GM, its partners, and its treasurer were convicted in the Chicago Federal Court of criminally conspiring to "replace electric transportation with gas-or-diesel powered buses and to monopolize

No one would say jobs should never move, but America's throwaway-city habit has grown way off the charts as we blather on about little efficiencies and look the other way on the big ones.

There are massive costs involved, but these are not costs paid by the corporation. In fact, we have no national capacity even to assess such costs intelligently, let alone to provide for a more rational solution. We have only very token tax and other incentives to locate jobs in areas of high unemployment—policies that no one even claims can make a significant dent in throwaway-city practices.[4]

The sad fact is that our political system is so dominated by corporate pressures in this area (and ideological fog about the free market, even as the companies chase after government incentives), we couldn't at this point implement a meaningful and efficient location strategy even if we knew what we wanted.

Moreover, given the political power imbalances, we also know that trying to use tax incentives, regulatory strategies, and the like has very little impact on the scale of the decisions that need to be made—even when they aren't simply a waste of taxpayer money (which, as we have seen, is all too often the case).

There's lots more to discuss on what it would really take to radically reduce throwaway-city costs (and to preserve intact human communities), but here's one way to think about it based simply on extending and expanding the Cleveland model we reviewed in part 2. As you'll recall, the model is one in which community stability is aided in part by changing ownership, and in part by stabilizing the market through purchases from larger institutions significantly funded by taxpayer dollars. (In the Cleveland case these are hospitals and universities.)

With that model in mind, consider what might have happened if the government and the UAW had used the General Motors stock they received because of the bailout to reorganize the company along full or joint public–worker ownership lines—and the new quasi-public General Motors' product

---

the sale of buses and related products to local transportation companies throughout the country." For the thousand-railways quote, see: Bradford Snell, "The Streetcar Conspiracy: How General Motors Deliberately Destroyed Mass Transit," *New Electric Railway Journal*, 1995, accessed February 14, 2011, www.lovearth.net/gmdeliberatelydestroyed.htm. For the Chicago court quote, see: Bradford Snell, *American Ground Transport: A Proposal for Restructuring the Automobile, Truck, Bus & Rail Industries*, 1974 (Prague, CR: Car Busters, March 2001), accessed February 14, 2011, www.worldcarfree.net/resources/freesources /American.htm. For more, see: Noam Chomsky, *Year 501: The Conquest Continues* (Cambridge, MA: South End Press, 1993), p. 226.

line were linked to a serious plan both to develop the nation's mass transit and rail system and to target jobs to economically distressed cities.

There are currently no US companies producing subway cars (although some foreign firms assemble subway cars in the United States).[5] Nor do any American-owned companies build high-speed rail. The American Public Transportation Association estimates that a $48 billion investment in transit capital projects could generate 1.3 million new green jobs in the next two years alone.[6] Transportation policy experts Richard Gilbert and Anthony Perl, projecting dramatic future increases in the cost of all petroleum-based transportation, have proposed building 15,500 miles of track devoted to high-speed rail between now and 2025.[7]

Whatever level of rail we one day decide to build, it will be paid for by taxpayers and commuters. Providing infrastructure and transportation will generate a long additional list of required equipment and materials that restructured companies could help produce—and (when the next big bailout occurs?) could at the same time help create new forms of ownership that might also help target, anchor, and stabilize the economies of the local communities involved.

For the moment, let's leave it at that—namely, simply another democratizing possibility to think about for the long haul.

CHAPTER EIGHTEEN

Public Enterprise Redux II

—— *Airline Foolishness and Endless Growth* ——

We're talking about big problems and big potential change and about the difference between narrow-minded efficiencies and large-order inefficiencies. Clarifying the "systemic design" required to sustain the values we affirm requires getting serious about such questions. Perhaps it will help if we take a look at another industry (airlines) and one problematic corporate goal (endless growth) in just a bit more detail.

Business journalists Phillip Longman and Lina Khan have recently given considerable study to the airline industry, particularly with regard to the impact of deregulation—the idea, implemented in the 1970s, that less regulation was a far better solution than the setting of schedules, routes, and fares that had been done up until that point by the Civil Aeronautics Board.[1] The problem with regulation (big surprise!) was that the big airlines had a great deal of influence on the regulators—just as the Chicago conservative economists had argued was inevitable. The result was protection from competition and de facto price floors rather than price ceilings (in the 1970s regulation guaranteed airlines a 12 percent return on flights with a target occupancy of just 55 percent).[2]

But the new answer of deregulation led to other problems.[3] For one thing, airfares fell more rapidly in the ten years *before* deregulation than they did during the following decade.[4] And this was only the tip of the iceberg. Indeed, since 1978 more than one hundred private airlines have gone bankrupt; they have either ceased operations or been bought up by competitors. Just a few of the once famous airlines no longer operating independently include Pan Am, TWA, Continental, Northwest, National, and Eastern.[5]

Moreover, during just the first ten years of the new century private US airlines posted cumulative losses of more than $60 billion.[6] All of the four major "legacy" airlines have been through bankruptcy proceedings, sometimes repeatedly—American (2011), Delta (2005), US Airways (2002 and 2004), and United (2002).[7]

From the vantage point of the overall economy, this use (misuse?) of resources is clearly wasteful and inefficient. Quite apart from the asset loss involved when companies are taken over by successor airlines in bankruptcy proceedings, the constant turmoil also means that the best minds in the industry are often more focused on fighting legal battles and reorganizing internal systems than delivering transportation services for passengers.

Furthermore, these private companies would be in a much more difficult position—and offering even worse service at even higher costs—were it not for the large-order government subsidies and bailouts they have received in recent years. Following the 9/11 attacks, for instance, the federal government provided $5 billion in direct "no-strings" aid to compensate airlines for their losses. It also provided insurance subsidies, and more than a billion in direct loans and loan guarantees to economically distressed airlines.[8] Again, Congress passed legislation in 2006 and 2007 that allows airlines to underfund their retirement plans, virtually ensuring that the public will be forced to assume ever-greater costs when private airlines fail in the future. (One estimate is that the legislation saved American Airlines $2.1 billion between 2006 and the time it filed for bankruptcy in 2011.[9])

In addition to the big federal bailouts and other subsidies, of course, the federal government provides logistic support through the Federal Aviation Administration (FAA)—at a cost of $15.9 billion in fiscal year 2012—and it provides security through the Transportation Security Administration (TSA), the latter charged to passengers through a tax they pay for every flight.[10] Many airports are also built and maintained by local governmental "authorities" that often have access to implicitly subsidized lower costs because municipal bonds are exempt from certain federal and state taxes.

Then there is this rather unpleasant problem: Have you noticed the way airlines price their tickets? Direct flights for even short trips now commonly run several hundred dollars, and indirect flights can take almost an entire day as travelers are required to transit through "hub" cities like Atlanta and Chicago. It can cost $900 to fly round-trip from Washington DC to Cleveland, Ohio—a distance of less than 350 miles. (At the same time a nonstop one-way flight from New York to Los Angeles, a distance at least five times as far, may run a mere $150.) Similarly, a one-way flight from Cleveland to Madison, Wisconsin, can cost $625, and although cheaper options exist—for instance, one that cost only $236—they may well take over nine hours and require a change of planes in St. Louis and Chicago. No one measures the cost to individuals and the economy in general of time wasted by thousands, indeed hundreds of thousands, of people forced to accept such practices.[11]

Much more important (if you are not narrow-minded about your efficiencies), if you go to a city like Cincinnati (and many others like Cincinnati) you will find that a number of firms are now closing down at great cost to the entire community because the cost of business travel is so high. Longman and Khan have analyzed the situation in some detail, but to give only one of their examples: In 2011 Chiquita Brands International was forced to relocate its headquarters from Cincinnati to Charlotte, North Carolina, due to lack of air service and rising travel costs after the city lost two-thirds of its flights over the previous decade.[12] Businesses thinking about moving *to* Cincinnati quickly realize that the transportation problem makes it a dubious proposition, to say the least.

Again, in such cases, for narrow and often temporary reasons that may or may not be (temporarily) efficient from the point of view of certain airline companies, we simply ignore the larger—often huge—community economic losses that occur when businesses shut down in a city like Cincinnati. And this is to say nothing of the overall waste involved from the point of view of the economy as a whole—in other words, the throwaway-city costs.

What in the world is going on in this industry?

(I haven't even mentioned, of course, how lousy airline food is, or how squeezed in we sardines are when we fly.)

In narrow-minded free-marketeering economics you close your eyes to everything but the specific firm involved—and when you open your eyes, you often see that not only have many businesses failed at great and unmeasured cost to specific communities and the economy in general, but few of the really massive public policy issues involved have even been confronted. And it's these, the ones we don't even discuss, that are where the real action is, or should be if we are serious about where we should be going in the twenty-first century.

Looking forward, it's useful to recall that the way we approached transportation matters was once far more broadly conceived—and ought to be again (especially as population increases). For instance, we built the railroads in significant part because we wanted to develop the country in general, and the West in particular. We invested in streetcars to build the inner suburbs and other roads and highways so as to build the outer suburbs in the days when this seemed important. The Interstate Highway System, for all its well-known limitations, was conceived on a large and positive scale.[13]

So here's a question to chew on as you think about transportation in general and the airlines in particular in coming years: The Census Bureau estimates we will have 130 million more people living in the United States by 2050, even plausibly growing to a population of a billion or more by 2100.[14] Where are all of these Americans going to live? And are we going to build cities with transportation to them? Indeed, might we use transportation policy to encourage healthy decentralization? Or are we going to continue to focus only (narrow-mindedly) on whether or not one or another airline operating in the market is efficient (until it goes bankrupt and skewers another dozen cities on the way as it cuts the transportation lifeblood they need to survive)?

The airline story gets even more interesting since, as we have seen, we've already tried both regulation and deregulation, with dismal results in both cases. Moreover, the token subsidies now in place to attempt to preserve at least some service to smaller cities were always meager and inadequate, and they are increasingly being targeted for reduction or elimination.[15]

Here's a case where a variation on the old Chicago School idea is really worth taking very seriously: If in fact you can't regulate an industry such as the airlines in the interests of both efficiency and the larger public considerations involved in major transportation issues, then probably the only logical answer, again, is public ownership. Fortunately, as we've seen, there are many, many good examples of publicly owned or partially owned airlines around the world, the best probably being Singapore Airlines, SAS, Air France, El Al, Etihad Airways, and Emirates Airlines.

Also, the federal and state governments currently do, in fact, attempt to locate public facilities and make their purchasing decisions (to a modest degree, to be sure) in ways that help local economic development—an approach that could be expanded upon were transportation policy to be used in a positive way that was less narrow-minded on matters of efficiency and more broad-minded on large-order population and other issues facing the nation.

Were we to follow the Chicago prescript and the example of many other nations, we might be in position to begin to coordinate the use of transportation policy and public procurement to provide real stability to our communities—not only now, but as time goes on and as our population expands and the need for a comprehensive overall strategy becomes more and more obvious.

* * * * *

Finally, here—for the moment!—is one additional general and really nasty issue that at least needs to be put on the table. One that explains why private corporations often don't act in anything but their own interests—and one that is particularly important as we enter an era of potentially constrained global resources in several key areas:

Large corporations must grow. They are subject to Wall Street's first commandment: Grow or die. "Stockholders in the speculation economy want their profits now," observes Lawrence Mitchell, author of *The Speculation Economy,* "and they do not much care how they get them."[16] If a corporate executive does not show steadily increasing quarterly earnings, the grim quarterly-returns reaper will cut her down sooner or later.

The "grow or die" imperative cannot be wished or regulated away. The problem is that the imperative runs directly counter to a series of increasingly serious global challenges. In addition to the overriding problem of global warming, countless studies have documented that limits to growth are fast being reached in such areas as energy, minerals, water, and arable land (among others).[17] The energy corporations are desperately trying to crash through some of these limits with technological fixes such as fracking, tar sands exploitation, and deep-water drilling, which are often equally or more environmentally costly than traditional methods.

Yet the trends continue: The United States, with less than 5 percent of global population, accounts for 22 percent of the world's consumption of oil, 13 percent of coal, and 21 percent of natural gas.[18] In the brief period between 1940 and 1976 alone Americans used up a larger share of the earth's mineral resources than did everyone in all previous history.[19] At some point a society like ours, which currently produces the equivalent of more than $190,000 for every family of four, must ask when enough is enough.[20]

Former presidential adviser James Gustave Speth puts it bluntly: "For the most part, we have worked within this current system of political economy, but working within the system will not succeed in the end when what is needed is transformative change in the system itself."[21] Which means somehow ultimately also developing economic institutions *that are not required* to grow.

Even though many public forms of enterprise are currently organized along profit-making lines, unlike private Wall Street–driven firms they clearly could, in fact, be restructured in ways that did not require growth if we so decided.

* * * * *

In all of this I am not arguing that public enterprise is inevitably better than private. Indeed, small local businesses and many medium-sized firms, especially high-tech businesses, are critical to the future of any serious economy. I am simply saying it's time to get our heads out of the sand on these issues in general—and also in particular in terms of the real world of efficiencies (including what to do about efficient use of scarce global resources).

There's lots more to say here, of course. For instance, there's no reason all public enterprise needs to be national; as previously noted some could be regional, some state-owned, and others even more locally based.*

The main point is to begin to ask the right questions:

- What are the total (rather than partial) efficiencies and inefficiencies in any given instance?
- What are the overall goals we want to achieve?
- What will it take *institutionally* to deal with the political power of the institutions that now control the action (and apparently cannot be adequately influenced by the usual policies we've been trying to use for the last several decades)?

Probably I don't really need to remind you that many of these problems and possibilities—except, probably, that involving the growth dynamic—could "in theory" be handled by trying to use incentives, tax deals, regulations, and the like to get private corporations to do what makes sense.

But the system that in theory had enough power to make such strategies work is the one that is decaying before our very eyes.

Yes, it may seem impossible to ever get a handle on these kinds of things in another way. But it is also obvious that if we (you and I) don't think about it, you and I will not have any ideas in our heads other than those that spin around big corporations—and the hope that you can regulate them in our next system, even though the basis of that politics is over.

Also (as we shall see) it just may be that even if what some folks like to term a total transformation of the overall system isn't possible (yet), some of

---

* During the 1930s a more populist form of the Tennessee Valley Authority (TVA) was under very serious consideration, and thereafter, in 1937, seven different regional public enterprise efforts were proposed by New Deal senator George W. Norris of Nebraska. See: William E. Leuchtenburg, "Roosevelt, Norris and the 'Seven Little TVAs,'" *Journal of Politics*, vol. 14, no. 3 (August 1952), pp. 418–41.

these ideas may still prove useful in a new progressive strategy in due course no matter what.

Especially as the failures and pain and frustration and difficulties of the ongoing system continue to force people to think new thoughts about where we might be going, and how we might find a better way.

Again, 'nuff said for now.

Part VI

THE EMERGING HISTORICAL ERA

CHAPTER NINETEEN

The Emerging
Historical Context

————— *And Why It's Critical to Your Theory* —————
————— *of Change and Your Strategy* —————

Okay, it's time to get serious.

So far we've talked about efficiency, public enterprise, and alternative policies. Now we need to begin to think about what these large-order issues really involve. But first let's revisit two very big points about the developing realities.

The first, which we discussed in part 1, is that the traditional system is in substantial stalemate. And a very significant part of that stalemate can be traced to the decline of labor (and the rise of corporate power). The old liberal system model let the corporations and elites largely own the system and hoped after the fact to use politics and reform to regulate, incentivize, and tax and spend for public purposes. *That model, give or take momentary blips, is fading away.*

The evidence is in the trends we reviewed in chapter 1—trends of growing inequality, declining ecological sustainability, declining liberty, and long-increasing concentrations of income, wealth, and corporate power. The evidence is also in the dismal economy.

Of course, the reasons behind the long-decaying trends and other systemic failings are more complicated than the dramatic decline of labor. They include globalization, racial discrimination, and many other factors (some of which we will consider a bit further shortly). There are also questions about the degree to which the model ever really worked—absent massive global-scale crisis developments like the Depression or worldwide war. The key point is simply but critically that the underlying power relationships have shifted in profound ways.

That is why the trends are what they are.

I know the idea that we face a fundamental fadeaway of traditional countervailing system-managing reform is difficult for some people to accept. (It certainly was difficult for me to accept when I first began to sense the painful realities!) But I don't think we get very far until and unless we face this distasteful and difficult challenge.

Note carefully, I didn't say that the old progressive model was no more, nor that some important things cannot be achieved. I said it was and is fading away—which is a different thing. In my opinion we need to do whatever we can in the old way, to the extent feasible—including trying to bolster labor wherever possible. These are very difficult times, people are in great pain, and no shred of power or potential power that can improve things should be ignored. Nonetheless, I don't think the fadeaway can be ducked. I also think lots of people know this, or sense it, but haven't yet found words to express the depth of the problem, or of their concern.

The second big reality we have discussed (in parts 2, 3, and 4) is that there are at least four interesting processes at work that have begun to generate different forms of change. These processes move in a direction that is not inherently corporate-dominated. Each has been creating new institutions, *and might in the future create major new institutions*—the critical characteristic of which is democratic ownership of productive wealth in one or another form. There are also many older institutions based on this principle that might be reinvigorated as part of a long-term rebuilding process.

Thus . . .

There are steadily building local changes, mostly developing out of stalemate, economic difficulties, pain, and frustration. These include cooperatives, worker-owned firms, land trusts, social enterprises, new forms of agriculture, B Corporations, and many, many other evolving efforts in communities across the nation. I have termed change of this kind evolutionary reconstruction to distinguish it from reform, on the one hand, and revolution on the other.

To recall: Traditional reform assumes that the ownership of wealth will remain largely in corporate hands and relies on policy to regulate and alter the impact of corporate behavior. Revolution commonly assumes a crisis collapse and a (usually violent) takeover of corporate institutions, democratizing their ownership through radical and abrupt shifts in power. Evolutionary reconstruction also democratizes ownership, but in an evolving, institution-developing way.

The second form of change is also different from traditional reform and traditional revolution. It involves what I called emerging checkerboard municipal and state strategies now under way that are democratizing the ownership of wealth in other very American ways, and also largely flying under the radar. They include municipal land development, municipal-owned electrical generation (and cable and Internet service), citywide efforts that capture methane and turn it into electrical power, and more. They also include state investment strategies, state land strategies, and even the investment of oil revenues on behalf of the public in conservative Alaska.

(A reminder, again simply to file away for the moment: Many of the national policies that became the New Deal largely involved upscaling programs that had been previously incubated in the state and local "laboratories of democracy.")

We also discussed what I dubbed (for lack of a better term) crisis transformations. Here the idea is straightforward and comes in two variations. One involves the slow buildup of cost and other pressures—as in connection with health care—that point ultimately toward public or quasi-public restructuring as the only long-term answer. The second—as in banking—involves the impossibility of achieving adequate regulation, which in turn appears likely to lead over time to crisis problems—and potentially, thereafter, some form of public or quasi-public solution.

Finally, we've considered big crisis transformations, as distinct from some of the more modest things happening at the state level (or possibly at both state and national levels). The model here builds on the General Motors and AIG takeovers, where very large bailouts took place and in the future likely will take place again. (And again? And perhaps with different long-term results.)

Also throughout I have pointed to the development of numerous forms of green development, institutionally in projects and organizing efforts; in culture, especially locally; in city and state and national strategy; and also in politics, particularly from the ground up. This development has dovetailed, too, with a growing interest by some entrepreneurs to push the envelope on social responsibility through triple-bottom-line efforts, impact investing, and related strategies.

The central question now is whether any of this might add up to anything serious—whether it might offer a significant way forward. And one way to get at the question is the following:

If the kinds of conditions that have produced the quietly developing evolutionary reconstructive trends, the checkerboard municipal and state ownership efforts, the crises that appear to be emerging in connection with banking and health care, and the large crises that have already created de facto nationalizations were complete aberrations—highly unusual, temporary, momentary bits of history—then probably the kinds of evolutionary, checkerboard, and other institution-changing processes could be understood as marginal, even inconsequential.

If, on the other hand, the kinds of painful, ongoing economic and political realities that have produced such developments in the past are likely to continue—and, indeed, if they were to define the dominant political-economic contextual reality of the future—then in all probability the kinds of processes we have discussed throughout part 2 would also likely continue.

Even more may be said: *They could potentially be aided and abetted at some point by a much more self-conscious and explicitly strategic political awareness that such processes matter.*

Indeed, matter a great deal.

Put another way: Evolutionary reconstructive change, on the one hand, and temporary and occasional crisis transformations, on the other, might become *strategic political ideas* rather than random developments and events.

To say nothing of checkerboard municipal and state efforts and big crisis transformations.

And all of this taken together might slowly begin to displace current institutional arrangements, build constituencies, and help build up new institutional sources of progressive political power.

Maybe!

I need to say a bit more about this so that my meaning is clear and the implications explicit.

First, the idea that the overarching social and economic environment is important—or, to be precise, the emerging historical context in which change will or will not occur is important—is a central idea not only of this book, but of any serious theory of change. That includes the one you, dear reader, embrace with all your conscious and unconscious might—including, for some, the idea that America is in such decline that nothing serious can be done.

Second, we are all forced to make judgment calls about what our reality really may allow, and what accordingly it makes sense to do. There is also no escape from the "maybe" problem. Since no one knows the future, we are all required to make our best guess (or informed assessment)—and then act. "You pays your money and you takes your chances."

For the most part, most people aren't clear about the necessity for explicit and informed judgments about the possibilities and the challenges ahead. Rather, most simply unconsciously remember the future (to recall historian Lewis Namier's insightful formulation). Their theory of change and their expectation of the emerging historical context are based on assumptions they have taken *from the past* about how change occurs in general—which they (usually unconsciously) project forward.

Which, of course, is what all traditional theories do: "Since we got reform the old way in the past, we can do it again," we might say. "All we need to do is reinvigorate the old ways through new efforts."

Let me again be clear: This way of proceeding—remembering the future—is very important. It often works successfully for long periods of time.

Nonetheless, the old way of proceeding is now coming slowly but steadily to an end. Which is to say remembering the future (even if you bolster it with traditional politically focused movement building) is unlikely to cut it, important as this all nonetheless is.

Nor will simple-minded (know it for sure) doom and gloom.

Nor does ill-defined, rhetoric-heavy use of the term *revolution* help.

So, going forward, given the fading away of traditional strategy, either there is likely to be no serious option . . .

. . . or some other way must be found.

And to get serious about some other way—about evolutionary reconstruction, checkerboard strategies, and crisis transformations at different levels of scale, and above all about democratizing ownership slowly throughout the system—we would have to offer reasons to believe that the processes described throughout parts 2, 3, and 4 might well continue.

Which is to say, we would have to understand *why* the emerging historical context might allow or favor this other way.

And why the emerging historic context might also continue to permit (or stimulate) the buildup of new forms of ownership both in practice and in the minds of lots of people as a real possibility.

Also maybe even begin to help create ideas about political strategy that might move such possibilities forward powerfully if the conditions that were producing the new forms of change continued.

And to do all this, step by step, as the system in general continues to flounder, creating not only great pain but disillusionment with the old ideas, a moral sense that something is powerfully wrong, and hunger for new ideas.

* * * * *

Now, obviously, the next step in the argument is to suggest to you precisely why I think the emerging historical context has the potential to nurture and support the new forms of change in an ongoing and powerful way.

Or might do so if we got serious about change that is deep enough to open up new political options and new ways to build power for those concerned about the direction the nation is taking, and might take.

CHAPTER TWENTY

Two Dogs That Are
Unlikely to Bark Again

The first and in many ways the most important thing to notice about the emerging historical context is that we are *not* likely to experience anything like the powerful shifts that allowed for—indeed, in many ways *produced*—the two massive, society-shaping eras of modern progressive change.

I'm talking, of course, about an economic collapse on the scale of the Great Depression, which made the New Deal possible, or a war on the scale of World War II, which not only brought the US economy back from its Depression-era brink but paved the way for the postwar boom era of great progressive achievement.

Another Great Depression–scale collapse is unlikely for five simple but basic reasons:

- The size of ongoing government spending stabilizing the economy is simply much, much larger than it was at the time of the Great Depression. Modern government spending now stands at roughly 30 to 35 percent of the economy.[1] This is three times the government share of the economy in 1929, when the Great Depression began.[2] The economy may decline rapidly, but such large and stable spending provides a much higher "floor" holding the system up when times are bad than was available during the 1930s.

- There are a number of built-in economic stabilizers—spending that ramps up to help offset the decline when recessions begin to get under way. Among the most obvious are unemployment insurance, income security for veterans, and food stamps (the Supplemental Nutrition Assistance Program). Even conservative politicians have added to such programs in recent years when the going got tough. In 2008 President Bush, with the support of both Republican and Democratic legislators, signed an Economic Stimulus Act that included $152 billion in tax rebates and incentives.[3] More recently, in December 2010, President Obama and congressional Republicans agreed on a deal to extend federal unemployment benefits as part of a compromise that also saw the Bush tax rates extended.[*4]

- We now know a great deal more about how the economy works than we did eight decades ago, in 1929. Even many conservative economists agree that more rather than less government spending is called for when things get really bad. Indeed, conservative economist Martin Feldstein, chairman of the Council of Economic Advisers under Ronald Reagan, criticized the Obama administration for not proposing a *larger* stimulus program. "Both its size and structure were inadequate to offset the enormous decline in aggregate demand," Feldstein wrote in 2011.[5]

- There has been a sea change in politics. The American public now holds that political leaders have a responsibility for making sure the economy works—or at least does not totally fail. Recessions and depressions were once thought to be like the weather, something you had to endure. Dealing with them—at least in some way—is now understood to be the job of government and government leaders. A very heavy political price can be paid by any politician who fails ultimately to deal with massive economic pain.

- Perhaps most important, when push comes to shove major corporate leaders now also support action to counteract truly major economic contractions. In January 2009, as Congress was gearing up for a vote on his $787 billion stimulus plan, President Obama received strong backing from major corporate leaders—including those of IBM, Honeywell, Google, Motorola, and Xerox.[6] "The business community needs action now . . . ," Google CEO Eric Schmidt declared. "It's time for government action."[7] Bruce Josten, chief lobbyist of the staunchly conservative US Chamber of Commerce, also backed the effort: "President Obama and Congress are right to take swift and bold action on the stimulus."[8]

---

* As we has seen, unemployment benefits were also extended (for one year) in the January 1, 2013, compromise legislation that made most of the Bush tax cuts permanent and increased tax rates for those making more than $400,000 (or $450,000 for couples).

Even so conservative a president as George W. Bush authorized massive government intervention (as you'll recall) out of fear that "this sucker could go down."[9] Asked if he was worried about being the Herbert Hoover of the twenty-first century, he declared: "I'm a free market guy. But I'm not gonna let this economy crater in order to preserve the free market system."[10]

I need to make a stop here—*a full stop*—to make sure I am not misunderstood.

The above facts and arguments do not mean that politicians are willing and able to manage the economy successfully, or that the best of all possible worlds can be achieved by political decision making of the kind we now get or are likely to get.

Quite the contrary.

What I am suggesting is a simple, limited, but extremely important point: *Truly massive—and sustained—economic collapse* of the kind that opened the way for unusual and far-reaching policy change in the decade of the 1930s, though not impossible, is no longer as likely as it was in the first third of the twentieth century.

This is emphatically not to say that great recessions, ongoing economic pain, stagnation, and high unemployment may not occur for long and extended periods of time. Indeed, as we will shortly explore, precisely such a reality—something like a continuation of the most recent decade's experience (give or take an up- or downtick)—appears to be highly likely.

But such an emerging historical context is very, very different in its political impact and meaning from that of a dramatic and extended Depression-scale collapse of the kind that opened the way politically to the New Deal.

Nor are we likely to experience the kind of massive world war that not only led the nation out of the Great Depression but paved the way for the extraordinary follow-on postwar boom that set the terms of reference for the second great modern era of progressive change. As we have seen, World War II brought with it an extended period of destruction for global economic rivals, increased spending on goods in our own economy to help former enemy nations get on their feet, and the deferred spending of wartime savings, or war-related programs like the GI Bill, which both supported veterans who wanted to go to college and stimulated the economy. The "boom" was the greatest period of economic growth in the entire twentieth century.

As we look to understand our emerging historical context, however, it is clear that the economy-stimulating realities that can flow from truly massive war are unlikely to create the kind of unusual conditions that permitted the boom era of progressive politics.

There is one profound and fundamental reason why: the advent of thermonuclear weapons. We may well destroy ourselves, along with much of the rest of the planet, if we engage in worldwide war. The kind of wars in which millions of men and machines fight for contested land areas (and in which nearly 40 percent of the US economy is devoted to war, as it was at the height of World War II) *are simply no longer likely.*[11]

Not when the main contenders have thermonuclear weapons.

Nor, it appears, are what might be called significant-scale small wars as likely to play a significant role in supporting the economy as they did in much of the second half of the twentieth century. The facts here are also dramatic.

Though large in absolute scale, the overall trend of military spending as a percent of the economy has gone down dramatically, on average, over the decades that began with the Korean War in the 1950s through Vietnam, Iraq, and Afghanistan. Such spending as a percentage of GDP was:

- 10.4 percent during the 1950s
  (peaking at 14.2 percent during the Korean War)
- 8.7 percent during the 1960s
  (peaking at 9.4 percent during the Vietnam War)
- 5.9 percent during the 1970s
- 5.8 percent during the 1980s
- 4 percent during the 1990s
- 3.8 percent during the 2000s.

It stands currently (2011) at 4.7 percent and is projected by the Office of Management and Budget to decline to 2.9 percent by 2017.*[12]

Military spending as an implicit way to support overall levels of employment, in short, also seems clearly to be on the decline. And it also appears—though it is obviously impossible to predict—that the American public is becoming less and less willing to send its sons and daughters to fight in what might be called significant-scale small wars.

Another way to understand the implications of these trends is to observe that by far the most important thing about the context that shaped the last several

---

* Note that in different economic times this would be lower. The 4.7 percent is high due, in part, to the low (recession-related) GDP denominator of the defense/GDP fraction.

decades—the decades of growing inequality and social and economic pain, *and also of the odd kinds of institutional developments explored in parts 2, 3, and 4*—was (in a variation of Sherlock Holmes's famous insight) that two very big dogs simply did not bark.

These were times when neither of the two extraordinary system-jolting events of the twentieth century—massive depression and world war— occurred again. The earlier frame of reference for shifting politics, and our economy, in powerful and dramatic ways no longer applied—a reality that remains *all but certain to continue for the ongoing era we are entering.*

Such a judgment does not, of course, offer answers to many, many other questions about the emerging historical context.

It is, quite simply, a place to begin any serious analysis.

CHAPTER TWENTY-ONE

Stagnation and
Punctuated Stagnation

The considerations outlined in the previous chapter suggest an even deeper difficulty that a number of important economists have begun to contemplate—namely, the possibility of a continued pattern of faltering economic growth, or what several now call stagnation, a term that suggests ongoing high unemployment and uneven, slow, and unsatisfactory economic forward motion, punctuated only occasionally by small upward gains.

The judgment is not to be taken lightly. Traditional economic theory holds that although the economy may experience up-and-down swings, it always resumes significant positive growth. That has, for decades, been a comforting thought for many. But that traditional theory no longer seems to hold. Rather, the judgment that we may have entered an era of stagnation suggests continuing economic decay with only minor ups and downs around a faltering longer-term trend.

In his book *From Financial Crisis to Stagnation* economist Thomas Palley, for instance, argues that "there is a high likelihood the Great Recession will be followed by the Great Stagnation."[1] Specifically, "the unemployment rate will remain high, wages will stagnate, and a general sense of economic disquiet will prevail."[2] Another book titled *The Great Stagnation* by Tyler Cowen became a 2011 best seller as the central theme resonated with the experience of very large numbers of Americans.

A critical element in the stagnation forecast is intimately related to the problem of growing economic inequality. The difficulty is that low- and moderate-income Americans spend a far greater share of their income than the rich and the very rich, thereby (in normal times) stimulating the economy when they make their purchases. When income becomes more and more concentrated at the top, however, the rich and very rich simply cannot (and do not) spend as great a percentage of what they get. Instead, they save—a useful thing to do in general, except that this also means that the purchase of goods and services declines, and with it economic growth.

As we have seen, the income share of the top 1 percent has gone from roughly 10 percent of all income to roughly 20 percent over the last thirty years. The share of everyone else has gone down, with the inevitable resulting decay in consumer spending.[3]

Nobel laureate Joseph Stiglitz minces few words: The relationship is "straightforward and ironclad: as more money becomes concentrated at the top, aggregate demand goes into a decline. Unless something else happens by way of intervention, total demand in the economy will be less than what the economy is capable of supplying—and that means that there will be growing unemployment, which will dampen demand even further."[4]

Another well-known economist, Dean Baker, underlines how dramatically things have changed since the era of postwar boom: In the "1950s, 1960s, into the 1970s, where you had productivity growth, very good in fact, that was passed on in wage growth pretty much up and down the income ladder, that led to increased consumption, increased demand; therefore increased investment, more productivity growth, etc., etc. That really broke down in the 1980s."[5]

Former labor secretary Robert Reich, focusing also on what changed, brings together a number of key factors in his assessment of the emerging reality. All have contributed to the declining wages and reduced purchasing power that are at the heart of the stagnation problem.

First, wages have been undermined both by global competition and technological change. Second, there has been a breakdown in three mechanisms that traditionally buffered the system:

- Although increasing numbers of women went to work to add to family wages during the postwar era, this trend has now gone about as far as it can go.
- Although workers put in more hours when they could, to receive additional pay, this also is no longer feasible given the reduced demand for labor.
- Although families borrowed to keep up purchases, they have also now reached the limit of what is feasible.[6]

The resulting decaying trend in family income and purchasing power has been all but impossible to deal with through the kinds of economic stimulus and other policies that are politically feasible. And the problem of political feasibility is itself made more difficult, Paul Krugman suggests, as growing inequality also works to weaken the political power of low-income groups (and, accordingly, their support for government spending programs to stabilize the economy).[7]

There are even further challenges—especially involving global trade.

Not only have America's traditional competitors long since returned to do battle in global markets, but increasingly very-low-cost producers—most important, China—have penetrated American markets. The challenges are more severe than are commonly understood. When considering jobs lost to China, we usually think only of low wages now earned by Chinese workers building cars or assembling iPhones at wages of $1.50 to $2.20 per hour (there are almost a million producing iPhones alone).[8] Though extraordinary, this is no longer the only difficulty. Apple also employs thirty thousand Chinese engineers, and engineers earn $41 an hour in the United States but only $6 in China and $4 in India.[9]

The once prevalent dream that the United States could win a global trade war by keeping ahead of the game educating engineering and other specialists is also fast becoming a nightmare. Indeed, China is now accelerating beyond the US in connection with solar and other renewable energy technologies.

In theory, it would be possible to enact legislation that would allow the federal government to put the economy into high gear through large-scale infrastructure, education, and other investments. That could offset the faltering demand caused by growing income inequality, on the one hand, and by challenges in global markets on the other.

However, in practice it is no longer politically possible to undertake large-scale Keynesian policies of this kind. On the one hand, the powerful labor-backed Democratic majorities that once made this possible have lost their ability to enact large-scale programs. On the other, the election of intensely conservative Republicans, especially to the House of Representatives, has created blocking power for any major new spending programs.

The result, to repeat, is not collapse, but rather an odd form of painful stagnation—the hallmark of which is economic decay, with occasional significant downturns and (at best) modest and temporary upticks around a sickening, uncertain, and debilitating norm.*

---

* Scholars in the Marxist tradition like the late Paul Sweezy long have held that absent major technological inventions, stagnation is the normal pattern of advanced capitalist nations. The argument—which emphasizes a different mechanism (the ability of large corporations to extract purchasing power through quasi-monopoly practices)—has been refined in a recent book by John Bellamy Foster and Robert W. McChesney, *The Endless Crisis: How*

There is a further set of difficulties as well, one that suggests we're entering an era not only of stagnation (give or take a major or minor economic uptick), but also of what might be called *"punctuated* stagnation," by which I mean a time in which major economic jolts regularly impact the economy, further intensifying the underlying difficulties.

By now it should be obvious that financial crises, both domestic and international, are part of our "new normal." You only have to go back and read the predictions of Nouriel Roubini, Simon Johnson, and Mark Mobius in chapter 13 to understand that all manner of serious economic thinkers believe we'll continue to face economic crashes until we address the fundamental system flaws that cause them.

But another problem is that we are also likely to experience massive economy-jolting price explosions in connection with a number of critical commodities, especially energy and key grains. "Oil markets will inevitably feature large and unavoidable price swings," observes Daniel P. Ahn of the Council on Foreign Relations, "and must be accepted as a natural feature of life."[10] Maria van der Hoeven, executive director of the International Energy Agency, stresses: "What has changed is that prices have risen significantly since 2002, so that a few percentage points up or down now represent multi-dollar swings."[11] And a British government report warns: "Global energy demand . . . is projected to increase by 45% between 2006 and 2030 and could double between now and 2050. Energy prices are projected to rise and become more volatile."[12]

Such price spikes impact the US economy in two powerful ways. First, and self-evidently, they increase costs, contributing to inflation. Second, by increasing the cost of everything from gasoline to food they also drain away spending from other sectors, contributing to unemployment.[13] A 2011 study by the Consumer Federation of America found that a $30-per-barrel increase in the price of oil resulted in a $200 billion reduction in consumer spending.[14]

War or even the threat of war—especially in oil-producing regions—can intensify and exacerbate the underlying price volatility problem. In early 2012, for example, war-related fears concerning Iran drove prices above $125 a barrel.[15] Natural disasters, such as the earthquake that led to the partial meltdown of Japanese nuclear facilities in Fukushima, can also cause oil prices to spike. Together the 2011 "Arab Spring," the temporary disruption of Libyan oil supplies, and the Fukushima accident in Japan brought global

Monopoly-Finance Capital Produces Stagnation and Upheaval from the USA to China (New York, NY: Monthly Review Press, 2012).

oil prices to a record annual *average* of more than $100 per barrel for the first time ever.[16]

World food prices, driven by increasing population, climate change, and limits to the availability of arable land, have also become increasing volatile. There have been three significant global food price spikes in the last six years alone (2007–08, 2011, 2012).[17] There is a strong likelihood that food crises will recur with greater frequency in the future (especially as global warming continues). The highly regarded research arm of Deutsche Bank states: "Spikes in food prices are expected to occur with increasing frequency in the future . . . intensified by climate change."[18]

Again, these problems are not likely to be easily solved in the new economic context we are entering. A growing global population (and wealth) has been steadily increasing the demand for food, even as resources are diminishing, soils are becoming depleted, and climate change is creating increasingly intense competition for water and land. Yields of rice and wheat—two of the world's most crucial staples—have been rising more slowly than demand. Shortages of key grains and high food prices can also contribute to explosive social and political challenges. More than sixty food riots occurred in thirty different countries in 2008 alone. Several analysts point to food price spikes in 2011 as important factors related to the Arab Spring protests and changes of government in North Africa and the Middle East.[19]

And we haven't even mentioned, yet, the impact of financial speculation in the world's energy and food markets. Suffice it to say that when investors attempt to profit off price fluctuations for these commodities, the impact of underlying shortages can multiply, creating even greater havoc.

In addition, certain rare earth elements and other less well-known minerals of special importance to modern electronics, medical devices, and modern automobiles are highly concentrated in a few countries. While the list includes Australia, South Africa, Brazil, Malaysia, Malawi, Russia, the United States, and India, it is dominated by China, estimated to hold half of the world's rare earth minerals and currently producing 97 percent of the global rare earth supply.[20] But as China looks to its own industrial future, it anticipates decreasing exports and increasing its consumption. The possibility that supplies can be cut off by political decision, especially if and when inventories for domestic consumption begin to run low, is another area of potential disruption.

Finally, some highly respected economists like Northwestern University professor Robert Gordon hold that we have run out of the productivity gains traceable to the last major round of high-power technological inventions—and that there is no reason to assume that a new burst of large-order inventions will automatically occur. If so, this would further complicate the stagnation forecast by reducing the underlying capacity of the economy to generate real income growth.[21]

The bottom line:

All things considered, economic and social pain are likely to deepen and persist. But as they do, they are also likely to produce precisely the kinds of conditions that, as we have seen, have been critical drivers for various forms of democratization—of ownership, of wealth, and of institutions. The challenge is to develop a system-changing strategy that can not only end the downward spiral but build forward on such possibilities and give rise to something different, something entirely American.

CHAPTER TWENTY-TWO

The Logic of Our Time in History

- *And What That Means for the Next American System* -

Yes, some form of change unique to our time may be possible. Yes, we need to look around and forward, not backward, to create it. And, yes, a great deal depends on the national and global factors we just discussed.

But other major factors are also powerfully impacting the emerging historical context. Factors that will also make it extremely difficult to achieve traditional solutions (rather than gestures) that respond to the scale of the many, many problems we face now, and the many more we are likely to face. Factors that also suggest the possibility of an entirely new political reality.

Take, for example, the Supreme Court's 2010 *Citizens United* decision, which has added enormously to the corporate-dominated system's capacity to block solutions to a number of critical social, economic, and environmental problems. The court's finding that unrestricted amounts of money can be contributed by corporate "persons" to affect politics, and its clarification that money spent on advertising by such "persons" is "speech" protected by the Constitution, opened powerful new flows of highly conservative political funding. A recent study tracking money in politics by the Center for Responsive Politics found that "business interests dominate, with an overall advantage over organized labor of about 15-to-1." Between 2009 and 2010 contributions by corporations and other businesses totaled $1.36 billion compared with a modest $96 million from labor groups.[1]

It is also clear that as time goes on, and as labor unions continue to decline, the politically important financial imbalances are likely to worsen—to say nothing of the fact that as the need for systemic change intensifies, those holding power and purse in the old system will likely up the scale and sophistication of their efforts to resist it.[2]

The faltering system's underlying difficulties will also be further intensi-fied, going forward, by profound fiscal challenges. Indisputably, projected costs (especially of health care) will put enormous pressure on the federal budget—and further pressure, too, on political decision making involving the expenditure of funds. On its current course, the Congressional Budget Office projects federal spending could rise from 24.1 percent of the economy in 2011 to 35.7 percent over the next twenty-five years.[3] (In the absence of large-scale tax increases, such spending could produce deficits in the range of 17.2 percent of GDP and debt of around 200 percent of GDP.[4])

Which means—quite apart from congressional deadlocks, growing fights between liberals and conservatives, and the like—the political capacity to allocate funds to deal with new problems as time goes on will be severely, not marginally, limited, no matter who holds office, and even assuming some partial successes in altering the developing fiscal trajectory.

Political journalist Thomas Edsall observes:

> We're entering a period of austerity, far different from anything we've ever seen before.
>
> With resources shrinking, the competition for them will inflame. Each party will find itself in a death struggle to protect the resources that flow to its base—and, since the game will be zero-sum, each will attempt to expropriate the resources that flow to the other side. This resource war will scramble our politics. Each party will be forced to dramatically change its calculus and remake its agenda.
>
> And if you thought our politics had grown nasty, you haven't even begun to consider the ugliness of the politics of scarcity.[5]

Economist Jeff Faux adds: "An extended era of low wages and austerity will continue to undercut the New Deal institutions—trade unions and public-safety nets—that provide American workers with protection from assaults on personal dignity from dog-eat-dog job competition . . . With these protections gone or greatly diminished, class lines will harden and social mobility in America— already below that of many other advanced nations—will decrease further."[6]

It is difficult in the extreme to grasp the possibility—*embrace and understand fully the likelihood*—that we may be entering a many-decades-long period in which the dominant reality is one of erratic growth, punctuated stagnation, commodity inflation, substantial political stalemate, and decay. Give or take an occasional political or economic uptick moment, that, however, appears to be the most likely long-term context in which the next era of political-economic change will be forged.

It is possible that the deteriorating deeper conditions will simply continue; that decay and more decay may be the result of ongoing political-economic failure; that like Rome our nation may simply be unable to come to terms with the challenges it faces.

On the other hand, conditions like these over the last several decades have steadily fostered the development of the many wealth-democratizing, institution-building changes now under way around the nation. As conditions worsen and as the lessons of new advances are passed along, it is likely that the pace will increase on its own—and potentially could intensify if a coherent strategy is developed and implemented. The key lines of ongoing development and vectors of potential strategic change include:

- Evolutionary reconstruction—including the development of local cooperatives, worker-owned companies, neighborhood corporations, land trusts, social enterprises, B Corps (and other sustainable businesses), and many other community-based forms.
- Checkerboard municipal and state development—including public land development and ownership, municipalization of utilities and Internet services, land trusts, sustainability planning and related public energy strategies, use of direct municipal and state investment strategies, et cetera.
- Crisis transformations—including especially state and national banking initiatives and moves toward state and ultimately national single-payer health programs.
- Big crisis transformations—including the possible nationalization of certain firms following the GM and AIG precedent, and potentially ultimately moving over time toward public, public-worker, or quasi-public national or regional Tennessee Valley Authority-style and related ownership forms.

How far such processes might develop as the pain deepens is clearly an open question—one that is intimately related to other lines of ongoing political development that the new era might give rise to.

And herein lies one of the biggest challenges. Even people with a shared vision for social, political, environmental, or financial justice commonly choose to travel many different paths toward change. That diversity can work both for and against the shared visions, and a number of longer-term approaches and possible outcomes:

Option Number One

Some observers offer what they hope may be a politically viable way out of the pain and a context that is likely to intensify the long decaying trends. The respected political analyst Ruy Teixeira, for instance, holds that growing numbers of minorities, especially blacks and Hispanics, and growing numbers of women and educated professionals are likely to produce increasing Democratic majorities over time. In Teixeira's view: "All this adds up to big change that is reshaping our country in a fundamentally progressive direction."[7] Others hope that divisions within the Republican Party may open the way to new possibilities.

But the question we face is not simply whether Democrats or even progressives can be elected. Commonly lost in predictions based on demographic changes and Republican divisions is that the question of who is elected (and even the question of whether they can do something useful) is radically different from the question of whether the decaying long trends, and the challenging economic management problems emerging throughout the system, can be dealt with.

Put another way: Given the underlying and ongoing changes in institutional power balances, the deepening economic difficulties, the growing fiscal crisis, and the Supreme Court's *Citizens United* decision there is little reason to believe such changes, important as they are, will easily be translated into a force sufficiently powerful to alter the long-decaying income, wealth, climate, and other trends even if the balance of party affiliations in Congress (and their relative political views) begins to shift.

Option Number Two

It is "possible," to state the hope of many others, that a massive and far-reaching populist or progressive form of political movement building, along with new labor organizing strategies, will produce a renewal of traditional reform capacities in ways that may achieve more than modest gains—in other words, that, again, may actually begin to alter the downward trends. Such movement building is good and useful no matter what. The question lies in how far down the road traditional reform strategies can take us, and what a serious movement needs to embrace to create trend change, to say nothing of larger systemwide change. Demonstrations, sit-ins, direct action, civil disobedience in relevant cases, labor–community alliances, and the like are important, but they are unlikely on their own to achieve trend-altering change in the face of the deepening systemic crisis—especially given the decline of traditional unions, the institutions that have historically given weight and muscle to progressive movement efforts.

In a variation of older "pendulum-swing" and "cycle" theories of history, some progressives all too easily cite late 19th- and early 20th-century populist- and progressive-era gains in the hope that these provide precedents for our own time in history. But many forget that populism, in fact, was largely defeated in its major policy proposals, and that despite important regulatory and other gains, progressive-era achievements were of a radically different order. The federal government was a mere 3.7 percent of GDP (compared with 24.1 percent in 2011)—even after most of the gains traceable to the progressive era and World War I's impact on political-economic change had been incorporated into public policy.*[8]

To repeat, none of these considerations suggest that reform efforts and progressive movement building should be abandoned. Quite the contrary; both are extremely important. The critical challenge is to find a way, as we move ever deeper into a much more profound systemic crisis than many have as yet confronted, to dig much deeper in the quest for a new way forward than we have previously been forced to do. The challenge is to begin to deal directly with the core issue of how wealth is owned and controlled at the heart of the system.

Option Number Three

It is also possible that in addition to traditional progressive movement-building efforts, new strategies created especially by the young, by new environmental activists, by Occupy Movement activists, by progressive new business groups like the Business Alliance for Living Local Economies (BALLE) and American Sustainable Business Council, along with the many others who are beginning to coalesce in the New Economy Movement, will add new energies and a different kind of developing thrust to a larger movement-building effort. Especially important are localist efforts, and building from the bottom both economically and ecologically to achieve greater local resilience.

---

* The modest size of the modern American welfare state compared with that of many European nations also reminds us of the weakness of traditional American reform capacities—even without considering the decline of labor and other fast-growing modern challenges. Among the factors commonly cited to explain our much weaker state-managing politics are racial and ethnic divisions, a complex history of immigrant rivalries often exploited by conservative forces, the huge scale of the nation, the absence of feudalism, and the fact that the United States did not experience massive war on its own territory during the twentieth century—a force (as the late historian Tony Judt powerfully demonstrated in his book, *Postwar: A History of Europe Since 1945* [New York, NY: Penguin Press, 2006]) that helped pull together the modern welfare states and political-economic capacities of many European states.

Again, important as such a direction is—and important as it is to build wherever possible—the power of such activism to address some of the large-order system-driven trends, and especially those involving climate change, is also all but certain to be severely limited unless and until it becomes possible to fundamentally alter the underlying institutional and systemic power imbalances and the growth-driven corporate institutions that both continue to produce the ongoing trends and stand in the way of change. And this, in turn, requires a much deeper approach, side by side with such efforts.

Option Number Four

It is also possible that the growing social and economic decay will lead to one or another form of violence on either left or right (or both), even over time to domestic terrorism from one or more directions. Explosions of urban unrest like those of the 1960s may well occur again as the pain deepens. It is also a mistake to forget that even more threatening possibilities may develop elsewhere in the system: The 1995 Oklahoma City bombing of the Alfred P. Murrah Federal Building was committed by an angry white terrorist, Timothy McVeigh.

If there is violence, there will also be repression and—depending upon which party is in power and the precise circumstances—the already deepening trends of ever-declining civil liberties are likely to be intensified. It is accordingly also possible that this logic may lead to what the late Bertram Gross termed "Friendly Fascism" or to a corporate state in which civil liberties and democratic processes are subverted as politicians exploit fear in the wake of violence.

(On the other hand, even massive repression almost certainly does not end the challenge. The dictators who dominated Latin America for many decades have disappeared in most countries—and progressive groups, once suppressed and tortured, are building anew. Their determination to continue to build through even very dark times stands as a reminder of what is also possible, and what might become necessary in the challenging historical context we may face.)

Option Number Five

It is also possible that the quietly developing wealth-democratizing, institution-building trends reviewed throughout parts 2, 3, and 4 will continue to build in scale and power over time, decade by decade, *precisely because of the pain of the emerging historical context*—and that as a result such institutions might begin in critical areas to slowly displace corporate institutions at the same time they slowly create new political constituencies. The developing longer-term processes might thereby (minimally) begin to achieve steadily expanding institutional capacities to bolster traditional progressive movements—and in turn such movements might ultimately help enact policies to nurture and expand the developing wealth-democratizing institutional thrust.

If so, although the resulting longer-term, decade-by-decade development path would not serve to replace the institutional power of the labor union in progressive strategy, it could slowly help create institutional alternatives and new associated constituencies that might help strengthen a revised strategy. First, it could provide alternatives to the corporation as the only significant choice for local municipal economic development. Second, it could slowly displace corporate institutions in a number of key areas we have reviewed (for instance, state single-payer health insurance, electric power development, large-scale banking in crisis, possibly national health insurance over time, plausibly other major corporations over time). And third, it could help create new institution-shifting *ideas* of what must ultimately be done, and how longer-term strategic approaches might be changed so that, when the opportunity arises, developments nurtured in the local, state, and in part national "laboratories of democracy" might one day be available for further, larger-scale implementation.

An obvious conclusion is that it is important to build forward on all fronts, over time, steadily—and in particular to self-consciously advance new wealth-democratizing, institution-building strategies that may add new forms of power, along with new vision, to a politics of reform. Over the long haul such a direction could help forge—slowly, agonizingly (and in significant part precisely because of the ongoing systemic failures)—new institutional foundations and related political efforts that might become sufficiently powerful to begin to alter the downward-moving direction of the great social, economic, and environmental trends that now define the decaying pattern of the corporate-dominated system. Even possibly to create some elements of a new "mixed" economy more favorable to progressive concerns.

And with all this, too, we might also begin to see the slow development of a new vision and wealth-democratizing culture and movement capable of beginning to challenge the dominant hegemonic ideology.

Which leads, of course, to a final option—and potentially a more comprehensive and effective way forward:

A strategic and self-conscious decision by committed activists to further an ongoing and longer course of institution-changing action—one linked to ongoing movement-building politics and explicitly understood as a way to potentially begin to lay the necessary groundwork for something more.

PART VII

CONCLUSION

CHAPTER 23

The Prehistory of the Next American Revolution

—— Toward a Community-Sustaining System ——

Histotry has a way of surprising us, especially in times when serious change seems impossible. The modern civil rights movement, the feminist movement, the gay rights movement, even the modern conservative movement (which was modest in the early postwar era), all rose to major power without benefit of pundit prediction. Indeed, the success of all these movements was quite contrary to the conventional wisdom at the time, which held that nothing serious could change.

Nor did anyone predict the Arab Spring revolutions in the Middle East, or the radical shifts in power that have overthrown conservative and authoritarian governments throughout Latin America in the last two decades. Farther back, how many people in 1989 predicted that the Berlin Wall would fall, or that within two years the Soviet Union would dissolve, or that within five years apartheid would finally end in South Africa?

The American Revolution itself stands as a reminder that a small and totally outgunned group of determined people could defeat the then most powerful empire in the world.

I am no utopian; I am a historian and political economist. I am cautious about predictions of inevitability—*including the assumed inevitability, dictated from on high, that nothing fundamental can ever change.*

It is possible—indeed, perhaps likely—that at some point the pain, tensions, loss of belief, and anger building up in America will lead to something far more explosive and transformative than business-as-usual politics. And it is our responsibility—yours and mine and other Americans'—in advance of such a time to openly consider what might make sense, how to proceed, and what our role in the matter might be.

The place to begin is with the profound challenge now confronting us in connection with the truly fundamental American values—equality, liberty, and democracy; and with the ongoing loss of belief in the corporate system's capacity to achieve and nurture these values, not to mention those involving global sustainability. I am not talking, simply, about the need to address social and economic and climate change pain, as important as they are. I am talking about addressing something much deeper.

A nation that proclaims a creed based on centrally important values but continues to violate them in practice is setting itself up for challenges much more serious than the problems of "normal" politics. If the trends continue to decay—and there is every reason to believe that most, in fact, are likely to—we will clearly be entering what social scientists term a "legitimation crisis": a time when the values that give legitimacy to the system no longer can, in fact, be achieved by the system.

The late Seymour Martin Lipset and William Schneider, cautious researchers studying the loss of belief in American institutions during the 1980s at a time even before the economic and social pain had begun to deepen, concluded:

> The situation is much more brittle than it was at the end of the 1920s, just before the Great Depression, or in 1965, immediately preceding the unrest occasioned by the Vietnam War and the outbreak of racial tension . . . The outcome could very well be substantial support for movements seeking to change the system in a fundamental way.[1]

Their conclusion, though premature, stands as a warning—and a challenge—to our own time. At minimum it is another reminder of the importance of considering strategies beyond the usual political routes to change—an "Option Six," if you like.

Put another way, the deepening difficulties also suggest the possibility that we may now be well into the prehistory of the next American revolution, that Option Six may ultimately involve longer-term changes much greater than many have contemplated. It is never possible to know in advance what may or may not occur. Nonetheless, such a time is a time when it is also our responsibility to begin to consider the fundamental question of how a "next system" might and should be organized, a time to begin to explore new ways to achieve the great American values that can no longer be achieved by the dying system.

Understood in this larger perspective, the various efforts under way that offer the possibility of democratizing the ownership of wealth may not only help bolster traditional progressive political strategy, but also help lay down critical building blocks for something far more fundamental.

Which also means it is time to begin to get serious about the question: *If you don't like corporate capitalism and you don't like state socialism, what do you want?* It is time to throw off the blinders that suggest we must always and forever be constrained by systemic alternatives whose main lines of development can be traced back more than a hundred years—indeed, far longer back in historical time. That the question may be of more than passing interest is also suggested by the fact that the words *capitalism* and *socialism* were the most-looked-up words in the Merriam-Webster online dictionary in 2012.[2]

A good way to start answering the question is to confront the profound challenge of community, and its practical requirements and systemic implications. *The institutional requirements of community pose fundamental issues that neither corporate capitalism nor state socialism ever took seriously.* The critical point of departure is the question: Can you ever have Democracy with a big *D* in any system if you don't have democracy with a small *d* in the actual experience and everyday community life of ordinary everyday citizens?

Especially at a time like ours when corporate power and money dominate?

I'm talking about genuine democracy, not just voting. Real participation, the kind political theorist Benjamin Barber calls "strong democracy." The kind where people not only react to choices handed down from on high, yea or nay, but actively engage, innovate, create options—and also decide among them.

There are increasing numbers of experiments with what this means— some that we've visited in earlier chapters, and many others in the United States and around the world that point to a new direction, building from the bottom up. In such efforts the outlines of a very different, more vital, more engaged democracy for the next system are beginning to be forged, developed, expanded—starting in specific communities.

There are also new, related theoretical outlines being generated by our leading scholars. The president of the American Political Science Association, Harvard professor Jane Mansbridge, writes: "Without an extensive program of decentralization and workplace democracy, few people are likely to have the political experiences necessary for understanding their interests." As she also observes, "They are most likely to come to understand their real interests in a small democracy, like a town or workplace, where members make a conscious effort to choose democratic procedures appropriate to the various issues that arise."[3]

141

Other scholars—including Barber, Stephen Elkin, and Robert Putnam—have elaborated on similar themes. The spirit of such a vision, however, can be traced back to Alexis de Tocqueville and John Stuart Mill, who best understood the importance of getting things right at the community level. Here is Tocqueville: "Local assemblies of citizens constitute the strength of free nations. Municipal Institutions are to liberty what primary schools are to science; they bring it within the people's reach, they teach men how to use and how to enjoy it."[4]

And here is Mill: "We do not learn to read or write, to ride or swim, by being merely told how to do it, but by doing it, so it is only by practicing popular government on a limited scale, that the people will ever learn how to exercise it on a larger."[*5]

I need to stop the flow here to sharpen a critical point: It is not enough to urge such change, even to experiment with it, though both are important. A systemic challenge goes deeper, much deeper, and it brings us back full circle to who controls wealth—and for more than one reason.

First, anyone who has considered the matter for more than five minutes knows that money influences elections big-time, that the distribution of power is intimately related to the distribution of income and wealth, and that democracy remains superficial and essentially compromised so long as this is so. But the hard place in the argument about how to achieve real change, the place that underscores the need for systemic change rather than mere policy and political change, is that the old system, the one dominated by corporations with the hope that traditional politics can significantly alter the distribution of income and wealth (*hence democracy!*), no longer can achieve such change.

Which means that either the next system will be built upon different ways to organize the ownership of wealth, or the ongoing trends will continue (with or without minor adjustments around the edges).

Another way to say this is that there is a difference between an abstract vision of democratic practice and the value of democracy, on the one hand, and what is best termed a systemic design capable of achieving and sustaining that vision and that value, on the other.

Which means, again: If you don't like state socialism and you don't like corporate capitalism, what do you want?

---

* The challenge such a vision presents to weak democracy understandings—and also to abstract slogans of "participatory democracy"—was captured by a wall poster during the 1968 uprisings in Paris: "Question: How do you conjugate the word 'participate'? Answer: I participate, you participate, we participate. *They decide!*"

And if you aren't willing to answer that question, or even engage it, why should we listen to your concerns about the failings of the current system?

Just to dig a bit deeper into the difference between defining our values and vision and creating a serious systemic design capable of achieving and sustaining them, here's a second challenge:

You can't have a genuine experience of meaningful local democracy if communities are continually disrupted, the people moved hither and yon, and municipal government so dependent on corporate help that there is no room for any serious form of democratic choice.[6]

Accordingly, if the next system takes community and democracy from the ground up seriously, it will have to deal with stabilizing the local economies of our communities.

And this in turn takes us back again to how wealth and capital are owned and organized. I have noted in chapters 6 and 17 several ways to think about this, based in part on how cities like Cleveland are exploring new models, but also on how large-scale industry might be organized to help stabilize communities as well (in chapter 17). As we have also noted, there is also plenty of room in such a vision for small business and for high-tech intermediate-scale enterprise.

I remind you: We are not "merely" talking about nurturing democratic community practice; we are talking about community practice *as the basis of fundamental experiences of critical importance to the nation as a whole and of democracy in general.* The answer to the question "Can you have genuine Democracy with a big *D* in a continental nation if its citizens have little genuine experience of democracy with a small *d* in their own lives?" is simple: No.

And turning this around requires structural and institutional support to reorganize how wealth is owned and controlled.

Beyond this, and again critically, if we are to counter the dangers both of corporate domination and of traditional forms of socialist statism, decentralization is essential—both of economic institutions and of political structure.

There are also important questions of function: Manufacturing involves different issues than dealing with land use or finance, health care, and many other city, state, and national level political economic matters.

I won't go further with the challenge of community and the challenge of genuine democracy at this point.* However, if you care about these matters, come on in: Get in the game. It is time (in this possible prehistory of the next

---

* See the afterword for further discussion.

American revolution) to get serious about systemic design. Especially, again, if you don't like corporate capitalism and you don't like state socialism.

The same challenge faces us in connection with one of our most vexing global issues. For anyone interested in climate change, halting ongoing global warming and creating a new ecologically supportive culture is not exempt from the system-change challenge. It is not possible to do more than marginal "sustainability planning" to achieve greater resilience in cities that are continually tossed hither and yon by uncontrolled economic pressures. Moreover, when—as is now common—we throw away cities like Detroit, Cleveland, St. Louis, and many others, having to rebuild them someplace else, it is not only the capital and human costs that are huge, but also the carbon costs.

We are back again by another route to the question of community—and communities. And back again to the requirement, in the new era, that we go beyond simply urging a mere "politics" against the power structure (important as that is), back to getting serious about creating the building blocks of what a different and practical systemic design that might do the job will entail.

The great Jewish theologian Martin Buber adds one further element that underscores a deeper point. It is not simply democracy in the abstract that is at stake; it is also the principle of community—of whether we see and understand each other, and our nation, *as a community*. The dying system gives lip service regularly to this idea, but in practice its institutional structures serve to divide and conquer. (And its traditional political capacities no longer serve to "overcome.")

Just after World War II, Buber offered his own approach to dealing with the issue, emphasizing wealth democratization, too, starting from community (and bringing together both worker and consumer cooperatives). "By the structure of a society," he wrote, "it is to be understood its social content or community-content: a society can be called structurally rich to the extent that it is built up of genuine societies."[7] We may or may not embrace Buber's particular formula, but the challenge he presents is the same: A systemic design that builds upon the principle of democratization of wealth opens up the possibility not only of democracy with a small *d* locally, and with a large *D* in the system as a whole, but ultimately also of slowly nurturing a new culture and rebuilding the essential understanding of ourselves and our nation *as a community*.

In so doing, perhaps we also may begin to create a new moral "North Star," a direction that is logical and developed in its structural argument, but also inspiring and empowering in its vision and hope.

Elsewhere—as described in the afterword—I have suggested other elements that any serious systemic design based on principles of democracy, individual liberty, community, and ecological sustainability must begin first to debate, and then to implement. Among the most important and challenging in the coming era is how a very large nation like our own (you can tuck Germany into Montana!) might ultimately be reorganized to give more power to various regions. There is a long history of regional thought to build upon, beginning with serious research done during the 1930s, and with the New Deal–era plan for seven TVAs, but there have also been several proposals with regional decentralization during the Johnson, Nixon, and Clinton administrations.

Quite apart from the fact that Congress is increasingly stalemated at the national level, and especially as population increases toward a possible Census Bureau "high" projection of around a billion by 2100, it is highly unlikely that a systemic design that aspires to meaningful democracy can be managed from Washington. And if most states are too small and the continent too big, the (intermediate-scale) regional question will also inevitably be on the table for anyone serious about the future of democratic participation.

We have also touched on the importance, for large industry, of moving beyond corporate structures that must inherently grow.[8] All in all a new overall systemic model might be called "a pluralist commonwealth" to capture the plural forms of common wealth-holding institutions it affirms. These include not only communitywide stabilizing efforts but also cooperatives, worker-owned companies, neighborhood corporations, small- and medium-sized independent firms, municipal enterprises, state health efforts, new ways of banking and investing, regional energy and other corporations, and in certain critical areas national public firms and related democratic planning capacities.[9]

Yes, of course, the possibility that we have entered the prehistory of the next American revolution is just that: a possibility. And for most people—as is the case, always, historically—such a possibility is too distant, too abstract, too far from ongoing experience to deal with.

No problem. It would be surprising if more than a small number of people were able and willing to engage seriously at this level. Moreover, it is possible, as I have argued in the preceding chapter, that at best the ongoing wealth democratization buildup will serve only to help bolster traditional strategies that reduce pain. Which itself is a positive step forward, no matter what. (And in any case, there is plenty of work to do in movement building, creating important projects, demonstrations, politics, and, in appropriate cases, civil disobedience and direct action.)

On the other hand, what is already happening is all but certain to continue to happen: first, a deepening of the fast-developing legitimation crisis and a loss of belief that the core values can be sustained; and second, the ongoing slow democratization processes (evolutionary reconstruction, checkerboard municipal and state development, crisis transformations, big crisis transformations). Because other strategies are failing, and because the pain is increasing.

Like a picture slowly developing in a photographer's darkroom, the potential elements of a new system, of something meaningful and very American, are beginning to emerge.

At the same time, three recent national surveys have found Americans under the age of thirty—*the people who will build the next system*—largely indifferent as to whether capitalism or socialism is better, and if anything slightly more favorable to the latter term.[10]

What confronting the possibility that we are entering the prehistory of the next American revolution offers is a chance to get serious about thinking through what we really want, and this itself may help us clarify new options for the long haul.

It is ultimately also likely to offer us new ways to deal with others around the world. It is unlikely that we will be able to significantly alter ongoing policies that do and do not contribute to global peace and the development of other nations until we become a different community ourselves, until the power structure changes, until we change.[11]

We may also gain perspective another way. America is the wealthiest nation in the history of the world. Over the course of the twentieth century alone, real income per capita (adjusted for inflation) increased roughly sevenfold in the United States.[12] As we have seen, so wealthy is our nation that were income divided equally today, all families of four would receive almost $200,000. (Alternatively, of course, the workweek could be cut in half, with family income reduced on average to $100,000—roughly two times current median family income.)[13]

We do not know the course of future change. It will almost certainly be determined by the direction taken by two powerful trends. On the one hand, the long trends of technological change, if continued, may be promising.

Indeed, if ongoing technological change continues to sustain the previous century-long sevenfold-increase trend, potential real (inflation-adjusted) income for families of four could in theory exceed $1 million per family (or, more likely, a radical reduction in the workweek).

The other trend involves resource limits, and it is a powerfully constraining trend, especially with regard to energy, but also many other things globally (including basic grains, water, fisheries, and arable land). All this will also be impacted by global population growth—or its reduction, as is happening now throughout Europe and Russia, another unknown. And, again, also by specific technologies that may potentially open new directions in certain areas, especially with regard to energy, but also, at this point, to an unknown extent.

What is striking is that in either case, the reconstruction of an American community is clearly the precondition for a decent and meaningful outcome: either to build forward in hopeful new ways on the basis of technological change, or, critically, to work together to manage, as a community, the challenge of resource constraints.

Finally, a place to end and a place to begin—and maybe to help us remember who, in fact, touched off the explosions that helped fuel the modern civil rights, feminist, gay rights, and other movements, to say nothing of the long history of work to make American democracy meaningful that goes back to before the Revolution itself.

As the late Margaret Meade famously reminded us, we should "never doubt that a small group of thoughtful, committed citizens can change the world. Indeed, it is the only thing that ever has."[14] And, of course, everything done in the new direction and to establish the fundaments of a new American community is positive no matter what.

The Question of
Long-Term Systemic Design

This book marks an important stage in a longer series of books and reports, the origins of which may be traced back to work first published in 1972.[1] Supporting research for the argument can be found in *America Beyond Capitalism: Reclaiming Our Wealth, Our Liberty and Our Democracy* (John Wiley & Sons, 2004); the extended introduction to the second edition of *America Beyond Capitalism* (Democracy Collaborative Press, 2011); *Unjust Deserts: How the Rich Are Taking Our Common Inheritance* (with Lew Daly, New Press, 2008); and *Making a Place for Community: Local Democracy in a Global Era* (with David Imbroscio and Thad Williamson, Routledge, 2002).

Additional supporting research can be found in the following coauthored reports and related work done under my supervision: *Building Wealth: The New Asset-Based Approach to Solving Social and Economic Problems* (Aspen Institute, with the Democracy Collaborative, 2005); *Climate Change, Community Stability, and the Next 150 Million Americans* (with Thad Williamson and Steve Dubb, Democracy Collaborative, 2010); *Rebuilding America's Communities: A Comprehensive Community Wealth Building Federal Policy Proposal* (with Steve Dubb and Ted Howard, Democracy Collaborative, 2010).*

---

* In addition, see detailed comprehensive 1968 legislation in support of one approach to the kind of broad community-building strategy suggested in part 2: the Community Self-Determination Act of 1968 (coauthored with John McClaughry and introduced by a bipartisan group of thirty-three senators). Available in *Congressional Record*, July 18, 1968. For early work on stagnation, see: Gar Alperovitz, Harold G. Vatter, and John F. Walker, "The Onset and Persistence of Secular Stagnation in the U.S. Economy: 1910-1990," *Journal of Economic Issues*, vol. 29, no. 2 (June 1995), pp. 591-600.

Detailed information related to many emerging models can be found at www.community-wealth.org, a project of the Democracy Collaborative. A guide to additional related resources can be found at http://whatthenmustwedo.org.

For those who want to dig deeper, the following offers a few guideposts to work where certain aspects of the conceptual frame presented here are dealt with in more detail, and where some of the theory that informs the overall argument is explored in greater depth.

An expanded discussion of political theory and three matters of particular importance to the argument presented in *What Then Must We Do?* is found in part 1 of *America Beyond Capitalism*: (1) local democracy and its relationship to systemwide democracy; (2) the institutional foundations of liberty; and (3) scale, decentralization in general, and regional decentralization in particular.

It may also be useful to note, as suggested in the conclusion, that the emphasis given to the centrality of community in any new systemic design rests on arguments concerning both the requirements of democracy and the requirements of ecological sustainability (and also of planning to achieve locally coherent responses to the challenge of global warming).[2] I have cited the work, particularly, of political theorists ranging from Alexis de Tocqueville and John Stuart Mill to Jane Mansbridge, Stephen Elkin, and Benjamin Barber—and also the theologian Martin Buber, especially in connection with the question of how a culture of community can be nurtured. Recent sophisticated Marxist work has also begun to focus on community as a focal point of concern (and on how it might be sustained and supported in any larger systemic design). See in particular the work of David Harvey and, in turn, his instructive return to earlier work by Murray Bookchin.[3] (Harvey also usefully challenges models that do not take into account questions of governance and structural systems "across a variety of scales" as part of any serious design.)*

In my judgment an emphasis on communitywide structures of ownership is likely to be of increasing analytic importance as time goes on and more

---

* Karl Marx, of course, also focused on community as an important element of his analysis in connection with the Paris Commune, and in his exploration of the significance of the Russian commune or *mir*. He also famously argued near the end of his life that a peaceful transition to socialism was possible in the United States, Britain, and "possibly" the Netherlands. On the Paris Commune see: Karl Marx, "The Paris Commune," in *The Civil War in France*, 1871. On the question of transition see: Karl Marx, "La Liberté Speech: Delivered September 8, 1872 in Amsterdam," published in Marx and Engles, *On Britain* (Moscow: Foreign Languages Press, 1962). On the question of the Russian *mir* see: Karl Marx, "First Draft of Letter to Vera Zasulich," 1881, MECW, vol. 24 (originally published: 1924), p. 346.

experience with various worker ownership and related experiments develops. As is evident throughout this volume, I believe both that such efforts are extremely important and also that (especially in the case of larger economic efforts) there are important reasons to explore joint worker–community structural designs. Among the problems that arise, especially in connection with larger enterprise, are the following: (1) differences between the interests of workers in specific worker-owned firms and the interests of the broader community—which, in turn, can lead to externalizing pollution and other costs to the detriment of the community;* (2) the pressure for larger firms operating in a market to develop expansive growth paths (especially when there are economies of scale) irrespective of longer-term national and global resource constraints; (3) how to resolve problems of inequality in situations where large firms may differ radically in their control of specific markets (as for instance the challenge to equality that might be presented by worker ownership in the oil industry versus worker ownership in the garbage collection industry). For further discussion of some of the issues see the "Brief Note" in the introductory section of the second (2011) edition of *America Beyond Capitalism*.†

It may also be instructive to note that in one of the first major modern efforts at significant-scale worker ownership (in Youngstown, Ohio, during 1977–78), this broader concept was also strongly supported. One of the leading participants and the historical chronicler of the Youngstown effort, Staughton Lynd, writes of the joint worker–community structure: "What was new in the Youngstown venture was the notion that workers and community residents could own and operate a *steel mill* . . . Employee–community ownership of the Campbell Works would have challenged the capitalist system on the terrain of the large-scale enterprises in basic industries . . . This was the ownership model the workers themselves chose."‡

---

* Technically, broader community-inclusive designs internalize many externalities.

† An assessment of these and related issues is also available in an extended joint exploration that David Schweickart and I presented at the International Confederation of Associations for Pluralism in Economics conference at the University of Massachusetts in November 2011, available at my website: http://www.garalperovitz.com/2012/04/icape.

‡ Martin Buber's *Paths in Utopia* also offers a useful analysis of the different implications of systemwide designs based on (1) worker cooperatives, (2) consumer cooperatives, and (3) what he termed a full cooperative integrating both in an overlapping communitywide structure. See: Martin Buber, *Paths in Utopia* (Boston, MA: Beacon Press, 1958). Related to this, Robert McChesney has called for widespread experimentation with new institutional models; also, Immanuel Wallerstein has suggested that nonprofit models (like hospitals) might play an important role in a new systemic design. See: Immanuel Wallerstein, "A Left Politics for the 21st Century? Or, Theory and Praxis Once Again," *New Political Science*, vol. xxii, no. 2 (June 2000), pp. 143–59.

Larger issues concerning the democratization of wealth are presented in my book *Unjust Deserts* (written with Lew Daly). The argument offered there challenges both liberal and conservative justifications for great inequality by stressing the historical (social and societywide) sources of the technological basis of all current income and wealth. Given that the work of any one generation stands upon a Gibraltar of socially created and inherited technological and scientific knowledge, the book distinguishes between the portion of current income and wealth that must be attributed to such societywide historical inheritance and the (much, much) smaller portion of current income and wealth that is attributable to current effort and current invention. While current work, innovation, and effort certainly can and should be rewarded, there is little justification, the book holds, for the fruits of historically inherited and socially created knowledge to be attributed to (and allocated to) elites in position to capture what are essentially unearned "rents." *Unjust Deserts* also draws upon the Nobel Prize–winning work of Robert Solow that demonstrated the extraordinarily large role played by technologically inherited gains in current economic production (especially as compared with current labor and capital).

Also, for those who may be interested in traveling farther down this path, the following suggests some of the issues that I believe are likely to be at the cutting edge of next-stage development.

The Challenges of Scale

I have noted that although the problem very large populations and geographic scales present to democracy and democratic participation has been neglected by many analysts, I do not believe serious work on systemic design can afford to neglect such issues for much longer—especially in the continental-scale American system that will likely reach a population of five hundred million over the next decades and, as noted in the text, could reach over one billion by 2100 if the high estimate projection of the US Census Bureau is reached.

James Madison, the architect of the US Constitution, understood the problem all too well. Madison is usually viewed as favoring constructing the nation on a large scale. What he urged, in fact, was that a nation of reasonable ("mean") size had advantages over a very small one. And writing to Jefferson at a time when the population of the United States was a mere four million, Madison expressed concern that if the nation grew too large, elites at the center would divide and conquer a widely dispersed population, producing "tyranny."*

Scale also significantly determines who has privileged access to the country's news media and who can largely shape its political discourse. In very large nations, television and other forms of political communication are extremely costly. This gives added leverage to elites, who have better corporate connections and greater resources than non-elites. And the priorities of such elites commonly differ from state and regional priorities. Simply to recall: The 2012 electoral campaign involved expenditures in the neighborhood of $6 billion.[5]

We rarely realize how large the United States is compared with other advanced countries. In fact, leaving aside three nations with large, unpopulated landmasses (Russia, Canada, and Australia), the United States is *larger geographically than all the other advanced industrial countries taken together.* In the late George F. Kennan's phrase, it is "a monster country."[6] As noted in the text, Germany is smaller than Montana; France could fit into Texas.

Again, the current US economy is over four and a half times the size of the German economy, and approximately six and a half times the economies of France and Britain. It is only slightly smaller than that of all twenty-seven countries of the European Union taken together.[7]

Beyond this, the most conservative projection model used by Social Security suggests that the US economy will almost double by midcentury, reaching twice the scale of the current European Union economy. Under more optimistic models it could triple, and could reach more than six and a half times its current size by the end of the century. If these models prove to be correct, the figure could easily be well over $100 trillion by 2100. Discounting either projection substantially, of course, still yields an extraordinary figure and an extraordinarily large system.[8]

These various considerations—and especially the challenges presented to democracy by large scale—call out for serious work on decentralization, and if most states are too small to manage major economic problems, and the continent too large, regional units become logically inevitable. Regional decentralization was a subject of significant research and debate during the

---

* "*Divide et impera*, the reprobated axiom of tyranny, is under certain qualifications, the only policy by which a republic can be administered on just principles. It must be observed however that this doctrine can only hold within a sphere of a mean extent. As in too small a sphere oppressive combinations may be too easily formed agst. the weaker party; so in too extensive a one, a defensive concert may be rendered too difficult against the oppression of those entrusted with the administration." James Madison to Thomas Jefferson, October 24, 1787, in *The Papers of James Madison*, vol. 10, ed. William T. Hutchinson et al. (Chicago, IL: University of Chicago Press, 1977), pp. 207–15.

1930s, and various theorists have contributed to the beginnings of an over-view theory that further work might build upon. Among some useful sources: Harvard professor William Bennett Munro (then president of the American Political Science Association) minced few words about the issues he believed needed to be confronted: "Most Americans do not realize what an imperial area they possess." "Many important issues and problems . . . are problems too big for any single state, yet not big enough for the nation as a whole . . . They belong by right to regional governments."[9]

A leading conservative theorist who urged the same logic during the 1930s was Harvard political scientist William Yandell Elliott: "Regional commonwealths would be capable of furnishing units of real government, adequate laborato-ries of social experiment, and areas suited to economic, not-too-cumbersome administration."[10] In recent times the late radical historian William Appleman Williams offered a converging argument in his book *The Great Evasion.*[11]

Research by economists Alberto Alesina of Harvard University and Enrico Spolaore of Tufts University also demonstrates that the larger the nation, the harder it becomes for the government to meet the needs of its dispersed population. Among other things their work suggests that regions that are not well served by a central government's distribution of goods and services have an incentive to take independent action.[12]

Finally, an intense exploration of regional constitutional changes has been under way throughout the world in recent decades—and in nations as diverse as Britain, China, Italy, Indonesia, the former Soviet Union, and Canada. As early as 1989 a comprehensive international report concluded that decentralization had become the "subject of discussion in all countries regardless of whether they are old or young states or whether they have a long unitary or federal tradition."[13] In 2009 another study found that "since the 1980s, concepts of region building . . . have diffused out from their Western European and North American origins and have become firmly entrenched in political discourses."[14] At this writing, intense struggles over regional (even possibly separatist) issues are under way in Spain, Belgium, and Britain.

The bottom line: It is time for a much deeper and more serious assessment of various options for long-term regional decentralization in general, and for longer-term systemic design in particular.

The Role of Planning

Finally, a brief word about the general question of planning, particularly in connection with economic issues. There have been a number of experiments with more participatory forms of planning at the local level.* Although these are highly instructive as to new directions in democratic participation, they have not, of course, as yet attempted to deal with a number of issues that a fully developed national systemic design would require.

Some of the larger challenges:

- A comprehensive planning approach oriented to sustaining community would necessarily have to be able to give priority to community stability, likely, at least in part, along the lines suggested in chapter 17 but also in accord with overall national priorities. The setting of such priorities is, of course, itself an implicit plan (whether called that or not, even under current haphazard and contradictory national budgeting procedures), and the development of a democratic and participatory approach to such planning would be critical in any new systemic design.† A serious participatory planning system would also have to establish criteria to ensure that ecological goals (especially related to climate change) were part and parcel of any plan. And to the degree that regional decentralization is developed over time, the planning system would also necessarily have to integrate regional considerations in the overall approach— or possibly, over time, begin with regional direction, and build up to national formal or informal coordination of regional efforts (depending on the degree of regionalization and its pace).

- Although the efficiency gains that a sophisticated planning approach may offer (see chapters 16, 17, and 18) are potentially of a very large order, a serious plan would also likely have to make appropriate use of the market to help check tendencies toward excessive centralization, bureaucracy, and waste. The essential model suggested for communities in the preceding pages attempts to use quasi-public procurement (hospital purchases, funded in

---

* Information on developing efforts in Porto Alegre, Brazil, and in Chicago and New York can be found at www.participatorybudgeting.org. See also Eric Olin Wright, *Envisioning Real Utopias* (New York, NY: Verso, 2010), pp. 155–67.

† Some possible general directions a more democratic and participatory planning process might take are offered in chapter 15 ("Toward Democratic Planning") of Gar Alperovitz and Jeff Faux, *Rebuilding America* (New York, NY: Pantheon Books, 1984). See also the discussion of national economic planning (specifically chapter 12, "The Need for Planning") in James Galbraith, *The Predator State: How Conservatives Abandoned the Free Market and Why Liberals Should Too* (New York, NY: Free Press, 2008).

significant part by Medicare and Medicaid, and university purchases in part paid for by other taxpayer-supported programs)
and in other areas, potentially, by way of illustration, public procurement of mass transit and high-speed rail (the public market
in general) to help stabilize comprehensive worker-community
structures—both in the Cleveland case (chapter 6) and in the
national illustration offered in chapter 17. Such planning should
not exclude the use of some private market competition to keep
the model in check (as in Cleveland), and perhaps in other areas.
Ultimately, implicit "yardstick" competition between different
regional structures might also serve to perform similar services.

- Part and parcel of any serious model is the question of trade. Open
economies allow the global market to significantly set the terms
of reference for internal development. Alternative approaches
suggestive of ways to manage trade in accord with both internally
coherent planning and community stability can be found in
sections 1 and 4 of Thad Williamson, David Imbroscio, and Gar
Alperovitz, *Making a Place for Community* (Routledge, 2003) as
well as chapter 3.6 of David Schweickart's *After Capitalism* (Row-
man & Littlefield Publishers, 2011).

- Lastly (for the moment), a comprehensive plan would necessarily
have to encompass monetary dimensions and requirements and
to subordinate monetary policy to the overall direction approved
in the plan. This in turn would require institutional changes to
subject monetary institutions to democratic control.[15]

For all these reasons and more, the subjects of planning in general and
participatory planning in particular are matters of great importance—and
also ones that call out for intense research and a rigorous process, both
experimental and theoretical, of development over the coming period.

Moving from Isolated Projects to Integrated Systems

Intimately related to the above is the need to distinguish clearly between the
development of new institutional models, on the one hand, and the requirements of an integrated systemic design, on the other. Worker cooperatives,
land trusts, municipal enterprise, and even the extraordinary Mondragon
effort all suggest institutional elements that might usefully be brought
together in an integrated systemic design. None, however, on its own attempts

to deal with the systemwide aspects listed above, or with many other issues a coherent systemic design would necessarily entail.

In a similar vein, and simply to note: The above listing does not include parliaments, regional legislatures, or other political institutions that might appropriately be reconsidered in a fully coherent long-term design—especially given some of the difficulties facing the substantially hobbled more-than-two-hundred-year-old American constitutional structure.

In the conclusion I suggested that "it is unlikely we will be able to significantly alter ongoing policies that do and do not contribute to global peace and the development of other nations until we become a different community ourselves, until the power structure changes, until we change." This judgment derives from my work both as a historian of American foreign policy and as someone who has participated in the development of policy at high levels in the Department of State and in the US Senate.

All too briefly, three matters are critical:

- American policy in its largest dimensions cannot be separated from the ways in which different corporate and other institutions help shape the fundaments of policy.
- The history of American policy, and its ongoing patterns, cannot be understood without considering the systemic sources of expansionism that have set the terms of reference for policy for more than a century.
- American policy cannot be understood without considering the nature of American culture, and the weakness of its capacity to generate a larger sense of commonality and community.

This book, and the proposals it offers for further work, may also be understood as an attempt to suggest some of the systemic requirements of a radically different foreign policy, one that is responsive to the challenges presented by these deeper considerations. See also the introduction to my *Cold War Essays* (Doubleday, 1970) and the conclusion of *The Decision to Use the Atomic Bomb* (Alfred A. Knopf, 1995) for an all-too-brief related discussion especially of the sources of expansionism, on the one hand, and the limits of traditional American culture, on the other. The overall strategy for US global economic management flowing from both, as it had developed by the 1940s and the end of World War II, is also discussed in my *Atomic Diplomacy: Hiroshima and Potsdam* (Simon & Schuster, 1965).

Acknowledgments

My wife teases me about how long it normally takes me to write a book. Five years? Ten years? Who knows? This book shocked us both; it took roughly three and a half months from first sketch to submission of the manuscript. The reason, obviously, is that it draws upon work done over more than forty years, and in a sense completes at least a certain phase of that work.

Accordingly, I have many people to thank and acknowledge!

First, two of my teachers, long ago:

I was fortunate as an undergraduate at the University of Wisconsin to encounter the great radical historian William Appleman Williams at the point in his career when he was developing some of his most powerful and instructive ideas. (He was testing on us undergraduates, I now realize, themes that became *The Tragedy of American Diplomacy*; other themes that later appeared in *The Contours of American History* were also being sketched in the extraordinary lectures he gave.) My debt to Williams is enormous, and I am pleased to be able to acknowledge it and him. (Indeed, some of the work presented in this book and its predecessors may be understood as a partial down payment on a joint project he and I kicked around some years after I left Wisconsin that somehow never came to fruition.)

The great left-Keynesian economist Joan Robinson was my PhD adviser at Cambridge, and my debt to Joan is also enormous. I left Wisconsin interested in the dynamics of imperialism, and also convinced that in some way those dynamics could not be understood without understanding a great deal more about economics than I then did. Joan's introduction to Rosa Luxemburg's *The Accumulation of Capital* was a powerful punch in the solar plexus; I gladly gave up a Marshall fellowship in London to work with her in Cambridge.* My first book, *Atomic Diplomacy: Hiroshima and Potsdam*, started out as a study of American economic planning for the post–World

---

* And with an extraordinary group of scholars that included Piero Sraffa, Nicholas Kaldor, Richard Kahn, E. H. Carr, Sir Denis Brogan, Maurice Dobb, and many others of great learning and great commitment who expertly helped guide a then-very-young graduate student through more than one intellectual minefield.

War II global economy. When I ran into Secretary of War Henry L. Stimson's diaries documenting the many ways US policy makers saw the atomic bomb as what Stimson called "the master card" in support of US policy, my work took a different turn. Joan didn't blink an eye, allowing and encouraging a study of the role of the atomic bomb in US policy as a PhD dissertation in political economy.

For the past twenty years I have had the extreme good fortune to work with my colleague and partner on matters related to the central theme of this book, Ted Howard. Ted is first and foremost a man of integrity and a committed and forthright friend, colleague, and comrade in arms; he defines the words *world-class mensch*. It has been a pleasure working with him, jointly creating the Democracy Collaborative and developing a strategic vision that begins with wealth democratization at the very local level (as in the work in Cleveland described in chapter 6, where Ted's central creative role has been extraordinary), but also in developing a new theory and strategy of system-wide political-economic change.

The staff of the Democracy Collaborative has also been of great importance, and wonderful to work with. Steve Dubb, who has been the linchpin of our team for the past ten years, is exceptional—both as a truly brilliant colleague and as a master of numerous fields of knowledge, practical and theoretical. Without Steve the center of gravity of our Washington organization could not exist. A special word of thanks and appreciation, too, to Thomas Hanna, whose research support has been topflight throughout, and whose knowledge, professionalism, and patience dealing with my often repetitive and detailed requests have been quite amazing (and very much appreciated!). My thanks and appreciation, too, to John Duda for his supportive communications work, for his intellectual contribution, and for an extremely impressive publication effort from the very start on a very tight timetable. My appreciation, too, to Benzamin Yi for his unflagging administrative and research support (and provocative and eye-catching graphic designs); to Keane Bhatt for help with a number of communications challenges, and in particular for helping arrange certain important media efforts; to David Zuckerman, who has recently joined the staff but has already helped nudge me in the right direction on certain issues; and to Joe Guinan, who worked with us some years ago and happily has recently returned to help with larger systemic design challenges— his contribution, especially to regional issues, was and is of great ongoing importance. Finally, my thanks to Laura Gilliam, who has somehow been able to keep me from excessively tangling up a host of financial and other records and has kept my administrative life (reasonably) orderly. Thad Williamson and Lew Daly, longtime allies and prior coauthors, contributed to specific elements of the argument that is further developed in *What Then Must We Do?* and also helped me keep perspective on many of the larger issues involved.

Friends and colleagues at the New Economics Institute have also been extremely helpful—especially discussions over the years with Gus Speth and Susan Witt, and, more recently, with Neva Goodwin, John Fullerton, Peter Victor, and Bob Massie, all of whom have helped in diverse ways, the importance of which they perhaps may not realize (but I do!). Eli Feghali and Rachel Plattus provided extremely insightful feedback at an important moment in the development of the argument. I am also indebted to *The Nation* and its editors, who over many years have encouraged me to experiment with themes that appear in more developed form in this book; and to the editors of *Dissent, Truthout, Alternet, Yes!, Huffington Post,* and *Common Dreams,* who have allowed me to explore other themes in their pages. My thanks, too, for intellectual stimulation and encouragement to all my colleagues in the New Economy Working Group, and especially to its cochairs, John Cavanagh and David Korten, and its coordinator, Noel Ortega.

A special word of appreciation to several people whose support has been of great significance, both financially and personally, over many, many years—to Lance Lindblom, who as president of the Nathan Cummings Foundation supported the final research and writing push that became this book; to Peter Teague of the same foundation, whose support (and searching questions and intellectual integrity!) contributed greatly to the work; to Jan Philip Reemtsma and my good friend Bernd Greiner, whose support in general—and at a particular moment of challenge—was crucial; and to Patricia Bauman and John Bryant, whose long-term support has been profoundly important: It gave me the gift of time, without which it is hard to see how the deep research immersion that led to this work would have been possible. My thanks, too, to the board of the Nathan Cummings Foundation. The support over many decades of my friends Marcus Raskin and Seymour Hersh has been an ongoing source of strength. My thanks, too, for his help over the years to my friend and agent Ronald Goldfarb. The contributions more recently by Dan Levinson and Kevin Jones have helped enrich the argument. I am indebted, too, to two other friends no longer with us, the late David Hunter and the late John Kenneth Galbraith, who helped launch and gave ongoing support to the institutional home for much of the work that ultimately produced this book.

The people at Chelsea Green have been a joy to work with. I am deeply appreciative of their help and support. (I know what serious publishing and great editing can mean from past experience, both positive and negative!) My editor, Joni Praded, has been special: a great professional eye, an open and warm person, and now a friend. Margo Baldwin has been a source of support and strength throughout (and offered the suggestion that led me to Tolstoy's book of the same title!). I am just beginning to know, learn from, and appreciate the depth of professional knowledge and supporting strength of Shay Totten. My appreciation, too, for their help in diverse areas to Darrell Koerner, Jenna Stewart, Jillian Leclerc, Lettie Stratton, Michael Weaver, Patricia Stone, and Melissa Jacobson. Special thanks to Evan Gaffney for so creative a cover design, and to Gail Leondar-Wright for her professionalism and dedication to making sure progressive ideas reach their audience.

Finally, my family: My children (Kari and David, along with their partners, Jamie and Joanna) and my grandsons (Noah and Ben) have patiently and lovingly supported me—allowing, too, for my writing escapes, sometimes, to "the little cabin" on vacations. My love and thanks to one and all! I cannot possibly acknowledge and thank my wife, Sharon, sufficiently for her love and support these all-too-brief past forty years. This book is dedicated to her. Indeed, it is her book as well as mine; her politics as well as mine. She understands and practices more deeply than anyone I know what a community-sustaining vision really entails. Quite simply, words fail: She has contributed far more than it is possible to acknowledge in this note.

Notes

INTRODUCTION: WHAT THEN MUST WE DO?

1. Leo Tolstoy, *What Then Must We Do?*, 1886, translated by Aylmer Maude in *The World's Classics* (London, UK: Oxford University Press, 1935), p. 54, accessed November 15, 2012, http://arvindguptatoys.com/arvindgupta/whatthenmustwedo.pdf. Tolstoy took his title ("Так что же нам делать?") from Luke 3:10–3:14, and may also have had in mind a well-known nineteenth-century populist novel by Nikolai Chernyshevsky with a similar but slightly different title ("Что делать?"), usually translated as "What Is to Be Done?" The latter became much more well known when Lenin borrowed it for a famous 1902 pamphlet.

2. Real average wages for production workers in manufacturing and nonsupervisory workers in other sectors (accounting for 80 percent of employment) were $18.74 an hour in 1973 ($690.63 per week) in 2011 dollars. In 2011 they were $19.47 an hour ($654.87 per week). See: Lawrence Mishel et al., "Table 4.3: Hourly Wage and Compensation Growth for Production/Non-supervisory Workers, 1947–2011," in *The State of Working America*, 12th ed. (Washington, DC: Economic Policy Institute, September 2012), p. 184.

3. The income share (including capital gains) for the top 1 percent was 9.16 percent in 1973. In 2010 it was up to 19.86 percent. See: Facundo Alvaredo et al., "The World Top Incomes Database," Paris School of Economics, no date, accessed September 17, 2012, http://g-mond.parisschoolofeconomics.eu/topincomes.

4. According to the Census Bureau's 2011 poverty report, "The Organization for Economic Co-operation and Development (OECD) uses a poverty threshold of 50 percent of median income. The European Union defines poverty as an income below 60 percent of the national median equalized disposable income after social transfers." Using the Census Bureau's "OECD equivalence scale" for below 50 percent of family median income results in 69 million Americans in poverty in 2011; using the same scale for below 60 percent of family *disposable* median income results in 73 million Americans in poverty in 2011. See: Carmen DeNavas-Walt, Bernadette D. Proctor, and Jessica C. Smith, *Income, Poverty, and Health Insurance Coverage in the United States: 2011* (Washington, DC: Census Bureau, September 2012), quote on p. 20, accessed November 8, 2012, www.census.gov/prod/2012pubs/p60-243.pdf; United States Census Bureau, *Current Population Survey (CPS) Table Creator* (Washington, DC: Census Bureau, 2011), accessed November 8, 2012, www.census.gov/cps/data/cpstablecreator.html.

5. It was 14.5 percent as of October 2012. See: Bureau of Labor Statistics, "Table A-15: Alternative Measures of Labor Underutilization" (Washington, DC: United States Department of Labor, November 2, 2012), accessed November 20, 2012, www.bls.gov/news.release/empsit.t15.htm.

6. CBS News Poll, "United States of Influence," CBS News, June 28, 2011, accessed October 23, 2012, www.cbsnews.com/stories/2011/06/27/politics/main20074879.shtml#ixzz1QbIxU6H4.

7. Pew Research Center for the People and the Press, "December 2011 Political Survey," Pew Research Center, December 15, 2011, p. 34, accessed August 2, 2012, www.people-press.org/files/legacy-questionnaires/12-15-11%20Topline%20for%20release.pdf.

8. Jeff Jones and Lydia Saad, "Gallup News Service: June Wave 1," Gallup, June 23, 2011.

1. HOW TO DETECT A SYSTEM PROBLEM WITHOUT REALLY TRYING

1. These are the OECD nations minus the former Soviet Bloc countries, Chile, Turkey, Mexico, South Korea, Luxembourg, Greece, and Israel. In many cases these less advanced countries actually have *better* outcomes than the United States. In some cases countries do not report certain comparable statistics. For life expectancy, mental health, infant mortality,

and obesity, see: Organisation for Economic Co-operation and Development, *Health Data 2012: Frequently Requested Data* (Paris, FR: OECD, June 28, 2012), accessed September 27, 2012, www.oecd.org/health/healthpoliciesanddata/oecdhealthdata2012.htm. For inequality, poverty, and social spending, see: Organisation for Economic Co-operation and Development, *Society at a Glance 2011: OECD Social Indicators* (Paris, FR: OECD, April 12, 2011), accessed September 27, 2012, www.oecd.org/els/socialpoliciesanddata/societyata glance2011-oecdsocialindicators.htm. For maternity leave, see: Organisation for Economic Co-operation and Development, "Table PF2.1.A: Calculating Full-Rate Equivalent of Paid Maternity, Paternity and Parental Leave, 2007/2008," in *PF2.1 Key Characteristics of Parental Leave Systems* (Paris, FR: OECD Family Database, April 15, 2011), accessed September 27, 2012, www.oecd.org/social/socialpoliciesanddata/oecdfamilydatabase.htm. For annual leave, see: Organisation for Economic Co-operation and Development, "Table PF2.3.A: Statutory and Collectively Agreed Annual Leave, 2007," in *PF2.3 Additional Leave Entitlements of Working Parents* (Paris, FR: OECD Family Database, January 1, 2010), accessed September 27, 2012, www.oecd.org/social/socialpoliciesanddata/oecdfamilydatabase.htm. For math scores, see: Organisation for Economic Co-operation and Development, *PISA 2009 Results: What Students Know and Can Do: Student Performance in Reading, Mathematics and Science* (Paris, FR: OECD, July 12, 2010), accessed September 27, 2012, www.oecd.org/pisa /pisaproducts/pisa2009/pisa2009resultswhatstudentsknowandcandostudentperformance inreadingmathematicsandsciencevolumei.htm. For environmental performance, see: Environmental Performance Index, "2012 EPI Rankings," Yale University, 2012, accessed September 27, 2012, http://epi.yale.edu/epi2012/rankings. For high school dropout rates, see: Organisation for Economic Co-operation and Development, "Table A2.1: Upper Secondary Graduation Rates (2009)," in *Education at a Glance 2011: OECD Indicators* (Paris, FR: OECD, 2011), accessed September 27, 2012, www.oecd.org/education/highereducation andadultlearning/48631582.pdf. For gender inequality, see: United Nations Development Program, *Human Development Report 2011—Sustainability and Equity: A Better Future for All* (New York, NY: UNDP, 2011), pp. 139–42, accessed September 28, 2012, http://hdr .undp.org/en/reports/global/hdr2011/download. For carbon dioxide and ecological footprint, see: United Nations Development Program, *Human Development Report 2011—Sustainability and Equity: A Better Future for All* (New York, NY: UNDP, 2011), pp. 146–49, accessed September 28, 2012, http://hdr.undp.org/en/reports/global/hdr2011/download. For the well-being of children, see: Organisation for Economic Co-operation and Development, "Table 2.1: Comparative Policy-Focused Child Well-Being in 30 OECD Countries," in *Doing Better for Children* (Paris, FR: OECD, 2009), accessed September 28, 2012, www.oecd .org/social/familiesandchildren/43570328.pdf. For military expenditures, see: Stockholm International Peace Research Institute, "Military Expenditure (% of GDP)," World Bank, 2012, accessed September 28, 2012, http://data.worldbank.org/indicator/MS.MIL.XPND.GD.ZS. For international agreements and international aid, as well as other trends, see: James Gustave Speth, "We're Number One!" *Yes! Magazine*, March 22, 2011, accessed September 28, 2012, www.yesmagazine.org/people-power/on-american-superiority.

2. The income share (including capital gains) for the top 1 percent was 9.16 percent in 1973. In 1980 it was 10.02 percent. In 2010 it was up to 19.86 percent. See: Facundo Alvaredo et al., "The World Top Incomes Database," Paris School of Economics, no date, accessed September 17, 2012, http://g-mond.parisschoolofeconomics.eu/topincomes.

3. Edward Wolff, using different methodology than Alvaredo, Piketty, et al., has calculated that in 2006 the top 1 percent of households had a 21.3 percent share of the nation's income. Correspondingly, the bottom 60 percent together had just 20.7 percent. The US Census Bureau reports that in 2006 there were 114.38 million households with an average size of

2.57 persons per household. Thus the top 1 percent (1.14 million households with 2.94 million people) had more income than 68.63 million households with 176.38 million people. See: Edward N. Wolff, *Recent Trends in Household Wealth in the United States: Rising Debt and the Middle-Class Squeeze—an Update to 2007*, Working Paper no. 589 (Annandale-on-Hudson, NY: Levy Economics Institute of Bard College, March 2010), accessed December 15, 2010, www.levyinstitute.org/pubs/wp_589.pdf; US Census Bureau, *America's Families and Living Arrangements: 2006* (Washington, DC: USCB, no date), accessed October 23, 2012, www.census.gov/population/www/socdemo/hh-fam/cps2006.html.

4. In January 2013 the top rate was raised back to the Clinton-era 39.6 percent rate, but only for individuals making more than $400,000 per year (or $450,000 for couples)—and only for income received above these figures. The changes affected approximately 7/10 of one percent of the population.

5. In 1964 the top marginal tax rate dropped from 91 to 77 percent. It dropped again in 1965 to 70 percent. It rose by 1968 to 75.25 percent and 77 percent by 1969, the last year Johnson was in office. Thereafter, the top marginal rate dropped, particularly quickly under Reagan to a low of 28 percent by 1988–89. Under Bush I the rate rose to a modest 31 percent, and under Clinton to 39.6 percent. See: *Historical Highest Marginal Income Tax Rates* (Washington, DC: Urban Institute and Brookings Institution, January 31, 2011), www.taxpolicycenter.org/taxfacts/displayafact.cfm?Docid=213.

6. Carmen DeNavas-Walt, Bernadette Proctor, and Jessica Smith, *Income, Poverty, and Health Insurance Coverage in the United States: 2011* (Washington, DC: US Census Bureau, September 2012), accessed October 23, 2012, www.census.gov/prod/2012pubs/p60-243.pdf.

7. An increase of around 0.1 percent per year. See: Lawrence Mishel et al., *The State of Working America*, 12th ed. (Washington, DC: Economic Policy Institute, September 2012), p. 184, accessed September 20, 2012, http://stateofworkingamerica.org/files/book/Chapter4-Wages.pdf.

8. Office of Management and Budget, "Table 2.2: Percentage Composition of Receipts by Source: 1934–2017," in *Historical Tables: Budget of the United States Government, Fiscal Year 2013* (Washington, DC: Government Printing Office, 2012), www.whitehouse.gov/omb/budget/Historicals.

9. Office of Management and Budget, "Table 2.3: Receipts by Source as Percentages of GDP: 1934–2017," in *Historical Tables: Budget of the United States Government, Fiscal Year 2013* (Washington, DC: Government Printing Office, 2012), www.whitehouse.gov/omb/budget/Historicals.

10. US Environmental Protection Agency, *Inventory of US Greenhouse Gas Emissions and Sinks, 1990–2010* (Washington, DC: EPA, April 15, 2012), pp. 4–6, accessed June 20, 2012, www.epa.gov/climatechange/Downloads/ghgemissions/US-GHG-Inventory-2012-Main-Text.pdf.

11. US Environmental Protection Agency, "Air Quality Trends," EPA, July 24, 2012, accessed October 25, 2012, www.epa.gov/airtrends/aqtrends.html.

12. For the 93 figure, see: Kathleen Maguire, ed., *Source Book of Criminal Justice Statistics: 2002* (Washington, DC: Government Printing Office, 2004), p. 495, accessed December 15, 2010, www.albany.edu/sourcebook/pdf/sb2002/sb2002-section6.pdf. For 2000 and 2009 figures, see: Bureau of Justice Statistics, "Key Facts at a Glance: Incarceration rate, 1980–2009," Office of Justice Programs, no date, http://bjs.ojp.usdoj.gov/content/glance/tables/incrttab.cfm. For 2010 figures, see: Paul Guerino et al., *Prisoners in 2010* (Washington, DC: US Department of Justice, February 2012), accessed June 8, 2012, http://bjs.ojp.usdoj.gov/content/pub/pdf/p10.pdf. For international comparisons, see: Roy Walmsley, *World Prison Population List*, 9th ed. (London, UK: International Centre for Prison Studies, May 2011), accessed June 8, 2012, www.idcr.org.uk/wp-content/uploads/2010/09/WPPL-9-22.pdf.

13. For 1980, see: Staff, "Data Points: Presidential Campaign Spending," *US News & World Report*, October 21, 2008, accessed July 6, 2012, www.usnews.com/opinion/articles/2008/10/21

/data-points-presidential-campaign-spending. For 2008, see: Center for Responsive Politics, "2008 Presidential Election: Banking on Becoming President," OpenSecrets.org, no date, accessed July 6, 2012, www.opensecrets.org/pres08/index.php. For 2012 estimates, see: Fredreka Schouten, "Deeper Pockets in Fashion for 2012 Presidential Race," *USA Today*, April 5, 2011, accessed July 6, 2012, www.usatoday.com/news/politics/2011-04-05-1Aprezmoney05 _ST_N.htm; Center for Responsive Politics, "2012 Presidential Race," OpenSecrets.org, no date, accessed November 15, 2012, www.opensecrets.org/pres12/index.php.

2. But Hasn't What We Normally Call Politics Done What Needs to Be Done in the Past?

1. Donella Meadows, "Things Getting Worse at a Slower Rate," *Progressive Populist*, vol. 6, no. 14 (August 2000).

2. In 1922 Benito Mussolini seized power in Italy amid severe economic problems. Inflation was rising at a faster rate than during World War I. The lira (Italian currency) was being decimated in international markets, and unemployment was high—exacerbated by the fact that hundreds of thousands of men had left the army and were searching for work. "So parlous was the situation that, early in 1920, there was semi-official talk of bankruptcy." See: R. J. B Bosworth, *Mussolini's Italy: Life Under the Fascist Dictatorship, 1915–1945* (New York, NY: Penguin Books, January 30, 2007). In 1926 the army came to power in Portugal on the back of economic turmoil and inflation wrought by both the Depression and the country's participation in World War I. By 1928 Antonio de Oliveira Salazar, an economics professor, had emerged as the regime's strongman. Salazar ruled the country until 1968, and "his dictatorship was the most insular and longest-lived clerical authoritarian regime of modern Europe." See: Robert Paxton and Julie Hessler, *Europe in the Twentieth Century* (Belmont, CA: Wadsworth Publishing, January 1, 2011), p. 225. In Spain, Francisco Franco seized power after a brutal civil war. That war commenced in part because the Spanish had experienced an unprecedented economic boom between the end of World War I and 1930, and the expectations that increasing prosperity would continue were ruthlessly dashed by the Depression—and a preceding agricultural downturn—that increased unemployment and decreased industrial production. See: Stanley G. Payne, *The Franco Regime, 1936–1975* (Madison, WI: University of Wisconsin Press, September 27, 2011), pp. 35–36; and: Stanley G. Payne, *Franco and Hitler: Spain, Germany, and World War II* (New Haven, CT: Yale University Press, January 28, 2008), p. 5. Most infamously, Adolf Hitler rose to power in 1933 after "inflation [had] undermined the political basis of the Republic and concentrated all real power in the hands of a few" and "the depression radicalized sections of the population which inflation had already rendered unstable." The result was that Germany returned "to the practice of authoritarian government." See: Stephen Lee, *European Dictatorships 1918–1945* (London, UK: Routledge, September 1, 2000), p. 163.

3. According to a recent biography, "Kennan insisted: the only solution lay along a path that few Americans were willing to contemplate, extending 'through constitutional change to the authoritarian state.'" See: John Lewis Gaddis, *George F. Kennan: An American Life* (New York, NY: Penguin, 2011), p. 114.

4. The far-reaching impact the Depression had on politics (and on the political-economic system) has been analyzed by Jacob Hacker and Paul Pierson in "Business Power and Social Policy: Employers and the Formation of the American Welfare State," *Politics & Society*, vol. 30, no. 2 (June 2002).

5. Stanley Lebergott, "Annual Estimates of Unemployment in the United States 1900–1954," in *The Measurement and Behavior of Unemployment*, ed. Universities-National Bureau (Washington, DC: National Bureau of Economic Research, 1957).

3. FLIES NUMBER TWO AND THREE
IN THE TRADITIONAL THEORY OF POLITICS

1. Annual real GDP growth rate from: Lawrence H. Officer and Samuel H. Williamson, "Annualized Growth Rate and Graphs of Various Historical Economic Series," Measuring-Worth, 2011, accessed November 15, 2012, www.measuringworth.com/growth. Median income data from 1947 ($2,685) and 1970 ($8,335) in 1970 dollars from: US Census Bureau, "Table 7: Families and Unrelated Individuals by Total Money Income in 1947 and 1950 to 1970," in *Income in 1970 of Families and Persons in the United States* (Washington, DC: Government Printing Office, 1971), p. 21.

2. Federal military spending in 1940 was around 1.7 percent of GDP. Federal military spending in 1944 was 37.8 percent of GDP. Thus, military spending as a result of World War II amounted to around 36 percent of GDP in 1944. The Obama stimulus package in 2009 amounted to $787 billion. With around $13.93 trillion in total GDP that year, this amounts to around 5.6 percent of the economy. All data from: Office of Management and Budget, *Historical Tables: Budget of the United States Government, Fiscal Year 2013* (Washington, DC: Government Printing Office, 2012), www.whitehouse.gov/omb/budget/Historicals.

3. For a detailed analysis of the so-called compression of wages during the war years, see: Claudia Goldin and Robert Margo, "The Great Compression: The Wage Structure in the United States at Mid-Century," *Quarterly Journal of Economics*, vol. 107, no. 1 (February 1992). For details of the GI Bill, see: "History of the GI Bill," Today's GI Bill, 2011, accessed October 24, 2012, www.todaysgibill.org/todays-gi-bill/history-of-the-gi-bill.

4. For the Truman-era programs, see: "American President: A Reference Resource—Harry S. Truman," Miller Center at the University of Virginia, no date, accessed August 7, 2012, http://millercenter.org/president/truman/essays/biography/9. For Eisenhower, see: Burton Kaufman and Diane Kaufman, *The A to Z of the Eisenhower Era* (Metuchen, NJ: Scarecrow Press, October 26, 2009). For Johnson, see: "American President: A Reference Resource—Lyndon Baines Johnson," Miller Center at the University of Virginia, no date, accessed August 7, 2012, http://millercenter.org/academic/americanpresident/lbjohnson/essays/biography/1.

5. Although many of the major environmental laws were enacted following 1970, they have roots in the political and social movements of the boom era. For instance, the Clean Air Act enacted in 1970 is widely considered the beginning of the modern incarnation of this massively important piece of environmental legislation (amended again in 1977 and 1990). However, it has its roots in the 1955 Air Pollution Control Act, the 1963 Clean Air Act, and the 1967 Air Quality Act. See: "History of the Clean Air Act," US Environmental Protection Agency, February 17, 2012, accessed October 24, 2012, http://epa.gov/oar/caa/caa_history.html. For the study on environmental laws and unemployment, see: Daniel J. Weiss, "Anatomy of a Senate Climate Bill Death," Center for American Progress, October 12, 2010, accessed August 27, 2012, www.americanprogress.org/issues/green/news/2010/10/12/8569/anatomy-of-a-senate-climate-bill-death/.

6. For federal defense spending, see: Office of Management and Budget, *Historical Tables: Budget of the United States Government, Fiscal Year 2013* (Washington, DC: Government Printing Office, 2012), www.whitehouse.gov/omb/budget/Historicals. For an analysis of the economic costs of US wars, see: Stephen Daggett, *Costs of Major US Wars* (Washington, DC: Congressional Research Service, June 29, 2010), accessed July 8, 2010, www.fas.org/sgp/crs/natsec/RS22926.pdf.

7. For the Lichtenstein quote, see: Nelson Lichtenstein, *State of the Union: A Century of American Labor* (Princeton, NJ: Princeton University Press, 2003), pp. 104–5.

8. For the quote and the National Council of Senior Citizens, see: Robert Ball, "What Medicare's Architects Had in Mind, Perspectives on Medicare," *Health Affairs*, vol. 14, no. 4

(1995), pp. 62–72. For more on union lobbying, see: Theodore Marmor, *The Politics of Medicare*, 2nd ed. (Hawthorne, NY: Aldine De Gruyter, 2000), pp. 17–21. For more on how seniors become politically active as they have more programs they are concerned with, see: Andrea Louise Campbell, *How Policies Make Citizens: Senior Political Activism and the American Welfare State* (Princeton, NJ: Princeton University Press, 2003).

9. Nelson Institute for Environmental Studies, "The UAW Steps Up for Earth Day," Wisconsin Historical Society, January 24, 2010, accessed August 29, 2012, www.nelsonearthday.net /collection/coalition-uawflyer.htm.

10. For union density rates, see: Gerald Mayer, *Union Membership Trends in the United States* (Washington, DC: Congressional Research Service, August 31, 2004), http://digitalcommons .ilr.cornell.edu/key_workplace/174; Barry T. Hirsh, *Sluggish Institutions in a Dynamic World: Can Unions and Industrial Competition Coexist*, IZA Discussion Paper no. 2930 (Bonn, Germany: Institute for the Study of Labor, July 2007), http://unionstats.gsu.edu/IZA _Unions&Competition_dp2930.pdf.

11. Many scholars have attempted to explain the decline of unions in the United States (and globally), including but not limited to: Robert Baldwin, *The Decline of US Labor Unions and the Role of Trade* (Washington, DC: Peterson Institute, June 1, 2003); Michael Goldfield, *The Decline of Organized Labor in the United States* (Chicago, IL: University of Chicago Press, May 15, 1989); Barry Bluestone and Bennett Harrison, *The Deindustrialization of America* (New York, NY: Basic Books, April 15, 1984); Nelson Lichtenstein, *State of the Union: A Century of American Labor* (Princeton, NJ: Princeton University Press, 2002); Richard Freeman, "What Can We Learn from NLRA to Create Labor Law for the 21st Century?," paper presented at the George Washington Law School symposium "The National Labor Relations Act at 75: Its Legacy and Its Future," Washington, DC, October 28, 2010.

12. For 2011 rates, see: Bureau of Labor Statistics, *2011 Union Members Summary* (Washington, DC: US Department of Labor, January 27, 2012), accessed October 24, 2012, www.bls.gov /news.release/union2.nr0.htm. For more, see: Harold Meyerson, "If Labor Dies, What's Next?" *American Prospect*, September 13, 2012.

13. Jefferson Cowie and Nick Salvatore, "The Long Exception: Rethinking the Place of the New Deal in American History," *International Labor and Working-Class History*, vol. 74 (Fall 2008), pp. 25–26.

14. Robert Reich, "The Final Health Care Vote and What It Really Means," Robert Reich blog, March 21, 2010, http://robertreich.org/post/463440906/the-final-health-care-vote-and -what-it-really-means.

4. The Fading Power of Traditional Politics

1. In 1943 the War Labor Board ruled that work benefits (such as insurance coverage) were excluded from wage and price controls. See: Henry J. Kaiser Family Foundation, *National Health Insurance—A Brief History of Reform Efforts in the US* (Menlo Park, CA: Kaiser Family Foundation, March 2009), accessed November 15, 2012, www.kff.org/healthreform/upload/7871.pdf.

2. The form of health care legislation that has so far been approved is regressively financed, organized in a manner that requires buying in the insurance, pharmaceutical, and other corporations at huge expense—and, finally, is by no means secure. (More about this in chapter 14.)

3. Michael Kazin, *American Dreamers: How the Left Changed a Nation* (New York, NY: Alfred A. Knopf, 2011), p. xiii.

4. The 1960 census reports that out of a total population of 179.32 million people, there were 54.97 million people living in the geographic area of the South. During the 1940s, '50s, and '60s, the KKK and other white supremacist groups were not active in every community in this region. Conversely, such groups were active in some communities outside of

this geographic region. US Census Bureau, "Table 55: Summary of Population Characteristics, for the United States, by Regions, Divisions, and States, and for the Commonwealth
of Puerto Rico: 1960," in *General Population Characteristics* (Washington, DC: Government Printing Office, 1961), p. 163, accessed August 30, 2012, www2.census.gov/prod2/
decennial/documents/09768103v1p1ch4.pdf.

5. According to a 2007 report by the Civil Rights Project, statistics show "remarkable progress
from the 1960s through the 1980s in desegregation of black students, but then a sharp turn
in the other direction that continues to this day ... Resegregation is now occurring in all sections of the country and is accelerating most rapidly [where] the most was achieved for black
students, in the South." As of 2005, majority-white schools in the South had just 27 percent
black students—the lowest ratio since 1968 (23.4 percent) and down from a historical high
in 1988 (43.5 percent). "Nearly 40 years after the assassination of Dr. Martin Luther King,
Jr.," the report concludes, "we have now lost almost all the progress made in the decades after
his death in desegregating our schools." Gary Orfield and Chungmei Lee, *Historic Reversals,
Accelerating Resegregation, and the Need for New Integration Strategies* (Los Angeles, CA:
Civil Rights Project at the University of California–Los Angeles, August 2007), accessed
August 30, 2012, http://civilrightsproject.ucla.edu/research/k-12-education/integration
-and-diversity/historic-reversals-accelerating-resegregation-and-the-need-for-new
-integration-strategies-1/orfield-historic-reversals-accelerating.pdf.

6. For historical rates, see: US Census Bureau, "Table 2: Poverty Status, by Family Relationship, Race, and Hispanic Origin," in *Historical Poverty Tables—People* (Washington,
DC: USCB, no date), accessed August 30, 2012, www.census.gov/hhes/www/poverty/data
/historical/people.html. For 2011, see: Carmen DeNavas-Walt, Bernadette Proctor, and
Jessica Smith, *Income, Poverty, and Health Insurance Coverage in the United States: 2011*
(Washington, DC: US Census Bureau, September 2012), accessed October 23, 2012, www
.census.gov/prod/2012pubs/p60-243.pdf.

7. David Garrow, *Bearing the Cross: Martin Luther King and the Southern Christian Leadership Conference* (New York, NY: Quill, 1999), pp. 591–92.

8. Nick Kotz, *Judgment Days: Lyndon Baines Johnson, Martin Luther King, Jr., and the
Laws That Changed America* (New York, NY: Houghton Mifflin Company, 2005), p. 382.

5. A NOTE ABOUT SYSTEMS AND HISTORY AND PREHISTORY

1. This statistic is based on data from 2009. That year the four hundred richest Americans had a
combined net worth of $1.27 trillion, with the total net worth of all American households being
$53.1 trillion. Using Edward Wolff's wealth breakdown estimates for 2009, the poorest 60
percent of American households had just 2.3 percent of the nation's total net worth—or $1.22
trillion. In 2009 there were 117.18 million households with an average of 2.57 people per household. Thus the top 400 individuals had more wealth than the bottom 180.69 million people put
together. Since 2009 the Forbes 400 have increased their wealth by 34 percent to $1.7 trillion,
and while comparable data for the bottom 60 percent are not yet available, it is unlikely that
they have seen a corresponding rise. Therefore, this statistic is likely highly conservative. For
an overview of the methodology and expert analysis, see: Tom Kertscher, "Michael Moore Says
400 Americans Have More Wealth Than Half of All Americans Combined," PolitiFact, March
10, 2011, accessed October 24, 2012, www.politifact.com/wisconsin/statements/2011/mar
/10/michael-moore/michael-moore-says-400-americans-have-more-wealth-. For the 2009
Forbes 400, see: Matthew Miller and Duncan Greenberg, eds., "The Forbes 400," *Forbes*,
September 30, 2009, accessed October 24, 2012, www.forbes.com/2009/09/29/forbes-400
-buffett-gates-ellison-rich-list-09-intro.html. For the 2012 Forbes 400, see: Luisa Kroll, "The
Forbes 400: The Richest People in America," *Forbes*, September 19, 2012, accessed October

24, 2012, www.forbes.com/sites/luisakroll/2012/09/19/the-forbes-400-the-richest-people
-in-america. For Edward Wolff's wealth breakdown, see: Edward N. Wolff, *Recent Trends
in Household Wealth in the United States: Rising Debt and the Middle-Class Squeeze—An
Update to 2007*, Working Paper no. 589 (Annandale-on-Hudson, NY: Levy Economics Institute of Bard College, March 2010), accessed December 15, 2010, www.levyinstitute.org/pubs
/wp_589.pdf. For 2009 household data, see: US Census Bureau, *America's Families and Living Arrangements, 2009* (Washington, DC: USCB), accessed October 24, 2012, www.census
.gov/population/www/socdemo/hh-fam/cps2009.html.

6. An Initial Way to Think About System Change

1. For more details, see: Gar Alperovitz and Jeff Faux, *Rebuilding America* (New York: Pantheon, 1984); and Staughton Lynd, *The Fight Against Shutdowns: Youngstown's Steel Mill
Closings* (San Pedro, CA: Singlejack Books, 1982).

2. Rob Witherell, Jim Anderson, and Michael Peck, "The United Steelworkers, Mondragon,
and the Ohio Employee Ownership Center Announce a New Union Cooperative Model to
Reinsert Worker Equity Back into the US Economy," *USW News*, March 26, 2012, www.usw
.org/media_center/releases_advisories?id=0523. For Cincinnati, see: "Cincinnati Union
Co-Op Initiative," Cincinnati Union Co-op Initiative, no date, accessed December 5, 2012,
www.cincinnatiunioncoop.org.

3. For Pittsburgh, see: "SVA Wins $250,000 Grant Award from Heinz Endowments for Clean/
Green Consortium to Build Green, Cooperatively-Owned Laundry," Steel Valley Authority,
May 18, 2011, accessed August 30, 2012, www.steelvalley.org/newsroom/in-the-news/130
-51811-sva-wins-250000-grant-award-from-heinz-endowments-for-cleangreen
-consortium-to-build-green-cooperatively-owned-industrial-laundry. For New York, see:
Joe, "A Brief History of Cooperative Home Care Associates," *American Worker Cooperative*,
March 8, 2011, accessed August 30, 2012, http://american.coop/content/brief-history
-cooperative-home-care-associates.

4. Deborah Groban Olson, "Groban Olsen Employee Ownership Case Studies," Law Office of Attorney Deborah Groban Olson, no date, accessed August 30, 2012, www.esoplaw.com/casestud
.htm; "Associated Wholesale Grocers Sells Stores to Employees," *Progressive Grocer*, December 28, 2011, accessed August 30, 2012, www.progressivegrocer.com/top-stories/headlines
/industry-intelligence/id34475/associated-wholesale-grocers-sells-stores-to-employees.

5. Mondragon consists of more than eighty thousand workers in a network of 109 cooperatives, 125 subsidiaries, and twenty-four support organizations. See: Jose Luis Lafuente
and Fred Freundlich, "The MONDRAGON Cooperative Experience: Humanity at Work,"
Management Innovation Exchange, October 17, 2012, accessed December 5, 2012, www.
managementexchange.com/story/mondragon-cooperative-experience-humanity-work.

6. Ronald Reagan, "Project Economic Justice," speech, the White House, August 3, 1987,
Center for Economic and Social Justice, no date, accessed December 5, 2012, www.cesj.org
/homestead/strategies/regional-global/pej-reagan.html.

7. Quiet Democratization Everywhere

1. "Company Overview," Isthmus Engineering and Manufacturing, 2008, accessed September 21, 2012, www.isthmuseng.com/wp-content/uploads/IsthmusEngBrochure.pdf.

2. Richard Chamberlain, "History: The First Twenty Years," Union Cab Cooperative, no date,
accessed October 7, 2012, www.unioncab.com/History.

3. Joanne Ivancic, "The Louisville Biodiesel Cooperative, MSD and the Green Triangle in
the 9th District Announce Waste Cooking Oil Recycling Partnership," Advanced Biofuels
USA, December 2, 2011, accessed November 16, 2012, http://advancedbiofuelsusa.info

/the-louisville-biodiesel-cooperative-msd-and-the-the-green-triangle-in-the-9th-district
-announce-waste-cooking-oil-recycling-partnership.

4. "Mission," Sandhills Farm to Table Cooperative, 2011, accessed September 20, 2012,
   https://coop.sandhillsfarm2table.com/about_us/mission.php.

5. Dave Zuckerman, "Partnership Brings Community Solar to Edmonds, WA," Community-
   Wealth.org, March 14, 2012, accessed September 20, 2012, http://community-wealth.org
   /blog/index.php/partnership-brings-community-solar-to-edmonds-wa.

6. "About Organic Valley," Organic Valley, no date, accessed November 16, 2012, www.organic
   valley.coop/newsroom/about-organic-valley.

7. Sally Kohn, "A New Grassroots Economy," *The Nation*, May 25, 2011, accessed November
   16, 2012, www.thenation.com/article/160948/new-grassroots-economy#.

8. Black Star Co-op, *Black Star Co-op 2011 Annual Report* (Austin, TX: Black Star Co-op,
   2011), accessed September 20, 2012, www.blackstar.coop.

9. As of November 2012, more than $500 million had been moved as part of the "Move Our
   Money" campaign alone. For up-to-date estimates, see: "Move Our Money," The New Bot-
   tom Line and The Other 98%, November 15, 2012, accessed November 15, 2012, www.move
   ourmoneyusa.org. In 2011, in the month between the beginning of October and "Bank
   Transfer Day," November 5, nearly two-thirds of a million Americans joined credit unions,
   depositing $4.5 billion in the month; see: Credit Union National Association, "CUNA
   Survey: 40k Members, $80M in Savings on BTD," *News Now*, November 9, 2011, accessed
   November 18, 2011, www.cuna.org/newsnow/11/wash110811-2.html.

10. Interview and e-mail exchanges between the author and Burlington organizer-activist Matt
    Cropp, June 8–21, 2012. See also: John Briggs, "Critic Wins Seat on Vermont Federal Credit
    Union Board," *Burlington Free Press*, June 8, 2012, accessed September 21, 2012, www
    .burlingtonfreepress.com/article/20120608/NEWS/306080014/Critic-wins-seat-on
    -Vermont-Federal-Credit-Union-Board; "Vermont Federal Credit Union Members
    Assembly Platform," Vermont Federal Credit Union Members Assembly, July 2, 2012,
    accessed November 16, 2012, http://vfcuma.blogspot.com/p/current-platform.html.

11. Pioneer Human Services, *2011 Annual Report* (Seattle, WA: PHS, 2011), www.pioneer
    humanservices.org/wp-content/uploads/2012/05/2011-PHS-annual-report.pdf; Mike Burns
    (CEO of Pioneer Human Services), interview by Steve Dubb, March 9, 2006; Pioneer Human
    Services, *Annual Report 2010: Pioneering the Possibilities* (Seattle, WA: PHS, 2010), accessed
    May 12, 2011, www.pioneerhumanservices.org/annual_report/10_annual_report.pdf; John
    Cowen, "Pioneer Human Services: 'A "Chance for Change,"'" *Chronicle of Social Enterprise*, vol. 1
    (Spring 2009), p. 5, accessed September 18, 2012, www.socialent.org/pdfs/THE_CHRONICLE
    _OF_SOCIAL_ENTERPRISE_VOLUME_ONE_SPRING_2009.pdf

12. John Golden, "The Zen of Brownies," *Westchester County Business Journal*, May 11, 2009.
    Quote on p. 29 of: Julius Walls, "A Successful Social Enterprise Responds to the Market,"
    in *Powering Social Change* (Washington, DC: Community Wealth Ventures, 2003), pp.
    26–29; "Community Gardens," Greyston Foundation, no date, accessed October 8, 2012,
    www.greyston.org/index.php?gardens. For information on Greyston, see their website:
    "Who We Are," Greyston Foundation, no date, accessed November 16, 2012, www.greyston
    .org/index.php?who_we_are.

13. "Social Enterprises Overview," Southwest Key Programs, no date, accessed November 16,
    2012, www.swkey.org/enterprise/overview.html; "Southwest Key Overview," Southwest
    Key Programs, no date, accessed November 16, 2012, www.swkey.org/about/overview.
    html; "Annual Report & Financials," Southwest Key Programs, 2012, accessed October 8,
    2012, www.swkey.org/about/financials.html.

14. The Democracy Collaborative, "Models and Best Practices: Community Development

Corporations," Community-Wealth.org, no date, accessed November 15, 2012, www .community-wealth.org/strategies/panel/cdcs/models.html.

15. "About New Community," New Community Corporation, no date, accessed November 15, 2012, www.newcommunity.org/about; "Frequently Asked Questions," New Community Corporation, no date, accessed November 15, 2012, www.newcommunity.org/about/questions.

16. Kaid Benfield, "The Remarkable Story of Oakland's Fruitvale Transit Village," NRDC Switchboard, February 7, 2011, accessed September 20, 2012, http://switchboard.nrdc.org/blogs /kbenfield/the_remarkable_story_of_oaklan.html; "Fruitvale Village," MVEI, no date, accessed November 15, 2012, www.mve-institutional.com/project.php?lID=197&subgID=.

17. Champlain Housing Trust, *Annual Report 2011* (Burlington, VT: CHT, 2011), www.champlain housingtrust.org/_literature_118080/Annual_Report_2011.

18. John Emmeus Davis, "Origins and Evolution of the Community Land Trust in the United States," in *The Community Land Trust Reader*, ed. John Emmeus Davis (Cambridge, MA: Lincoln Institute of Land Policy, 2010) pp. 4–47.

19. For the number of community land trusts in the United States: "US Directory of CLTs," National Community Land Trust Network, no date, accessed August 20, 2012, www .cltnetwork.org/index.php?fuseaction=Main.MemberList; "About Us," Irvine Community Land Trust, no date, accessed August 31, 2012, www.irvineclt.org/about.

20. For B Corp legislation updates, see: B Lab, "Passing Legislation," Certified B Corporation, 2012, accessed November 15, 2012, www.bcorporation.net/what-are-b-corps/legislation. The Oglala Sioux Tribe and the Crow Indian Nation of Montana also designate L3Cs; see: "Laws," Americans for Community Development, no date, accessed November 15, 2012, www .americansforcommunitydevelopment.org/legislation.html. For the Louisiana initiative, see: Andrew Wolk, "Leading the Advancement of Social Entrepreneurship," Social Edge, June 11, 2008, accessed December 7, 2012, www.socialedge.org/blogs/government-engagement /archive/2008/06/11/leading-the-advancement-of-social-entrepreneurship.

21. For more on Market Creek, see: Annie E. Casey Foundation, *Building Community Ownership in Neighborhood Revitalization* (Baltimore, MD: AECF, 2005), pp. 12–13; Gar Alperovitz, Steve Dubb, and Ted Howard, "Asset Building Comes of Age," *Shelterforce*, is. 149 (Spring 2007), pp. 24–25 and 44–45; Doug Sherwin, "Community Members Purchase Shares of Market Creek Plaza IPO," *San Diego Daily Transcript*, November 13, 2006, accessed March 5, 2009, www.marketcreekplaza.com/news-11-13-06.html; "Project Overview," Market Creek Plaza, no date, accessed March 5, 2009, www.marketcreekplaza.com/mcp_project.html; "Market Creek Partners, LLC," Jacobs Center for Neighborhood Innovation, no date, accessed December 7, 2012, www.jacobscenter.org/whatwedo_economic_mccv_llc.htm.

8. Worker Ownership Redux

1. National Center for Employee Ownership, "Study 3: ESOP Trends and Characteristics," *Employee Ownership Report*, vol. 32, no. 2 (March–April 2012), p. 7.

2. Though growing in number, there are currently less than five hundred firms structured as traditional worker co-ops. For the origins of ESOPs, see: Todd S. Snyder, *Employee Stock Ownership Plans (ESOPs): Legislative History* (Washington, DC: Congressional Research Service, May 20, 2003), accessed May 23, 2011, http://digitalcommons.ilr.cornell.edu/cgi /viewcontent.cgi?article=1004&context=crs.

3. "About Appleton," Appleton, no date, accessed September 28, 2012, www.appletonideas .com/Appleton/jsps/ourcompany.do?langId=-1.

4. For W. L. Gore, see: Karen M. Young, Corey Rosen, and Edward J. Carberry, *Theory O: Creating an Ownership Style of Management* (Oakland, CA: National Center for Employee Ownership, 1999); "About Gore," W. L. Gore, no date, accessed October 10, 2012, www.gore.com

/en_xx/aboutus/index.html; "Fast Facts about Gore," W. L. Gore, no date, accessed October 10, 2012, www.gore.com/en_xx/aboutus/fastfacts/index.html. W. L. Gore is number thirty-eight on the 2012 Fortune Best Companies to Work For list; see: Fortune, "100 Best Companies to Work For," CNN Money, February 6, 2012, accessed October 10, 2012, http://money.cnn.com/magazines/fortune/best-companies/2012/full_list.

5. For Hy-Vee employees, revenues, and stores, see: "About Hy-Vee," Hy-Vee, no date, accessed October 24, 2012, www.hy-vee.com/company/about-hy-vee/default.aspx; for the Forbes ranking, see: "$48 Hy-Vee," *Forbes*, no date, accessed October 24, 2012, www.forbes .com/lists/2011/21/private-companies-11_Hy-Vee_ABYQ.html.

6. For Lifetouch employment, see: National Center for Employee Ownership, *The Employee Ownership 100: America's Largest Majority Employee-Owned Companies* (Oakland, CA: NCEO, June 2012), accessed October 24, 2012, www.nceo.org/articles/employee-ownership-100; "About Us," Lifetouch, 2011, accessed May 16, 2011, www.lifetouch.com/overview-about-us. Latest revenue estimates are from 2007; see: "#402 Lifetouch," *Forbes*, November 8, 2007, accessed October 24, 2012, www.forbes.com/lists/2007/21/biz_privates07_Lifetouch_KH8H.html.

7. The tax benefits are also available when such a transfer is made to a co-op.

8. The 2002 declaration of bankruptcy by United Airlines has sometimes mistakenly been attributed to the fact that it was significantly owned by employees. Aside from the fact that most airlines experienced extraordinary difficulties in the wake of September 11, 2001—and that most ESOPs have been organized in (and work best in) small- and medium-sized non-publicly traded firms, not hundred-thousand-person publically traded firms such as United— many worker ownership experts judge that United's failure to deal with participation and related organizational issues such as multiple centers of power (not its ownership structure) were major factors in its poor performance. Southwest, which also has significant worker ownership—and a strong participatory culture—is one of the few profitable bright spots in the airline industry. Another "bad apple" example is the *Chicago Tribune*. In 2007 billionaire Sam Zell used an ESOP as part of a massive leveraged buyout of the Tribune Company. The resulting structure was composed of an ESOP with a majority ownership stake, Zell with stock warrants worth about 40 percent of the company, and management with synthetic equity rights of 8 percent. The purchase left the Tribune Company saddled with enormous debts, and when the financial crisis and recession hit in 2008 the company was forced into Chapter 11 bankruptcy reorganization. In March 2011 a US district court judge allowed a class-action lawsuit to proceed against the Tribune Company ESOP trustee—GreatBanc Trust Co.—for failure to fulfill its fiduciary duty to the ESOP members when it purchased $250 million in unregistered shares from the Tribune Company rather than on the open market during the buyout. In November 2010 the same judge ruled that GreatBanc had indeed violated its fiduciary duty. According to a study by the ESOP Association, like United Airlines, the Tribune Company made no real effort to create an ownership culture at the company—and even if it had done so, "the best culture, however, may have made no difference given the deeply troubled state of the newspaper business." See: J. Michael Keeling, "Statement Regarding United Airlines," ESOP Association, 2003; Christopher Mackin and Loren Rodgers, "'But What About United Airlines?' Answering Tough Questions," in *The ESOP Report* (Washington, DC: ESOP Association, January 2003), p. 3, accessed May 23, 2011, www.ownershipassoci ates.com/united_questions.shtm; James Flanigan, "United Is a Poor Model for Employee Ownership," *Los Angeles Times*, December 4, 2002; Corey Rosen, "The Tribune Company Transaction: Things to Know in Assessing What Happened," National Center for Employee Ownership, May 2009, accessed May 23, 2011, www.nceo.org/main/column.php/id/316; "Michaels, Wood Named Officers at Tribune Co.," *Business Courier*, December 20, 2007, accessed May 23, 2011, www.bizjournals.com/cincinnati/stories/2007/12/17/daily39.html;

Julie Johnsson, "Judge OKs Class-Action Against Tribune ESOP Trustee," *Chicago Tribune* "Breaking Business," March 6, 2011, accessed May 23, 2011, http://archive.chicagobreaking-business.com/2011/03/judge-oks-class-action-suit-against-tribune-co.html.

9. Jacquelyn Yates and John Logue, "Democratic Employee Ownership and Economic Performance: Preliminary Results of a New Study," paper prepared for the 2004 Annual Meeting of the American Political Science Association (APSA), Chicago, IL; *The ESOP Association: 2000 Survey*, Washington DC, cited in *Building Wealth: The New Asset-Based Approach to Solving Social and Economic Problems* (Washington, DC: Aspen Institute, 2005), pp. 63–64.

10. For democratizing the ESOP form, see: John Logue and Jacquelyn Yates, *The Real World of Employee Ownership* (Ithaca, NY: ILR Press, 2001). For the Employee Ownership Act, see: "Will America Be 30% Employee Owned in 2010?" Ohio Employee Ownership Center, 1999, accessed December 24, 2010, http://dept.kent.edu/oeoc/publicationsresearch/Sum1999/EOOwnedSum1999.html. Another seeming maverick-style oddity: Under very conservative leadership in 2010 the state of Indiana established a $50 million "linked deposit" program to encourage banks to finance ESOP transactions. See: Office of Indiana Treasurer Richard Mourdock, "Indiana's ESOP Initiative," State of Indiana, no date, accessed April 12, 2012, www.in.gov/tos/2343.htm.

11. H. Con. Res. 204 was co-sponsored by eleven representatives including Rohrabacher (R-CA), and two Democrats, Pomeroy (D-ND) and Courtney (D-CT). It is titled: Expressing Continued Support for Employee Stock Ownership Plans. For the resolution, see: Expressing Continued Support for Employee Stock Ownership Plans, HR Res. 204, 111th Congress (2009).

12. In 1987 the General Accounting Office (now the Government Accountability Office) found that while ESOPs did not necessarily increase profits, ESOPs with participatory management did increase their productivity growth rate by 52 percent per year. Due to controversial assumptions regarding overall compensation, it is believed that these conclusions are actually relatively conservative. See: US General Accounting Office, *Employee Stock Ownership Plans: Little Evidence of Effects on Corporate Performance* (Washington, DC: GAO, 1987), accessed October 25, 2012, www.gao.gov/assets/150/145909.pdf. In 2000 the largest study to date, by Douglas Kruse and Joseph Blasi of Rutgers University, found that "ESOPs increase sales, employment, and sales/employee by about 2.3% to 2.4% per year over what would have been expected absent an ESOP. ESOP companies are also somewhat more likely to still be in business several years later." For this and other studies confirming the positive economic impacts of ESOPs, see: National Center for Employee Ownership, "Research on Employee Ownership, Corporate Performance, and Employee Compensation," NCEO, no date, accessed October 25, 2012, www.nceo.org/articles/research-employee-ownership-corporate-performance.

13. Douglas L. Kruse, Richard B. Freeman, and Joseph R. Blasi, eds., *Shared Capitalism at Work: Employee Ownership, Profit and Gain Sharing, and Broad-Based Stock Options* (Chicago, IL: University of Chicago Press, April 2010).

14. "Business Philosophy," New Belgium Brewing Company, no date, accessed March 24, 2012, www.newbelgium.com/culture/alternatively_empowered/sustainable-business-story/business-philosophy.aspx.

15. "Carris Reels: Governance and Management Design," Praxis, no date, accessed September 24, 2012, www.praxiscg.com/case-study/carris-reels; "Carris Reels Is Employee Owned," Carris Reels, accessed September 24, 2012, www.carris.com/employeeownership.html.

16. "Working at Litecontrol," Litecontrol, no date, accessed November 1, 2012, www.litecontrol.com/working-at-litecontrol.

17. Christopher Mackin, "Employee Stock Ownership Plan (ESOP) Companies," presentation, Jobs Creation Commission meeting, February 29, 2012, in *Job Creation Commission Final*

Report: January 2011–September 2012, Appendix, vol. 2 (Boston, MA: Commonwealth of Massachusetts, 2012); American Rights at Work, *Litecontrol Corporation* (Washington, DC: American Rights at Work, no date), accessed March 14, 2012, www.americanrightsatwork .org/labor-day-list/2010-companies/litecontrol-corporation-20100830-913-195-195.html.

18. Mary Hoyer et al., "The Role of Unions in Worker Co-op Development," *Grassroots Economic Organizing,* vol. 2, is. 8 (Summer 2011), accessed October 25, 2012, www.geo.coop/node/630.

19. "Our Story," Recology, no date, accessed November 1, 2012, www.recology.com/index.php /about-us.

20. "Recology Pursues Zero-Waste in Bay Area," Blue Green Alliance, no date, accessed September 24, 2012, www.bluegreenalliance.org/apollo/signature-stories/recology-pursues -zero-waste-in-bay-area; "Employee Ownership," Recology, no date, accessed September 24, 2012, www.recology.com/index.php/employee-ownership.

21. Among others. Examples include: Homeland Acquisition Corp., a large grocery chain with seventy-six locations in Oklahoma and Texas. In late 2011 Homeland's employees—with the assistance of their union, the United Food and Commercial Workers (UFCW) Local 1000—purchased the company and are transitioning it to 100 percent employee owner-ship. See: Deborah Groban Olson, "Groban Olson Employee Ownership Case Studies," Law Offices of Deborah Groban Olson, no date, accessed September 24, 2012, www.esoplaw. com/casestud.htm. The Gledhill Road Machinery Company—a snowplow manufacturer based in Galion, Ohio—began to transition to a 100 percent employee-owned company in 1999, and its forty employees are unionized by the International Association of Machin-ists and Aerospace Workers (IAM) Local 1151. See: Gledhill Road Machinery Company, *Snowplows and Road Maintenance Equipment* (Galion, OH: Gledhill, no date), accessed September 28, 2012, www.gledhillonline.com/brochure.pdf; "Machinists: Manufactur-ing," Union Facts, 2010, accessed September 28, 2012, www.unionfacts.com/contracts /Machinists/Manufacturing. Marland Mold—a Pittsfield, Massachusetts–based manufac-turer of steel molds used by the plastics industry—was unionized by the International Union of Electronic, Electrical, Salaried, Machine and Furniture Workers Local 225 in 1977. In 1992 the company was bought by its employees. In 1994 and 1996 it was voted New England ESOP of the year, and in 1998 it became a 100 percent ESOP company. See: "About Marland," Marland, no date, accessed September 28, 2012, www.marlandmold.com/aboutmain.html.

10. How the Conservatives Buried Adam Smith

1. Milton Friedman, "On Freedom and Free Markets," interview, Public Broadcasting System, October 1, 2000, accessed September 13, 2012, www.pbs.org/wgbh/commandingheights /shared/minitextlo/int_miltonfriedman.html#1.

2. Hayek quoted in Jeff Barnes, *Children of Liberty* (Bloomington, IN: Xlibris, 2011), p. 116. For more on Hayek, see: John Cassidy, "Annals of Money: The Price Prophet," *The New Yorker,* February 7, 2000.

3. Economic development researcher Greg LeRoy notes that a 2002 study of the Connecticut Development Agency found that companies receiving tax incentives "had created only 9 per-cent of the jobs they had forecast. The average subsidy for each new job: $367,910." See: Greg Leroy, *The Great American Jobs Scam* (San Francisco, CA: Berrett-Koehler Publishers, 2005), p. 34. See also: Marc Breslow, *Connecticut's Development Subsidies: Job Growth Far Short of Projections, High Costs Per Job* (Boston, MA: Northeast Action, February 28, 2002). In 2011, in connection with Illinois incentives to Evraz Inc. that amounted to $61,000 per job, LeRoy asserted that he was pleasantly surprised because many states "offer more than $100,000 per job. A company in upstate New York," he added, "got a package worth $1 million per job." Alejan-dra Cancino, "Illinois Promises Evraz Nearly $61,000 Per Job," *Chicago Tribune,* November

25, 2011, accessed February 22, 2012, http://articles.chicagotribune.com/2011-11-25/business/ct-biz-1125-edge-jobs--20111125_1_evraz-group-tax-credits-packages.

4. Greg LeRoy, *The Great American Jobs Scam* (San Francisco, CA: Berrett-Koehler Publishers, 2005), pp. 14–16.

5. Ibid., pp. 35–36.

6. The more-than-$200,000 figure is calculated by dividing a low-end estimate of $200 million by the nine hundred workers actually employed at the plant. State and local officials demanded repayment of the subsidies, but in the end only managed to "claw back" $26 million in local subsidies and a $1.5 million state grant. Philip Mattera et al., *Money-Back Guarantees for Taxpayers: Clawbacks and Other Enforcement Safeguards in State Economic Development Subsidy Programs* (Washington, DC: Good Jobs First, January 2012), p. 1, accessed March 5, 2012, www.alignny.org/wp-content/uploads/2012/01/moneyback.pdf.

7. Susan E. Clarke and Gary L. Gaile, *The Work of Cities* (Minneapolis, MN: University of Minnesota, 1998), p. 84.

8. Peter K. Eisinger, *The Rise of the Entrepreneurial State: State and Local Economic Development Policy in the United States* (Madison, WI: University of Wisconsin, 1988), pp. 333–34.

9. David Ebersole, "Funding Evergreen Initiatives: City of Cleveland," presentation, National League of Cities, July 25, 2012.

10. Section 108 is the loan guarantee portion of HUD's Community Development Block Grant (CDBG) program. It allows local governments to convert some of their CDBG money into loans in order to, according to HUD, "pursue physical and economic revitalization projects that can renew entire neighborhoods." The Brownfields Economic Development Initiative is a grant program operated by HUD that enables community development by assisting cities with the cleanup and redevelopment of former commercial and industrial facilities that may be environmentally contaminated. The New Markets Tax Credit program was created by Congress in 2000 to facilitate new or increased investment in low-income communities. In exchange for making equity investments in special financial organizations called Community Development Entities, investors receive a tax credit to use against their federal income tax return. Ohio Solar Renewable Energy Certificates are five-year state verifications that all Ohio retail electricity suppliers must obtain under a 2008 law that requires all utilities (except public utilities and cooperatives) to provide 25 percent of their energy from renewable sources by 2025. They can be bought or traded. The Neighborhood Stabilization Program was created by Congress in 2008 to provide states and local governments with funds to help reverse the effect of the housing collapse and financial crisis. Through three rounds, Cuyahoga County was allocated nearly $50 million in funds, some of which has been used for a developer loan program targeted at lower-income neighborhoods suffering from foreclosures and economic deprivation.

11. The tax benefits from the Southeastern Economic Development Corporation consist of property tax reimbursements for bridges, walkways, and thoroughfares in the plaza. As a result 60 percent of the funds used for the construction of these improvements will be returned to JCNI to support other community work. The loan program developed by the California Southern Small Business Development Corporation allows interest-only loans for two years (followed by interest and principal) to businesses in the plaza. See: "Public–Private Partnerships (Financing)," Market Creek Plaza, no date, accessed September 13, 2012, www.marketcreekplaza.com/mcp_financing.html; US Department of Housing and Urban Development, "State Supports Innovative Catalyst Projects," *Housing and Urban Development Newsletter*, vol. 10, no. 4 (July 2011), www.huduser.org/portal/rbc/newsletter/vol10iss4_3.html; Jacobs Center for Neighborhood Innovation, "Gold Level Catalyst," Village at Market Creek, 2011, accessed October 16, 2012, http://thevillageatmarketcreek.com/plan_catalyst.htm.

12. In 2006 the Government Accountability Office released an updated list of federal economic development programs. It included eighty-six programs administered by thirteen departments, agencies, administrations, commissions, and authorities. See: US Government Accountability Office, *Rural Economic Development: More Assurance Is Needed That Grant Funding Information Is Accurately Reported* (Washington, DC: GAO, February 2006), pp. 4 and 39–54.

13. Office of Community Services, *CED Grantees* (Washington, DC: US Department of Health and Human Services, 2012), accessed October 16, 2012, www.acf.hhs.gov/programs/ocs/programs/ced/ced-grantees.

14. John Logue (director of Ohio Employee Ownership Center), interview by Steve Dubb, the Democracy Collaborative, May 2008, accessed November 15, 2012, www.community-wealth.org/content/john-logue.

15. Bureau of Planning and Sustainability, *2011–2013 Strategic Plan* (Portland, OR: City of Portland, no date), accessed September 13, 2012, www.portlandoregon.gov/bps/article/336131.

16. "About the Green Impact Zone," Green Impact Zone of Missouri, no date, accessed January 30, 2012; "Green Impact Zone Programs," Green Impact Zone of Missouri, no date, accessed November 2, 2012, www.greenimpactzone.org/Plan/programs.aspx.

17. "Homegrown Prosperity," City of Austin: Office of Sustainability, no date, accessed January 30, 2012, www.austintexas.gov/department/homegrown-prosperity.

18. "Austin Green Business Leaders," City of Austin: Office of Sustainability, no date, accessed March 22, 2012, www.austintexas.gov/department/austin-green-business-leaders.

19. Office of Sustainability, *Climate Action Report* (Austin, TX: City of Austin, 2010–11), accessed March 22, 2012, www.austintexas.gov/sites/default/files/files/Sustainability/CityofAustin_ClimateActionReport_Final_Small_RR.pdf.

20. "Programs," City of Austin: Office of Sustainability, no date, accessed January 30, 2012, www.austintexas.gov/department/sustainability/programs.

21. David Orr, "The Oberlin Project and 'Full-Spectrum Sustainability,'" ThinkProgress, April 6, 2011, http://thinkprogress.org/climate/2011/04/06/207826/the-oberlin-project-and-full-spectrum-sustainability/?mobile=nc; David Orr, "The Oberlin Project," *Oberlin Alumni Magazine*, vol. 106, no. 4 (Fall 2011).

22. One interesting initiative is the Mayors Innovation Project, a network of city leaders "committed to 'high road' policy and governance: shared prosperity, environmental sustainability, efficient democratic government." See: "Mayors Innovation Project," Mayors Innovation Project, 2012, accessed November 15, 2012, www.mayorsinnovation.org.

11. Everyday Socialism, All the Time, American-Style

1. American Public Power Association, *APPA Annual Directory and Statistical Report 2012–2013: US Electric Utility Industry Statistics* (Washington, DC: APPA, June 2012), accessed October 25, 2012, www.publicpower.org/files/PDFs/USElectricUtilityIndustryStatistics.pdf.

2. American Public Power Association, *Public Power: Shining a Light on Public Service* (Washington, DC: APPA, November 2010), accessed September 4, 2012, www.publicpower.org/files/PDFs/PPFactSheet.pdf.

3. For public power authority salaries, see: American Public Power Association, *Survey of Management Salaries in Local Publicly Owned Electric Utilities* (Washington, DC: APPA, 2011), p. 4, accessed February 10, 2012, www.publicpower.com/pdf/APPA_2011SalariesReport.pdf. In 2011 the CEO of the largest public utility in the country—the Tennessee Valley Authority, with more than $11 billion in annual revenue—made less than half ($3.2 million) as much in total compensation as the average CEO ($7.1 million) of a directly comparable very large private utility (one with more than $6 billion in revenue). For private-sector salaries, see: Robert J. Gormley, "Executive Compensation—FY2011:

Consultant's Report," Towers Watson, November 4, 2010, accessed February 10, 2012, www.tva.com/abouttva/board/pdf/towers_watson_ceo_comp_11-10.pdf. Note that the $6 million figure includes salaries and other forms of compensation, the largest of which is typically stock bonuses. Public utility CEOs may receive additional compensation in the form of cash bonuses, but do not receive stock bonuses.

4. American Public Power Association, *Payments and Contributions by Public Power Distribution Systems to State and Local Governments, 2010 Data* (Washington, DC: APPA, February 2012), www.publicpower.org/files/PDFs/PilotReport2010.pdf.

5. "The Utility's Future," City of Ashland, no date, accessed March 5, 2012, www.ashland.or.us /Page.asp?NavID=37; "Public Power," City of Ashland, no date, accessed March 5, 2012, www.ashland.or.us/Page.asp?NavID=32.

6. "The NPU Business Model," Norwich Public Utilities, 2012, accessed October 16, 2012, www .norwichpublicutilities.com/index.php/about-npu/business-model. In the latest budget, $7.45 million of the city's $114.7 million budget was utility income. City of Norwich, *City Council's Adopted Budget, Fiscal Year 2012-2013* (Norwich, CT: City of Norwich, June 4, 2012), pp. 50–51, www.norwichct.org/filestorage/43/97/5133/5135/5143/2012-13_Adopted_Budget.pdf.

7. "Environment: Climate Change," Sacramento Municipal Utility District, no date, accessed March 6, 2012, www.smud.org/en/about-smud/environment/climate-change.htm.

8. Deborah B. Warren and Steve Dubb, *Growing a Green Economy for All: From Green Jobs to Green Ownership* (College Park, MD: Democracy Collaborative, June 2010), pp. 40–41; "About Us: Environmental Initiatives," Austin Energy, no date, accessed January 30, 2012, www.austinenergy.com/About%20Us/Environmental%20Initiatives/index.htm.

9. Austin Energy, *Austin Energy Resource, Generation, and Climate Protection Plan to 2020* (Austin, TX: Austin Energy, April 22, 2010), pp. 3–4, accessed March 6, 2012, www.austin energy.com/about%20us/Environmental%20Initiatives/climateProtectionPlan/generation BriefingSummary.pdf; "Homegrown Prosperity," City of Austin: Office of Sustainability, no date, accessed January 30, 2012, www.austintexas.gov/department/homegrown-prosperity. Public utilities have a mixed record on environmental matters—and there is clearly room for major improvement. For example, according to the National Renewable Energy Laboratory, Austin Energy has ranked first nationally in kilowatt-hours (kWh) sold for nine years in a row. Another large-scale example is the Los Angeles Department of Water and Power. Historically a legendary environmental offender for draining the Owens Valley, today the LA DWP looks much different; in 2005, only 3% of its power supply came from green sources; by 2008, that number had jumped to 8.5% with a goal of 35% by 2020. See: US Environmental Protection Agency, Green Power Leadership Awards: 2012 Award Winners (Washington, DC: EPA, 2012), accessed December 22, 2012, www.epa.gov/greenpower/awards /winners.htm; Kristen Underwood, "How to Get Green in LA," Planet Green, 2012, accessed December 22, 2012, http://tlc.howstuffworks.com/home/greenenergy-los-angeles.htm. For further information both on the record and on positive examples, see: Democracy Collaborative, Building Wealth: The New Asset-Based Approach to Social and Economic Problems (Washington, DC: Aspen Institute, 2005), pp. 89–92; Deborah B. Warren and Steve Dubb, Growing a Green Economy for All: From Green Jobs to Green Ownership (College Park, MD: The Democracy Collaborative at the University of Maryland, June 2010), pp. 39–46.

10. Gayle Fee and Laura Raposa, "Faneuil Hall Marketplace Sale," *Boston Herald*, December 19, 2008.

11. B. J. Frieden and L. B. Sagalyn, *Downtown, Inc.* (Boston, MA: MIT Press, 1989), p. 169. See also: Steven C. Bourassa and Yu-Hung Hong, eds., *Leasing Public Land: Policy Debates and International Experiences* (Cambridge, MA: Lincoln Institute of Land Policy, 2003). The lease in Boston was recently sold, although there do not appear to be any negative

repercussions for the city or merchants. See: Gayle Fee and Laura Raposa, "Faneuil Hall Attracts Big Apple Buyer," *Boston Herald*, May 10, 2011.

12. Irene D. Ferradaz (public information officer at Miami-Dade Transit), interview by Benzamin Yi, December 11, 2012.

13. "Property Development," Bay Area Rapid Transit, accessed February 10, 2012, www.bart .gov/about/business/development; BART Property Development, *BART Transit-Oriented Development Program* (San Francisco, CA: BART, November 1, 2010), accessed February 10, 2012, www.bart.gov/docs/BART_TOD_121510.pdf.

14. Washington Metropolitan Area Transit Authority, *Comprehensive Annual Financial Report for the Fiscal Year Ended June 30, 2011* (Washington, DC: WMATA, December 20, 2011), p. 66, accessed February 9, 2012, www.wmata.com/about_metro/docs/FY11_CAFR _Combined_01-06-12.pdf.

15. "Joint Development Completed Projects," Valley Transportation Authority, no date, accessed November 12, 2012, www.vta.org/realestate/devandleasing/projects/completed; "Almaden Lake Village," City of San Jose Department of Housing, no date, accessed November 12, 2012, www.sjhousing.org/project/alv.html.

16. Christopher Mitchell, *Publicly Owned Broadband Networks: Avoiding the Looming Broadband Monopoly* (Minneapolis, MN: New Rules Project, March 2011), p. 1.

17. Kent Lassman and Randolph J. May, "A Survey of Government-Provided Telecommunications: Disturbing Growth Trend Continues Unabated," *Progress on Point: Periodic Commentaries on the Policy Debate*, vol. 10, no. 17 (October 2003), pp. 2–3, 10, 16–28; American Public Power Association, *Digital Future of the United States: Part VI: The Future of Telecommunications Competition*, written statement of the American Public Power Association to the House Energy and Commerce Committee, Subcommittee on Telecommunications and the Internet (Washington, DC: APPA, October 2, 2007).

18. Sharon Kyser (marketing director at BVU Optinet), interview by Benzamin Yi, March 23, 2012. See also: MI-Connection, "BVU OptiNet: A Success Story," Town of Davidson, North Carolina, May 2007, www.ci.davidson.nc.us/DocumentCenter/Home/view/1711; "Municipal FTTH Snapshot: Bristol, Virginia," *Broadband Properties*, August 2008, pp. 28–30, accessed November 13, 2012, www.bbpmag.com/2008issues/aug08/AugSep08 _MuniSnapshot.pdf.

19. Christopher Mitchell, *Broadband at the Speed of Light: How Three Communities Built Next-Generation Networks* (Minneapolis, MN: Institute for Self Reliance, April 2012), p. 9, www.ilsr.org/wp-content/uploads/2012/04/muni-bb-speed-light.pdf.

20. For an overview, see: Christopher Mitchell, *Broadband at the Speed of Light: How Three Communities Built Next-Generation Networks* (Minneapolis, MN: Institute for Self Reliance, April 2012), p. 9, www.ilsr.org/wp-content/uploads/2012/04/muni-bb-speed-light.pdf. For price comparisons, see: Phillip Dampier, "Community Broadband Works: Knoxville's High-Tech Jobs Move South for Chattanooga's Fiber Broadband," Stop the Cap!, January 11, 2012, accessed March 6, 2012, http://stopthecap.com/2012/01/11/community-broadband-works -knoxvilles-high-tech-jobs-move-south-for-chattanoogas-fiber-broadband.

21. To be sure, Amazon is hardly a model of democratized ownership (to say the least). On the other hand, in some instances public strategies of the kind that helped attract Amazon may bring benefits to communities that are worth the effort—at least until other, more powerful strategies become possible. For information on Amazon and Chattanooga, see: Mike Pare, "Amazon's Chattanooga Distribution Center Plans to Expand," *Chattanooga Times Free Press*, January 8, 2012, accessed March 6, 2012, http://timesfreepress.com /news/2012/jan/08/amazons-chattanooga-distribution-center-plans-expa.

22. "Dallas City Council Approves Convention Center Hotel," *Dallas Business Journal*, May

14, 2008, accessed November 13, 2012, www.bizjournals.com/dallas/stories/2008/05/12/daily38.html.

23. Aman Batheja, "Leppert Takes Mayoral Record into Senate Race," *New York Times*, May 19, 2012, accessed November 13, 2012, www.nytimes.com/2012/05/20/us/politics/leppert-takes-dallas-mayoral-record-into-texas-senate-race.html?pagewanted=all&_r=0.

24. Steven R. Thompson, "Omni Dallas Hotel Preps for Opening Day," *Dallas Business Journal*, November 4, 2011, accessed February 15, 2012, www.bizjournals.com/dallas/print-edition/2011/11/04/commercial-real-estate-omni-preps-for.html. As in all business ventures, these various efforts are not without risk. For instance, the city-owned Marriott Hotel in Trenton, New Jersey, was powerfully impacted by the Great Recession. The city has received almost no income from hotel operations, and the value of the building has fallen dramatically. See: Matt Fair, "Trenton Council Grants Marriot $500K to Support City's Struggling Hotel," *Times of Trenton*, February 3, 2012, accessed April 5, 2012, www.nj.com/mercer/index.ssf/2012/02/trenton_grants_marriott_5_hund.html.

25. Taressa Fraze et al., *Public Hospitals in the United States, 2008* (Rockville, MD: Healthcare Cost and Utilization Project, September 2010), accessed November 13, 2012, www.hcup-us.ahrq.gov/reports/statbriefs/sb95.pdf.

26. Dylan Scott, "Denver Health Becomes Profitable After Using Toyota as a Template," *Governing Magazine*, February 2012, accessed November 13, 2012, www.governing.com/topics/health-human-services/gov-denver-health-becomes-profitable-after-using-toyota-as-a-template.html.

27. Ibid.; "About Us: Board of Directors," Denver Health, no date, accessed November 30, 2012, http://denverhealth.org/AboutUs/WhoWeAre/BoardofDirectors.aspx.

28. Denver Health, *2011 Annual Report: Serving a Diverse Community* (Denver, CO: Denver Health, 2012), accessed November 13, 2012, http://denverhealth.org/Portals/0/docs/pr/2011-Annual Report.pdf; Dylan Scott, "Denver Health Becomes Profitable After Using Toyota as a Template," *Governing Magazine*, February 2012, accessed November 13, 2012, www.governing.com/topics/health-human-services/gov-denver-health-becomes-profitable-after-using-toyota-as-a-template.html.

29. Brad Schweikert, "Don't Mind the Smell," Sustainable City Network, October 25, 2010, updated November 8, 2010, accessed February 2, 2011, www.sustainablecitynetwork.com/topic_channels/solid_waste/article_8976ace8-e03f-11df-b84a-00127992bc8b.html.

30. "Riverview Gas Producers, LLC," DTE Biomass Energy, 2012, accessed October 16, 2012, www.dtebe.com/aboutus/successStories/riverview.html; City of Riverview, *Proposed Operating Budget, Fiscal Year 2012/13* (Riverview, MI: City of Riverview, 2012), p. 186; "Riverview Energy Systems," Landfill Energy Systems, no date, accessed November 13, 2012, www.landfillenergy.com/proven-solutions/projects/michigan/riverview-energy-systems.

31. Brad Schweikert, "Is Your Wastewater Going to Waste?" Sustainable City Network, November 2, 2010, accessed February 2, 2011, www.sustainablecitynetwork.com/topic_channels/water/article_86c69e9c-e6af-11df-9dc9-0017a4a78c22.html.

32. California Public Employees' Retirement System, *Facts at a Glance: Investments* (Sacramento, CA: CalPERS, June 2012), accessed November 13, 2012, www.calpers.ca.gov/eip-docs/about/facts/investments.pdf.

33. "Global Governance: Investing with a Sustainable Framework," California Public Employees' Retirement System, 2012, accessed November 13, 2012, www.calpers-governance.org.

34. California Public Employees' Retirement System, *California Investments* (Sacramento, CA: CalPERS, September 25, 2012), accessed October 16, 2012, www.calpers.ca.gov/index.jsp?bc=/investments/assets/califinvestments.xml.

35. Retirement Systems of Alabama, *2011 Annual Report* (Montgomery, AL: RSA, 2011), www.rsa-al.gov/About%20RSA/Pubs%20and%20forms/RSA%20Pubs/Annual%20Report

/Annual%20Report%202011.pdf; University of Alabama, *Economic Impacts of RSA-Owned Investments on Alabama* (Tuscaloosa, AL: University of Alabama, December 2008), accessed April 12, 2012, www.rsa-al.gov/About%20RSA/Pubs%20and%20forms/RSA%20Pubs/RSA%20Inv%20EI%20Final%20Report.pdf.

36. Dividends are paid to individuals who have lived in the state for one year. See: "Annual Dividend Payouts," Alaska Permanent Fund Corporation, 2012, accessed April 12, 2012, www.apfc.org/home/Content/dividend/dividendamounts.cfm.

37. Arkansas, California, Connecticut, Illinois, Indiana, Iowa, Maryland, Massachusetts, Michigan, Missouri, Montana, New Hampshire, New Jersey, New York, Ohio, Oregon, Vermont, Washington, and Wisconsin. See: Corporation for Enterprise Development, "Incentives for Employee Ownership," Assets and Opportunity Scorecard, 2012, accessed April 12, 2012, http://scorecard.assetsandopportunity.org/2012/measure/incentives-for-employee-ownership.

38. "US State-Supported Venture Capital Funds," National Association of Seed and Venture Funds, March 2008.

39. Maryland Department of Business and Economic Development, *Annual Financial Status Report Fiscal Year 2011* (Baltimore, MD: Office of Finance Programs Investment Finance Group, October 18, 2011), www.choosemaryland.org/aboutdbed/Documents/ProgramReports/2011/IFGAnnualReportFY11.pdf.

40. "Company Overview of Plasmonix, Inc.," *Bloomberg Businessweek*, no date, accessed April 11, 2012, http://investing.businessweek.com/research/stocks/private/snapshot.asp?privcapId=134579357; "Advanced BioNutrition Corp. Company Information," Hoovers, no date, accessed April 11, 2012, www.hoovers.com/company/Advanced_BioNutrition_Corp/rrycjri-1.html.

41. Texas Permanent School Fund, *Annual Report—Fiscal Year Ending August 31, 2011* (Austin, TX: TPSF, December 2011), accessed April 12, 2012, www.tea.state.tx.us/index4.aspx?id=2147489178&menu_id=2147483695.

12. Checkerboard Strategies, and Beyond

1. Sweeney, from T. S. Eliot, "Sweeney Agonistes," in *Collected Poems 1909-1962* (Orlando, FL: Harcourt Brace & Company, 1963), p. 123.

2. Ken Silverstein, "Tea Party in the Sonora," *Harper's Magazine*, July 2010, accessed January 3, 2013, http://harpers.org/archive/2010/07/tea-party-in-the-sonora/; Sasha Abramsky, "Arizona's Private Prisons: A Bad Bargain," *The Nation*, April 4, 2012, accessed December 2, 2012, www.thenation.com/article/167216/arizonas-private-prisons-bad-bargain#; Tim Murphy, "Arizona Wants to Buy Back State Capitol It Inexplicably Sold," *Mother Jones*, January 11, 2012, accessed December 2, 2012, www.motherjones.com/mojo/2012/01/arizona-wants-buy-back-state-capitol-it-inexplicably-sold.

3. Toluse Olorunnipa, "Lobbying Pays Off Big for Business in Florida's 2012 Session," *Tampa Bay Times*, March 12, 2012, accessed December 2, 2012, www.tampabay.com/news/business/lobbying-pays-off-big-for-business-in-floridas-2012-session/1219536; Jim Saunders, "Budget Whacks $562M from Health," *Health News Florida*, February 8, 2011, accessed December 2, 2012, www.healthnewsflorida.org/top_story/read/scott_budget_whacks_562m_from_health; Pat Garofalo, "Florida Doles Out Billions in Corporate Tax Breaks While Slashing College Funding and Laying Off Thousands," ThinkProgress, March 13, 2012, accessed December 2, 2012, http://thinkprogress.org/economy/2012/03/13/443827/floridas-budget-handouts; Nicholas Johnson et al., "An Update on State Budget Cuts" (Washington, DC: Center on Budget and Policy Priorities, February 9, 2011), accessed December 2, 2012, www.cbpp.org/cms/index.cfm?fa=view&id=1214.

4. California Budget Project, "Governor Signs 2012–13 Spending Plan," CBP, July 9, 2012, www.cbp.org/documents/120629_Final_Budget_Agreement.pdf. In November 2012 California

voters approved Proposition 30, a ballot measure designed to raise an estimated $6 billion in new revenue from income and sales tax increases. As a result, an estimated $6 billion in additional mandatory cuts (more than 80 percent to education) was avoided. See: Mike Rosenberg, "Proposition 30 Wins: Gov. Jerry Brown's Tax Will Raise $6 Billion to Prevent School Cuts," *San Jose Mercury News*, November 29, 2012, accessed November 29, 2012, www.mercury news.com/elections/ci_21943732/california-proposition-30-voters-split-tax-that-would.

5. Max Taves, "Private Fix for Public Parks," *Wall Street Journal*, June 17, 2012, accessed September 24, 2012, http://online.wsj.com/article/SB10001424052702303410404577464724255828622.html; Legislative Analyst's Office, *2012–13 Budget: Strategies to Maintain California's Park System* (Sacramento, CA: LAO, March 2, 2012), accessed November 14, 2012, www.lao.ca.gov/analysis/2012/resources/state-parks-030212.aspx.

6. Stacy Curtin, "Three California Cities Bankrupt: 'This Is the Tip of the Iceberg,' Says Fmr. Statesman," *Daily Ticker*, July 13, 2012, accessed September 24, 2012, http://finance.yahoo.com/blogs/daily-ticker/three-california-cities-bankrupt-tip-iceberg-says-fmr-155121281.html; CBS News/Associated Press, "Moody's: More Calif. Cities Could Go Brankrupt," CBS/AP, August 17, 2012, accessed November 14, 2012, www.cbsnews.com/8301-505123_162-57495674/moodys-more-calif-cities-could-go-bankrupt.

7. Kendall Taggart, "Legislators Pass Bills That Would Revive Redevelopment," California Watch, August 31, 2012, accessed September 24, 2012, http://californiawatch.org/daily report/legislators-pass-bills-would-revive-redevelopment-17808; Ian Lovett, "Voters in California Back Pension Cuts for City Workers," *New York Times*, June 6, 2012, accessed November 14, 2012, www.nytimes.com/2012/06/07/us/politics/voters-in-california-approve-pension-cuts-results-suggest.html?_r=0.

8. According to a 2012 Brookings Institution report, between 2009 and 2012 eight states had raised taxes on corporate income by more than 5 percent (Alabama, California, Connecticut, Delaware, Illinois, Iowa, Montana, and Oregon). Seven more had raised taxes on corporate income between 1 and 5 percent (Florida, Kansas, Maine, New Jersey, North Carolina, Tennessee, and Virginia). See: Tracy M. Gordon, *What States Can, and Can't, Teach the Federal Government About Budgets* (Washington, DC: Brookings Institution, March 2012), accessed November 14, 2012, www.brookings.edu/~/media/research/files/papers/2012/3/states%20budgets%20gordon /03_states_budgets_gordon.pdf. A 2011 report by *Forbes* magazine revealed that "during the recent recession-related state budgets mess, Connecticut, Hawaii, Maryland, New Jersey, New York, North Carolina, Oregon, and Washington DC all hit high-income folks with targeted rate hikes, most of them billed as temporary." See: Ashlea Ebeling, "Tax the Rich, State Edition," *Forbes*, November 16, 2011, accessed November 14, 2012, www.forbes.com/sites/ashleaebeling /2011/11/16/tax-the-rich-state-edition. Some cities have also proposed raising or actually raised taxes on the wealthy. In 2011 Washington DC enacted a modest temporary increase (from 8.5 to 8.95 percent) in income tax for those making $350,000 or more per year. In New York City comptroller John Liu has proposed an ambitious plan to raise taxes by 15 percent on those making more than $1 million per year and 31.5 percent for those making $5 million a year. This in turn would allow cutting taxes for 99 percent of residents while simultaneously reducing the city's budget shortfall. See: Tim Craig, "DC Council Agrees to Raise Taxes on City's Wealthiest Residents," *Washington Post*, September 20, 2011, accessed September 24, 2012, www .washingtonpost.com/local/dc-politics/dc-council-agrees-to-raise-taxes-on-citys-wealthiest -residents/2011/09/20/gIQAHKVQjK_story.html; John C. Liu, "New York City Tax Relief Proposal," Office of the New York City Comptroller, June 2012, accessed September 24, 2012, www.comptroller.nyc.gov/bureaus/opm/reports/2012/NYC_PIT_FactSheet_v13.pdf.

9. Rick Jacobus and Mike Brown, "City Hall Steps In," *Shelterforce*, is. 149 (Spring 2007), accessed February 20, 2009, www.nhi.org/online/issues/149/cityhall.html; "Chicago

CommunityLandTrust,"CityofChicago,2010,accessedMarch8,2011,www.cityofchicago.org /city/en/depts/dcd/supp_info/chicago_communitylandtrust0.html; John Emmeus Davis and Rick Jacobus, *The City–CLT Partnership: Municipal Support for Community Land Trusts* (Cambridge, MA: Lincoln Institute of Land Policy, 2008), p. 35.

13. Banking

1. US Department of the Treasury, *The Financial Crisis Response: In Charts* (Washington, DC: US Department of the Treasury, April 2012), www.treasury.gov/resource-center/data -chart-center/Documents/20120413_FinancialCrisisResponse.pdf; Sarah Childress, "How Much Did the Financial Crisis Cost?" *Frontline*, May 31, 2012, accessed November 30, 2012, www.pbs.org/wgbh/pages/frontline/business-economy-financial-crisis/money -power-wall-street/how-much-did-the-financial-crisis-cost.

2. David M. Herszenhorn, Carl Hulse, and Sheryl Gay Stolberg, "Talks Implode During a Day of Chaos; Fate of Bailout Plan Remains Unresolved," *New York Times*, September 25, 2008, accessed September 3, 2012, www.nytimes.com/2008/09/26/business/26bailout.html?pagewanted=all.

3. Geraldine Tan, "Global Economy Will Suffer More Financial Crises in Next 10 Years: Roubini," CNBC, September 27, 2010, accessed May 27, 2011, www.cnbc.com/id/39375262.

4. David J. Lynch, "Simon Johnson, Kenneth Rogoff Weigh In on Financial Overhaul," *USA Today*, June 25, 2010, accessed November 22, 2010, www.usatoday.com/money/economy /2010-06-25-regulation25_ST3_N.htm.

5. Kana Nishizawa, "Mobius Says Another Financial Crisis 'Around the Corner,'" Bloomberg, May 30, 2011, accessed June 21, 2011, www.bloomberg.com/news/2011-05-30/mobius-says -fresh-financial-crisis-around-corner-amid-volatile-derivatives.html.

6. Carmen M. Reinhart and Kenneth Rogoff, *This Time Is Different: Eight Centuries of Financial Folly* (Princeton, NJ: Princeton University Press, 2009).

7. Peter Boone and Simon Johnson, "Shooting Banks: Obama's Impotent Assault on Wall Street," *The New Republic*, February 24, 2010, accessed November 14, 2012, www.tnr.com /article/politics/shooting-banks.

8. As of June 30, 2012, the top six bank holding companies had assets of $9.48 trillion. The 2012 estimated GDP is 15.60 trillion. See: Federal Reserve System, *Top 50 Bank Holding Companies as of June 30, 2012* (Washington, DC: National Information Center, September 30, 2012), accessed November 6, 2012, www.ffiec.gov/nicpubweb/nicweb/Top50Form.aspx; Office of Management and Budget, "Table 10.1: Gross Domestic Product and Deflators Used in the Historical Tables: 1940–2016," in *Historical Tables: Budget of the United States Government, Fiscal Year 2013* (Washington, DC: Government Printing Office, 2012).

9. Center for Responsive Politics, "Lobbying Sector Profile: FIRE, 2010 and 2011," OpenSecrets .org, October 31, 2012, accessed November 30, 2012, www.opensecrets.org/lobby/indus.php ?id=F&year=2011.

10. Glenn Greenwald, "Top Senate Democrat: Bankers 'Own' the US Congress," *Salon*, April 30, 2009, accessed October 17, 2012, www.salon.com/2009/04/30/ownership.

11. For the number of banks and average size through 2008, see: David C. Wheelock and Paul W. Wilson, *Do Large Banks Have Lower Costs? New Estimates of Returns to Scale for US Banks*, Working Paper 2009-054C (St. Louis, MO: Federal Reserve Bank of St. Louis, May 2011), p. 1, http://research.stlouisfed.org/wp/2009/2009-054.pdf.

12. Kenneth D. Jones and Tim Critchfield, "Consolidation in the US Banking Industry: Is the 'Long, Strange Trip' About to End," *FDIC Banking Review*, vol. 17, no. 4 (2005), p. 35, accessed July 12, 2011, www.fdic.gov/bank/analytical/banking/2006jan/article2/article2.pdf.

13. As of June 30, 2012, the top four banks had $3.281 trillion out of a total of $8.95 trillion in total deposits. See: "Top 50 Bank Holding Companies by Total Domestic Deposits," Federal

Deposit Insurance Corporation, June 30, 2012, accessed November 14, 2012, www2.fdic
.gov/sod/sodSumReport.asp?barItem=3&sInfoAsOf=2011; "State Totals," Federal Deposit
Insurance Corporation, June 30, 2012, accessed November 14, 2012, www2.fdic.gov/sod
/sodSumReport.asp?barItem=3&sInfoAsOf=2011.

14. Richard A. Posner, *Antitrust Law* (Chicago, IL: University of Chicago Press, 2001), p. 107.

15. "Exxon-Mobil Merger Done," CNN Money, November 30, 1999, accessed November 16,
2012, http://money.cnn.com/1999/11/30/deals/exxonmobil.

16. Hoover's Incorporated, *Hoover's Handbook of American Business 2007* (Short Hills, NJ:
Hoover's Inc., 2006), p. 205.

17. "History of Sohio," British Petroleum, no date, accessed November 16, 2012, www.bp.com
/sectiongenericarticle.do?categoryId=9014450&contentId=7027728; "History of Amoco,"
British Petroleum, no date, accessed November 16, 2012, www.bp.com/sectiongenericarticle
.do?categoryId=9014823&contentId=7027814.

18. Brad Reed, "Does the AT&T Breakup Still Matter 25 Years On?" *Network World*, December 19,
2008, accessed December 2, 2010, www.networkworld.com/news/2008/121908-att-break.html.

19. "A Step Back for Derivatives Regulation," *New York Times*, November 19, 2012, accessed January
3, 2012, www.nytimes.com/2012/11/20/opinion/a-step-back-for-derivatives-regulation.html.

20. H. C. Simons, *Economic Policy for a Free Society* (Chicago, IL: University of Chicago
Press, 1948), p. 59.

21. George Stigler, "The Theory of Economic Regulation," *Bell Journal of Economics and
Management Science*, vol. 2, no. 1 (1971), pp. 3–21; Milton Friedman, "The Business Com-
munity's Suicidal Impulse," *Cato Policy Report*, vol. 21, no. 2 (March/April 1999), accessed
December 6, 2012, www.cato.org/pubs/policy_report/v21n2/friedman.html.

22. H. C. Simons, *Economic Policy for a Free Society* (Chicago, IL: University of Chicago
Press, 1948), p. 57.

23. Ibid., p. 51.

24. Ronnie J. Phillips, *The Chicago Plan and New Deal Banking Reform* (Armonk, NY: M. E.
Sharpe, Inc., 1995), pp. 47–48.

25. For the "root canal" comment, see: Walter Shapiro, "Bank Bailout Bingo: How Both Parties
Exploit Populist Anger," *Politics Daily*, August 2010, accessed December 2, 2010, www.politics
daily.com/2010/08/19/bank-bailout-bingo-how-both-parties-exploit-populist-anger-over. For
the pitchforks comment, see: Eamon Javers, "Inside Obama's Bank CEOs Meeting," *Politico*,
April 3, 2009, accessed March 23, 2011, www.politico.com/news/stories/0409/20871.html.

26. For survey results, see: CBS News Poll, "Bailing Out Banks and Financial Institutions: March
12–15, 2009," CBS, March 16, 2009, accessed December 2, 2010, www.cbsnews.com/htdocs
/pdf/MAR09A-Banks.pdf. For the Gallup poll, see: Dennis Jacobe, "Americans' Confidence in Banks Remains at Historical Low," Gallup, April 6, 2010, accessed December 2,
2010, www.gallup.com/poll/127226/americans-confidence-banks-remains-historic-low.
aspx. For the Elliot and McArdle quote, see: Editors, "Banks: Real Reform and Pitchforks,"
New York Times, December 14, 2009, accessed March 23, 2011, http://roomfordebate
.blogs.nytimes.com/2009/12/14/banks-real-reform-and-pitchforks.

27. Credit Union National Association, *Monthly Credit Union Estimates* (Washington, DC: CUNA,
September 2012), accessed November 16, 2012, www.cuna.org/research/download/mcue.pdf.

28. For the 140 formulation, see: Robert Pollin, "Tools for a New Economy: Proposals for a
Financial Regulatory System," *Boston Review*, January–February 2009, accessed November 30, 2010, http://bostonreview.net/BR34.1/pollin.php.

29. Among many others who have urged such change, economist Fred Moseley has proposed
that for banks deemed too big to fail "permanent nationalization with bonds-to-stocks
swaps for bondholders is the most equitable solution." Nationally owned banks, he argues,

would provide a basis for "a more stable and public-oriented banking system in the future." Banking expert Ellen Brown maintains: "It could be time to take the next logical step and nationalize not just the losses but the banks themselves, and not just temporarily but permanently." Professor George Irvin asserts that "if banking scandals multiply, if the advanced economies continue to stagnate, if jobs are scarce and unemployment grows—and particularly, if the taxpayer is asked once more to bailout the banks in the wake of another financial crash—then it is a near certainty that within a decade, the largest banks will become public utilities." Author Les Leopold urges: "Rather than bust them up into smaller privately owned pieces, I think it's time to take them over and run them as public utilities, paying decent civil service salaries and no more." And Matthew Rothschild of *The Progressive* believes that while nationalization may include certain problems, "we've had enough bumps on the road marked 'private.' If we're going to be shelling out the money, we might as well run the store." See: Fred Moseley, "Banks: Time for Permanent Nationalization?" *AlterNet*, March 3, 2009, accessed November 16, 2012, www.alternet.org/story/129700/banks%3A_time_for_permanent_nationalization; Ellen Brown, "Foreclosuregate Could Force Bank Nationalization," *Web of Debt*, November 5, 2010, accessed November 16, 2012, www.webofdebt.com/articles/force_nationalization.php; George Irvin, "Time to Nationalise the Big Banks," *Social Europe Journal*, July 19, 2012, accessed November 16, 2012, www.social-europe.eu/2012/07/time-to-nationalise-the-big-banks; Les Leopold, "There's Only One Solution That Might Fix Our Corrupt Financial System," *AlterNet*, August 14, 2012, accessed November 16, 2012, www.alternet.org/economy/theres-only-one-solution-might-fix-our-corrupt-financial-system; Matthew Rothschild, "Nationalize the Banks," *The Progressive*, March 2009, accessed November 16, 2012, www.progressive.org/mag/wx021109.html.

30. Willem Buiter, "The End of Capitalism as We Knew It," *Financial Times*, September 17, 2008, accessed June 2, 2011, http://blogs.ft.com/maverecon/2008/09/the-end-of-american-capitalism-as-we-knew-it.

31. "Bank of North Dakota," Institute for Local Self-Reliance, May 5, 2011, accessed November 7, 2012, www.ilsr.org/rule/bank-of-north-dakota-2. See also: Center for State Innovation, *Washington State Bank Analysis* (Madison, WI: CSI, 2010), accessed February 2, 2012, http://stateinnovation.org/Initiatives/State-Banks-Materials/CSI-Washington-State-Bank-Analysis-020411.aspx.

32. For One PacificCoast, see: "Our Mission," One PacificCoast Bank, no date, accessed November 16, 2012, www.onepacificcoastbank.com/mission.aspx. For Bremer Bank, see: "About Bremer," Bremer Bank, no date, accessed November 16, 2012, www.bremer.com/Home/AboutBremer.aspx. For Southern Bancorp, see: "Mission," Southern Bancorp, no date, accessed November 16, 2012, https://banksouthern.com/mission.

33. Since 2010, twenty states have considered or are considering legislation to form a state bank. One state—Colorado—has a citizen's initiative to do the same. See: "State Activity, Resource and Contact Info," Public Banking Institute, 2012, accessed September 19, 2012, http://publicbankinginstitute.org/state-info.

34. For Portland, see: Rich Goward and Jennifer Yocom, "Draft for Public Discussion—Responsible Banking," Office of the Mayor of Portland, February 3, 2012, accessed April 10, 2012, www.portlandonline.com/shared/cfm/image.cfm?id=384250. For San Francisco, see: Jonathan Nathan, "Supervisors Hear from San Franciscans About City Finance Options," *Beyond Chron*, February 9, 2012, accessed April 10, 2012, www.beyondchron.org/articles/Supervisors_Hear_From_San_Franciscans_About_City_Finance_Options_9884.html; Luke Thomas, "Supervisor Avalos Declares Re-Election Bid," *Fog City Journal*, March 18, 2012, accessed April 10, 2012, www.fogcityjournal.com/wordpress/3494/supervisor-avalos-declares-re-election-bid.

35. Communities Creating Opportunity, "City Council Passes CCO-Supported Responsible Banking Resolution," CCO, February 2012, accessed April 10, 2012, http://myemail.constant contact.com/A-CCO-Victory--City-Council-Passes-Responsible-Banking-Ordinance .html?soid=1101339995598&aid=KbY9HXioUy8.
36. Chad Houck, "Responsible Banking Act Vote Delayed by Pittsburgh Council," 90.5 WESA, March 28, 2012, accessed April 10, 2012, www.essentialpublicradio.org/story/2012-03-28/responsible -banking-act-vote-delayed-pittsburgh-council-10607; Brad Lander, "NYC Needs a Responsible Banking Act," *Huffington Post*, November 30, 2010, accessed April 10, 2012, www.huffingtonpost .com/brad-lander/nyc-needs-a-responsible-b_b_789625.html. Minnesota Neighborhoods Organizing for Change (NOC) has also called for Minneapolis public schools to divest funds from Wells Fargo bank after completing a study showing that foreclosures conducted by the bank had cost the school district $28 million. See: Hawthorne Hawkman, "Groups Call for Responsible Banking from Public Institutions," *North by Northside*, November 4, 2011, accessed April 10, 2012, http://north-by-northside.blogspot.com/2011/11/groups-call-for-responsible-banking .html; Joe Smydo, "City Council Encourages Banks to Invest in Neighborhoods," *Pittsburgh Post-Gazette*, April 18, 2012, accessed September 19, 2012, www.post-gazette.com/stories/local /neighborhoods-city/city-council-encourages-banks-to-invest-in-neighborhoods-631901.
37. Molly, "NCRC Responsible Banking Campaign: 'Our Community, Our Money,'" Northside Community Reinvestment Coalition, July 27, 2011, accessed April 10, 2012, http://northsidereinvestment .org/2011/07/27/ncrc-responsible-banking-campaign-our-community-our-money.

14. HEALTH CARE

1. Centers for Medicare & Medicaid Services, *National Health Expenditure Projections 2011–2021* (Baltimore, MD: CMS, 2012), accessed November 16, 2012, www.cms.gov /Research-Statistics-Data-and-Systems/Statistics-Trends-and-Reports/NationalHealth ExpendData/Downloads/Proj2011PDF.pdf.
2. Data is from 2010 or nearest available year. See: Organisation for Economic Co-operation and Development, *OECD Health Data 2012* (Paris, FR: OECD, June 28, 2012), accessed October 20, 2012, www.oecd.org/health/healthpoliciesanddata/oecdhealthdata2012.htm.
3. For detailed comparisons in many areas, see Karen Davis, Cathy Schoen, and Kristof Stremikis, *Mirror, Mirror on the Wall: How the Performance of the US Health Care System Compares Internationally, 2010 Update* (New York, NY: The Commonwealth Fund, June 2010).
4. Organisation for Economic Co-operation and Development, *OECD Health Data 2012* (Paris, FR: OECD, June 28, 2012), accessed October 20, 2012, www.oecd.org/health /healthpoliciesanddata/oecdhealthdata2012.htm.
5. Ibid.
6. Ibid., p.7.
7. Sophie Quinton, "Report: Health Insurance Profits Rise Despite Health Care Reform," *National Journal*, January 5, 2012, accessed October 20, 2012, www.nationaljournal.com /healthcare/report-health-insurance-profits-rise-despite-health-care-reform-20120105.
8. See: Steffie Woolhandler, Terry Campbell, and David U. Himmelstein, "Costs of Health Care Administration in the United States and Canada," *New England Journal of Medicine*, vol. 349 (2003), pp. 768–75. "In 1999, health administration costs totaled at least $294.3 billion in the United States, or $1,059 per capita, as compared with $307 per capita in Canada. After exclusions, administration accounted for 31.0 percent of health care expenditures in the United States and 16.7 percent of health care expenditures in Canada. Canada's national health insurance program had overhead of 1.3 percent; the overhead among Canada's private insurers was higher than that in the United States (13.2 percent vs. 11.7 percent). Providers' administrative costs were far lower in Canada." The authors report that "between

1969 and 1999, the share of the US health care labor force accounted for by administrative workers grew from 18.2 percent to 27.3 percent. In Canada, it grew from 16.0 percent in 1971 to 19.1 percent in 1996. (Both nations' figures exclude insurance-industry personnel.)"

9. Michael M. Rachlis, "A Canadian Doctor Diagnoses US Healthcare," *Los Angeles Times*, August 3, 2009, accessed August 14, 2012, http://articles.latimes.com/2009/aug/03 /opinion/oe-rachlis3.

10. With a 2011 GDP of $14.958 trillion, health expenditures similar to those of Canada (11.4 percent of GDP) would amount to just $1.7 trillion compared with $2.63 trillion in actual spending—a savings of $930 billion. Health expenditures similar to those of the United Kingdom (9.6 percent of GDP) would amount to just $1.43 trillion—a savings of $1.2 trillion.

11. In 2011, federal revenues were $2.3 trillion and federal expenditures were $3.6 trillion. See: Office of Management and Budget, "Table 1.1: Summary of Receipts, Outlays, and Surpluses of Deficits—1789–2017," in *Historical Tables: Budget of the United States Government, Fiscal Year 2013* (Washington, DC: Government Printing Office, 2012), pp. 21–23.

12. Bill Keller, "More Myths of Obamacare," *New York Times*, July 18, 2012, accessed September 20, 2012, http://keller.blogs.nytimes.com/2012/07/18/more-myths-of-obamacare.

13. Herbert Stein, "Herb Stein's Unfamiliar Quotations," *Slate*, May 16, 1997, accessed August 14, 2012, www.slate.com/articles/business/it_seems_to_me/1997/05/herb_steins_unfamiliar _quotations.single.html#pagebreak_anchor_2.

14. For "stop-loss" insurance, see: Wendell Potter, "New Scheme to Subvert Obamacare Would Hike Premiums for Many Consumers and Businesses," *Huffington Post*, December 3, 2012, accessed December 4, 2012, www.huffingtonpost.com/wendell-potter/new-scheme-to-subvert -oba_b_2230723.html. For avoidance of premium percentage requirements, see: Drew Armstrong, "Maine Wins First Waiver to Health Insurance Premium Rules," Bloomberg, March 8, 2011, accessed December 4, 2012, www.bloomberg.com/news/2011-03-08/maine-wins-first -waiver-to-health-insurance-premium-rules.html. For premiums and deductibles, see: Cathy Schoen et al., *State Trends in Premiums and Deductibles, 2003–2010: The Need for Action to Address Rising Costs* (New York, NY: Commonwealth Fund, November 2011), accessed December 4, 2012, www.commonwealthfund.org/~/media/Files/Publications/Issue %20Brief/2011/Nov/State%20Trends/1561_Schoen_state_trends_premiums_deductibles _2003_2010.pdf; Wendell Potter, "'Reframing' the Debate to Make Insurers Look Poor," WendellPotter.com, March 15, 2011, accessed December 4, 2012, http://wendellpotter.com /2011/03/%e2%80%98reframing%e2%80%99-the-debate-to-make-insurers-look-poor.

15. Andrew Taylor, "Medicare, Social Program Cuts: Will Democrats Go Along?" *Christian Science Monitor*, November 28, 2012, accessed January 4, 2013, www.csmonitor.com/Business /Latest-News-Wires/2012/1128/Medicare-social-program-cuts-Will-Democrats-go-along.

16. George J. Annas, "Your Money or Your Life: 'Dumping' Uninsured Patients from Hospital Emergency Wards," *Public Health and the Law*, vol. 76, no. 1 (January 1986), pp. 74–77. See also: Woodrow Jones Jr., "The Uninsured and Patient Dumping: Recent Policy Responses in Indigent Care," *Journal of the National Medical Association*, vol. 83, no. 10 (October 1991), pp. 874–80. See especially pp. 203–4 of: Thomas A. Gionis, Carlos A. Camargo Jr., and Anthony S. Zito Jr., "The Intentional Tort of Patient Dumping: A New State Cause of Action to Address the Shortcomings of the Federal Emergency Medical Treatment and Active Labor Act (EMTALA)," *American University Law Review*, vol. 52, is. 1 (December 2002), pp. 173–308; Karen Markus, "Patient Dumping: It's Illegal and You Should Know How to Spot It," *Nurse Week*, May 31, 1999, accessed October 27, 2010, www.nurseweek.com/features/99-5/legal531.html.

17. KABC-TV and City News Services, "Homeless Dumping Case Settled," *Kaiser Papers*, May 15, 2007, www.kaiserpapers.org/news/ca/may15.html, accessed October 27, 2010.

18. Sarah Anne Hughes, "James Verone Robs Bank to Receive Free Health Care," *Washington*

Post, June 21, 2011, accessed August 30, 2011, www.washingtonpost.com/blogs/blogpost /post/james-verone-robs-bank-to-receive-free-health-care/2011/06/21/AGxDrTeH_blog .html; Mansfield Frazier, "Prison's Cheap Health-Care Secret," *Daily Beast*, June 23, 2011, accessed August 30, 2011, www.thedailybeast.com/articles/2011/06/23/need-healthcare -go-to-prison-behind-richard-james-verone-s-thinking.html.

19. Associated Press, "Report: US Health Care System Is a Liability," MSNBC, March 12, 2009, accessed November 4, 2010, www.msnbc.msn.com/id/29641091.

20. On the business support coalition for the Clinton health care plan and its demise, see: John B. Judis, "Business and the Failure of Health Reform," *American Prospect*, November 30, 2002. See also press articles of the time, including: Kathleen Day, "Corporate America at Odds Over Curing Health Care System," *Washington Post*, April 13, 1993, p. D1; Jane Baird, "Reformers' Ad Blitz Rips Health Insurers; All Sides Intensifying Their Lobbying," *Houston Chronicle*, January 25, 1994, p. 1; Bennett Roth, "2 Business Groups Differ on Key Health Plan Mandate," *Houston Chronicle*, April 15, 1994, p. A-5.

21. Humphrey Taylor, "Oil, Pharmaceutical, Health Insurance, Banking, Tobacco and Utilities Top the List of Industries That People Would Like to See More Regulated," Harris Polls, December 15, 2011, accessed October 17, 2012, www.prnewswire.com/news-releases /oil-pharmaceutical-health-insurance-banking-tobacco-and-utilities-top-the-list-of -industries-that-people-would-like-to-see-more-regulated-135645908.html.

22. Physicians for a National Health Program, e-mail correspondence with author's staff, Democracy Collaborative, September 15, 2011.

23. "FAQ," Vermonters for Health Care Freedom, no date, accessed August 14, 2012, http:// vthealthcarefreedom.org/faq.

24. "Senate Rejects SB 810—Bill Solving Healthcare & Budget Crisis," Campaign for a Healthy California, February 2, 2012, accessed August 14, 2012, http://healthycaliforniacampaign.org /2012/02/02/senate-rejects-sb-810-bill-solving-healthcare-budget-crisis-coalition-gears -up-to-build-statewide-grassroots-movement-and-win-universal-healthcare.

25. "About Us," Healthcare4Every1, no date, accessed October 20, 2012, www.healthcareforevery 1.org/aboutus.

26. Kevin Sack, "A Lesson on Health Care from Massachusetts," *New York Times*, March 28, 2009, accessed December 3, 2012, www.nytimes.com/2009/03/29/weekinreview/29sack .html?pagewanted=all; Abby Goodnough, "Massachusetts Aims to Cut Growth of Its Health Costs," *New York Times*, July 31, 2012, accessed December 3, 2012, www.nytimes .com/2012/08/01/health/policy/vote-looms-in-massachusetts-on-bill-to-limit-health -care-costs.html?ref=sunday.

27. Paul Krugman, "The Swiss Menace," *New York Times*, August 17, 2009, accessed October 21, 2012, www.nytimes.com/2009/08/17/opinion/17krugman.html; Nelson D. Schwartz, "Swiss Health Care Thrives Without Public Option," *New York Times*, September 30, 2009, accessed December 3, 2012, www.nytimes.com/2009/10/01/health/policy/01swiss. html?pagewanted=all.

28. Ultimately, perhaps, over the long haul an even more rationalized system like that of the Veterans Administration, where several studies have demonstrated far greater cost reduction at the same time benefits have been increased, because the entire system can be managed as an integrated whole. See: Alison Percy, *Quality Initiatives Undertaken by the Veterans Health Administration, A CBO Paper* (Washington, DC: Congressional Budget Office, August 2009); Phillip Longman, *Best Care Anywhere: Why VA Health Care Is Better Than Yours*, 2nd ed. (San Francisco, CA: Berrett-Koehler Publishers, 2011). For an overview, see also: Paul Krugman and Robin Wells, "The Health Care Crisis and What to Do About It," *New York Review of Books*, March 23, 2006.

15. BEYOND COUNTERVAILING POWER

1. John Kenneth Galbraith, *American Capitalism: The Theory of Countervailing Power* (Cambridge, MA: Riverside Press, 1956), p. 114.

2. John Kenneth Galbraith, *The Essential Galbraith* (New York, NY: Houghton Mifflin, 2001), p. 125.

3. John Kenneth Galbraith, *The Anatomy of Power* (Boston, MA: Houghton Mifflin, 1983), p. 77; John Kenneth Galbraith, *American Capitalism: The Theory of Countervailing Power* (Cambridge, MA: Riverside Press, 1956).

4. John Kenneth Galbraith, *American Capitalism: The Theory of Countervailing Power* (White Plains, NY: M. E. Sharpe, 1980), p. vii.

5. John Kenneth Galbraith, "The Heartless Society," *New York Times Magazine*, September 2, 1984.

16. BIGGER POSSIBILITIES AND PRECEDENTS

1. "Bailout Tracker," ProPublica, December 3, 2012, accessed December 3, 2012, http://projects .propublica.org/bailout/list/index.

2. Incidentally, the fund is an estimated $20 billion short compared with the expected cost of promised benefits. Establishing the trust was a way for auto companies to reduce their health insurance costs (and put the industry on a firmer financial footing). See: Sharon Terlep and Matthew Dolan, "Pension Funds Strapped," *Wall Street Journal*, November 7, 2011, accessed October 17, 2012, http://online.wsj.com/article/SB1000142405297020370 7504577011901934288534.html. Sustained nationalization, of course, under either direct public or some form of joint ownership with workers, would simply establish and maintain the firm under the new ownership. In the case of both GM and Chrysler, the government bailed out and took the companies through bankruptcy before reestablishing them and beginning the process of selling them off. For an in-depth look at the takeover process, see: Steven Rattner, *Overhaul: An Insider's Account of the Obama Administration's Emergency Rescue of the Auto Industry* (New York: Houghton Mifflin Harcourt, 2010).

3. Robert Millward, "State Enterprise in Britain in the Twentieth Century," in *The Rise and Fall of State-Owned Enterprise in the Western World*, ed. Pier Angelo Toninelli (Cambridge, UK: Cambridge University Press, 2000), pp. 157–84.

4. Former IMF chief economist Simon Johnson writes that in any event "there are no economies of scale or scope in banks with over $100 billion of total assets," and as such there are no "efficiency enhancements" for banks bigger than this size. See: Simon Johnson, "One Man Against the Wall Street Lobby," *The Baseline Scenario*, August 25, 2012, accessed September 5, 2012, http://base linescenario.com/2012/08/25/one-man-against-the-wall-street-lobby; Simon Johnson, "Why Are the Big Banks Suddenly Afraid?" *New York Times*, August 30, 2012, accessed September 5, 2012, http://economix.blogs.nytimes.com/2012/08/30/why-are-the-big-banks-suddenly-afraid.

5. For example, in 2000 Tel Aviv University professor Yair Aharoni concluded that "the assumption that ownership per se creates an environment that is conducive to high or low performance is not proven, and empirical research on this point has yielded conflicting results." See: Yair Aharoni, "The Performance of State-Owned Enterprise," in *The Rise and Fall of State-Owned Enterprise in the Western World*, ed. Pier Angelo Toninelli (Cambridge, UK: Cambridge University Press, 2000), p. 50.

6. Francisco Flores-Macias and Aldo Musacchio, "The Return of State-Owned Enterprises," *Harvard International Review*, April 4, 2009, accessed January 9, 2012, http://hir.harvard .edu/the-return-of-state-owned-enterprises?page=0,0.

7. Ian Bremmer, "The Long Shadow of the Visible Hand," *Wall Street Journal*, May 22, 2010, accessed September 5, 2012, http://online.wsj.com/article/SB10001424052748704852004575258554875590852.html.

8. International Union of Railways High Speed Department, *High Speed Around the World: Maps* (Paris, FR: UIC, December 15, 2010). For France, see: "EPIC Status," SNCF, no date, accessed November 6, 2012, www.sncf.com/en/meet-sncf/epic-status. For Spain, see: "The Company," Renfe, no date, accessed November 6, 2012, www.renfe.com/EN/empresa/index.html. For Belgium, see: "About Thalys," Thalys, no date, accessed November 6, 2012, www.thalys.com /fr/en/about-thalys/presentation. For Germany, see: Deutsche Bahn AG, "2000 to 2008: Restructure and Invest," DB, January 25, 2012, accessed November 6, 2012, www.deutschebahn .com/en/group/history/chronology/2000_2008.html. For Italy, see: "Italy: Trenitalia," Rail Europe, no date, accessed November 6, 2012, www.raileurope-world.com/about-us-23/railways /article/italy-trenitalia. For the Netherlands, see: "Netherlands Railways (NS) (Netherlands), Railway Systems and Operators," in *Jane's World Railways*, 52nd ed., ed. Ken Harris (Surrey, UK: IHS Jane's, January 24, 2012), accessed November 6, 2012, http://articles.janes.com /articles/Janes-World-Railways/Netherlands-Railways-NS-Netherlands.html. For China, see: Keith Bradsher, "High-Speed Rail Poised to Alter China," *New York Times*, June 22, 2011, accessed November 6, 2012, www.nytimes.com/2011/06/23/business/global/23rail.html?pagewanted =all. For South Korea, see: "KORAIL Innovation Way," Korail, 2007, accessed November 6, 2012, http://info.korail.com/2007/eng/ekr/ekr03000/w_ekr03100.jsp.

9. For Air France–KLM, see: "Capital Structure and Equity Threshold Declarations," Air France–KLM, 2012, accessed November 6, 2012, www.airfranceklm-finance.com/en/Shares/Capital -structure-and-equity-threshold-declarations. For SAS, see: "Largest Shareholders: Principal Shareholders in SAS AB on 31 March 2012," SAS Group, 2012, accessed November 6, 2012, www.sasgroup.net/SASGROUP_IR/CMSContent/20%20largest%20shareholders.htm. For El Al, see: "Shareholders: As of June 30, 2012," El Al, accessed November 6, 2012, www.elal .co.il/ELAL/English/AboutElAl/InvestorRelations/shareholders.htm. For Singapore Airlines, see: "Stock and Shareholding Information," Singapore Airlines, 2012, accessed November 6, 2012, www.singaporeair.com/jsp/cms/en_UK/global_header/shareholdinginfo.jsp.

10. "Capital Structure as of 31 December 2011," EADS, 2011, accessed August 25, 2012, www.eads .com/eads/int/en/investor-relations/share-information/shareholder-structure.html.

11. Mathias Schmit et al., *Public Financial Institutions in Europe* (Brussels, BE: European Association of Public Banks, March 15, 2011).

12. Ellen Brown, "Japan Post's Stalled Sale a Saving Grace," *Asia Times*, April 1, 2011, accessed June 8, 2011, http://atimes.com/atimes/Japan/MD01Dh01.html.

13. Organisation for Economic Co-operation and Development, "Table 2.9: Government Ownership of Public Telecommunication Network Operators," in *OECD Communications Outlook 2011* (Paris, FR: OECD, June 2011), pp. 78–80, http://dwmw.files.wordpress.com /2011/06/oecd-commoutlook-2011.pdf.

14. Luciana Pontes, *Ownership Policy and SOE Autonomy*, presentation at second meeting of the OECD Global Network on Privatisation and Corporate Governance of State-Owned Enterprises (Paris, FR: Organisation for Economic Co-operation and Development, March 2–3, 2010).

15. Adrian Wooldridge, "State Capitalism: Special Report—New Masters of the Universe," *The Economist*, January 21, 2012.

17. PUBLIC ENTERPRISE REDUX I

1. A different set of efficiency questions comes up in discussions of markets versus one or another form of government involvement (ranging from tax deals and regulations to explicit planning). Here the problem is not so much narrow-mindedness as obstinacy—by which I mean obstinate refusal to acknowledge that in the real world businesses commonly work very hard to alter the market in their favor. As we began to explore in chapter 9, markets that are genuinely "free" of special tax incentives, loans, loan guarantees, regulatory preferences, and the

like are rare in many important contexts, both locally and nationally. Adam Smith, however, was on to this big-time. Smith wrote: "People of the same trade seldom meet together, even for merriment and diversion, but the conversation ends in a conspiracy against the public, or in some contrivance to raise prices." See also chapter 9 of this book and Adam Smith, "Of Wages and Profit in the Different Employments of Labour and Stock," in *An Inquiry into the Nature and Causes of the Wealth of Nations*, 1776 (London, UK: George Bell and Sons, 1887), p. 134.

2. Rich Exner, "2010 Census Population Numbers Show Cleveland Below 400,000; Northeast Ohio Down 2.2 Percent," Cleveland.com, March 9, 2011, accessed November 20, 2012, www .cleveland.com/datacentral/index.ssf/2011/03/2010_census_figures_for_ohio_s.html.

3. Time Newsfeed, "Vanishing City: The Story Behind Detroit's Shocking Population Decline," *Time*, March 24, 2011, accessed November 20, 2012, http://newsfeed.time.com/2011/03/24 /vanishing-city-the-story-behind-detroit%E2%80%99s-shocking-population-decline.

4. For a review of such programs, see: Greg LeRoy, *The Great American Job Scam: Corporate Tax Dodging and the Myth of Job Creation* (San Francisco, CA: Berrett-Koehler Publishers, 2005).

5. Jonathan Michael Feldman, "From Mass Transit to New Manufacturing," *American Prospect*, March 23, 2009.

6. John Neff and Matthew Dickens, eds., "Table 9: Revenue Vehicles by Mode," in *2009 Public Transportation Fact Book*, 60th ed. (Washington, DC: American Public Transportation Association, April 2009), p. 16; John Neff and Matthew Dickens, eds., "Table 17: Capital Expense by Mode and Type, Millions of Dollars," in *2009 Public Transportation Fact Book*, 60th ed. (Washington, DC: American Public Transportation Association, April 2009), p. 20; American Public Transportation Association, *Legislative Updates and Alerts* (Washington, DC: APTA, January 7, 2009), www.apta.com/gap/legupdatealert/2009/Pages/2009january07.aspx.

7. Richard Gilbert and Anthony Perl, *Transport Revolutions: Moving People and Freight Without Oil* (London, UK: Earthscan, 2008), p. 285.

18. PUBLIC ENTERPRISE REDUX II

1. Phillip Longman and Lina Khan, "Terminal Sickness," *Washington Monthly*, March–April 2012, accessed October 17, 2012, www.washingtonmonthly.com/magazine/march _april_2012/features/terminal_sickness035756.php.

2. Robert D. Hershey, "Alfred E. Khan Dies at 93; Prime Mover of Airline Deregulation," *New York Times*, December 28, 2010, accessed December 7, 2012, www.nytimes .com/2010/12/29/business/29kahn.html; Severin Borenstein and Nancy L. Rose, *How Airline Markets Work . . . Or Do They? Regulatory Reform in the Airline Industry* (Cambridge, MA: National Bureau of Economic Research, October 2008), accessed December 7, 2012, www.nber.org/chapters/c12570.pdf.

3. John Berlau, "Ted Kennedy's Deregulatory Legacy on Airlines and Trucking," OpenMarket .org, August 26, 2009, accessed December 7, 2012, www.openmarket.org/2009/08/26 /kennedys-deregulator-legacy-on-airlines-and-trucking.

4. Phillip Longman and Lina Khan, "Terminal Sickness," *Washington Monthly*, March–April 2012, accessed October 17, 2012, www.washingtonmonthly.com/magazine/march _april_2012/features/terminal_sickness035756.php.

5. Airlines for America, *US Airline Bankruptcies and Service Cessations* (Washington, DC: A4A, September 29, 2012), accessed December 4, 2012, www.airlines.org/Pages/U.S. -Airline-Bankruptcies-and-Service-Cessations.aspx.

6. Phillip Longman and Lina Khan, "Terminal Sickness," *Washington Monthly*, March–April 2012, accessed October 17, 2012, www.washingtonmonthly.com/magazine/march _april_2012/features/terminal_sickness035756.php.

7. Airlines for America, *US Airline Bankruptcies and Service Cessations* (Washington, DC:

A4A, September 29, 2012), accessed December 4, 2012, www.airlines.org/Pages/U.S.-Airline-Bankruptcies-and-Service-Cessations.aspx.

8. Margaret M. Blair, "The Economics of Post–September 11 Financial Aid to Airlines," *Indiana Law Review*, vol. 35 (2002), pp. 1 and 20–21; Reuters, "US Sees Profit on Airline Loan Guarantee Program," *USA Today*, January 30, 2006, accessed February 23, 2011, www.usatoday.com/travel/news/2006-01-30-loan-profits_x.htm; Daniel Gross, "Bailing for Dollars," *Slate*, May 7, 2004, accessed February 23, 2011, www.slate.com/id/2100198.

9. Steven Mufson, "'American Airlines' Plan for Pension Bailout Draws Criticism," *Washington Post*, February 3, 2012, accessed June 11, 2012, www.washingtonpost.com/business/economy/american-airlines-request-for-pension-bailout-draws-criticism/2012/02/03/gIQAu1m1nQ_story.html.

10. Federal Aviation Administration, *The Economic Impact of Civil Aviation on the US Economy* (Washington, DC: US Department of Transportation, August 2011), p. 4; William L. Painter, *Department of Homeland Security: FY 2013 Appropriations* (Washington, DC: Congressional Research Service, August 3, 2012), p. 49; "Summary of the President's FY 2013 Budget Request for the FAA," Arent Fox, February 13, 2012, accessed October 17, 2012, www.arentfox.com/publications/index.cfm?fa=legalUpdateDisp&content_id=3564.

11. All prices cited above were based on Expedia price quotes as of October 17, 2012: "Plan Your Trip on Expedia," Expedia, Inc., October 17, 2012, accessed October 17, 2012.

12. Phillip Longman and Lina Khan, "Terminal Sickness," *Washington Monthly*, March–April 2012, accessed October 17, 2012, www.washingtonmonthly.com/magazine/march_april_2012/features/terminal_sickness035756.php. See also: James Pilcher, "Why CVG Lost Half of All Flights," *Cincinnati Enquirer*, May 23, 2010, accessed October 17, 2012, http://news.cincinnati.com/article/20100524/EDIT03/5230393/Why-CVG-lost-half-all-flights. For the relocation of Chiquita, see: *Cincinnati Enquirer* Staff and Wire Reports, "Chiquita CEO Thanks Cincinnation Way Out," Cincinnati.com, November 29, 2011, accessed December 7, 2012, http://news.cincinnati.com/viewart/20111129/BIZ01/311290018/Chiquita-CEO-thanks-Cincinnati-way-out.

13. The point of importance in the case of the outer suburbs and interstate system is that large-order population distribution issues were central to the planning decisions. That private corporate interests shaped and misshaped these programs has long been well established; that alternative results might be achieved by a different constellation of institutions is the central argument of this book. For more, see: Kenneth T. Jackson, *Crabgrass Frontier: The Suburbanization of the United States* (New York, NY: Oxford University Press, 1985); Owen D. Gutfreund, *20th Century Sprawl: Highways and the Reshaping of the American Landscape* (New York, NY: Oxford University Press, 2004).

14. Thad Williamson, Steve Dubb, and Gar Alperovitz, *Climate Change, Community Stability and the Next 150 Million Americans* (College Park, MD: Democracy Collaborative at the University of Maryland, 2010). For 2050 projections, see: US Census Bureau, "Table 9: Resident Population Projections by Sex and Age: 2010 to 2050," in *Statistical Abstract of the United States 2012* (Washington, DC: USCB, 2012), accessed November 20, 2012, www.census.gov/compendia/statab/2012/tables/12s0009.pdf. For 2100 projections, see: Leon Kolankiewicz, "Immigration, Population, and the New Census Bureau Projections," *Center for Immigration Studies*, June 2000, accessed November 20, 2012, www.cis.org/CensusBureauProjections-Immigration%2526Population.

15. Josh Mitchell, "Air Subsidies Hit Turbulence," *Wall Street Journal*, July 28, 2011, accessed October 17, 2012, http://online.wsj.com/article/SB10001424053111904800304576472472698042018.html#printMode; Tad DeHaven, "'Essential' Air Subsidies Survive in the House," *Cato at Liberty*, June 27, 2012, accessed October 17, 2012, www.cato-at-liberty.org/essential-air-subsidies-survive-in-the-house.

16. Lawrence E. Mitchell, *The Speculation Economy: How Finance Triumphed over Industry* (San Francisco, CA: Berrett-Koehler Publishers, 2008), p. 275.

17. See: Robert *Costanza* et al., *RIO+20: Building a Sustainable and Desirable Economy-in-Society-in-Nature* (New York, NY: United Nations Division for Sustainable Development, 2012). See also: Richard Heinberg, *The End of Growth: Adapting to Our New Economic Reality* (Gabriola Island, BC: New Society Publishers, 2011); Dennis Pirages and Ken Cousins, eds., *Exploring New Limits to Growth* (Cambridge, MA: MIT Press, 2005); Michael Moyer and Carina Storrs, "How Much Is Left? The Limits of Earth's Resources," *Scientific American*, August 24, 2010, accessed November 21, 2012, www.scientificamerican.com/article.cfm?id=how-much-is-left.

18. According to the US Energy Information Administration, in 2010 the United States consumed 19.18 million barrels of oil per day, while the world consumed 87.04 million barrels per day (22.03 percent); the US consumed 1.048 billion short tons of coal, while the world consumed 7.995 billion short tons (13.1 percent); and the US consumed 23,775 billion cubic feet of natural gas, while the world consumed 112,971 billion cubic feet (21.04 percent). See: Energy Information Administration, *International Energy Statistics 2010* (Washington, DC: EIA, 2011), www.eia.gov/cfapps/ipdbproject/IEDIndex3.cfm?tid=1&pid=1&aid=2.

19. Ralph C. Kirby and Andrew S. Prokopovitsh, "Technological Insurance Against Shortages in Minerals and Metals," *Science*, vol. 191, no. 4228 (February 20, 1976), pp. 713–19.

20. In any serious long-term scenario, of course, there would be variations in income among groups and different associated consumption patterns—though hopefully not the extreme income variations we now experience. The point here is simply that we are already an extraordinarily wealthy society and can already afford extremely generous lifestyles for all citizens without having to grow at traditional rates, or indeed, grow indefinitely. US GDP in 2011 was $14.958 trillion. US population was around 312.78 million people. Thus per-capita GDP was approximately $47,822 or $191,288 for a family of four. For GDP information, see: Office of Management and Budget, "Table 10.1: Gross Domestic Product and Deflators Used in the Historical Tables: 1940–2016," in *Historical Tables: Budget of the United States Government, Fiscal Year 2013* (Washington, DC: Government Printing Office, 2012). For population, see: Robert Schlesinger, "US Population 2012: Nearly 313 Million People," *US News & World Report*, December 30, 2011, accessed November 21, 2012, www.usnews.com/opinion/blogs/robert-schlesinger/2011/12/30/us-population-2012-nearly-313-million-people.

21. Quote on page 555 of: James Gustave Speth, "Letter to Liberals: Liberalism, Environmentalism, and Economic Growth," *Vermont Law Review*, vol. 35 (2011), pp. 547–61.

20. Two Dogs That Are Unlikely to Bark Again

1. Total government spending was around 30 percent in the years preceding the Great Recession. In 2009 it jumped up to 37.1 percent before settling at 35.4 percent in 2010 and 2011. See: Office of Management and Budget, "Table 15.3: Total Government Expenditures as Percentages of GDP: 1948–2011," in *Historical Tables: Budget of the United States Government, Fiscal Year 2013* (Washington, DC: Government Printing Office, 2012).

2. Total government spending in 1929 was approximately 11.3 percent of GDP. See: Christopher Chantrill, ed., "Total Government Spending in the United States, Federal, State, and Local: Fiscal Year 1929," USGovernmentSpending.com, no date, accessed November 21, 2012, www.usgovernmentspending.com/breakdown_1929USpt_13ps5n.

3. As well as another $16 billion in fiscal year 2009. Through 2018, the program is estimated to cost $125 billion as "firms will claim less depreciation for investments made in 2008 than they otherwise would have." See: Roberton Williams, "Economic Stimulus: What Is the Economic Stimulus Act of 2008?" Tax Policy Center, March 13, 2008, accessed September 10, 2012, www.taxpolicycenter.org/briefing-book/background/stimulus/2008.cfm.

4. David M. Herszenhorn, "Congress Sends $801 Billion Tax Cut Bill to Obama," *New York*

Times, December 16, 2010, accessed November 21, 2012, www.nytimes.com/2010/12/17/us/politics/17cong.html?pagewanted=all.

5. Martin Feldstein, "The Economy Is Worse Than You Think," *Wall Street Journal*, June 8, 2011, accessed July 16, 2012, http://online.wsj.com/article/SB10001424052702303657404576363984173620692.html.

6. Andrew Ward and Alan Beattie, "Democrats Force Through Stimulus Bill," *Financial Times*, January 28, 2009, accessed September 11, 2012, www.ft.com/cms/s/0/c94d5f7e-ed66-11dd-bd60-0000779fd2ac.html#axzz26B6bW2my.

7. Jennifer Parker, "Google CEO to Congress: Pass Stimulus Now," ABC News, February 1, 2009, accessed September 11, 2012, http://abcnews.go.com/blogs/politics/2009/02/google-ceo-to-c.

8. Andrew Ward and Alan Beattie, "Democrats Force Through Stimulus Bill," *Financial Times*, January 28, 2009, accessed September 11, 2012, www.ft.com/cms/s/0/c94d5f7e-ed66-11dd-bd60-0000779fd2ac.html#axzz26B6bW2my.

9. David M. Herszenhorn, Carl Hulse, and Sheryl Gay Stolberg, "Talks Implode During a Day of Chaos; Fate of Bailout Plan Remains Unresolved," *New York Times*, September 25, 2008, accessed September 3, 2012, www.nytimes.com/2008/09/26/business/26bailout.html?pagewanted=all.

10. "Transcript: Bret Baier Interviews President Bush," Fox News, December 17, 2008, accessed May 7, 2012, www.foxnews.com/politics/2008/12/17/transcript-bret-baier-interviews-president-bush.

11. Federal defense spending alone during World War II reached as much as 37.8 percent of GDP in 1944. See: Office of Management and Budget, "Table 3.1: Outlays by Superfunction and Function: 1940–2017," in *Historical Tables: Budget of the United States Government, Fiscal Year 2013* (Washington, DC: Government Printing Office, 2012).

12. Office of Management and Budget, "Table 3.1: Outlays by Superfunction and Function: 1940–2017," in *Historical Tables: Budget of the United States Government, Fiscal Year 2013* (Washington, DC: Government Printing Office, 2012). The Congressional Budget Office has estimated that the Department of Defense's base budget will decline to 3 percent of GDP in 2017 and then to 2.5 percent of GDP by 2030. See: John Skeen, ed., *Long-Term Implications of the 2013 Future Years Defense Program* (Washington, DC: Congressional Budget Office, July 11, 2012), www.cbo.gov/publication/43428.

21. Stagnation and Punctuated Stagnation

1. Thomas I. Palley, *From Financial Crisis to Stagnation: The Destruction of Shared Prosperity and the Role of Economics* (New York, NY: Cambridge University Press, 2012), p. 125.

2. Ibid., p. 3.

3. The income share (including capital gains) for the top 1 percent was 9.16 percent in 1973. In 2010 it was up to 19.86 percent. See: Facundo Alvaredo et al., "The World Top Incomes Database," Paris School of Economics, no date, accessed September 17, 2012, http://g-mond.parisschoolofeconomics.eu/topincomes.

4. Joseph Stiglitz, "The 1 Percent's Problem," *Vanity Fair*, May 31, 2012, accessed June 21, 2012, www.vanityfair.com/politics/2012/05/joseph-stiglitz-the-price-on-inequality.

5. Russ Roberts, "Dean Baker on the Crisis," *Library of Economics and Liberty*, January 9, 2012, accessed June 21, 2012, www.econtalk.org/archives/2012/01/dean_baker_on_t.html.

6. Robert Reich, "The Truth About the American Economy," *OB Rag*, May 30, 2011, accessed June 12, 2012, http://obrag.org/?p=38708.

7. Paul Krugman and Robin Wells, "Economy Killers: Inequality and GOP Ignorance," *Salon*, April 15, 2012, accessed June 22, 2012, www.salon.com/2012/04/15/economy_killers_inequality_and_gop_ignorance.

8. For Foxconn hourly wages in Chinese factories making iPhones, see: *Economix* Editors, "The iEconomy: How Much Do Foxconn Workers Make?" *New York Times*, February 24,

2012, accessed October 19, 2012, http://economix.blogs.nytimes.com/2012/02/24/the-ieconomy-how-much-do-foxconn-workers-make.

9. Jeff Faux, "Apple's Low-Wage Path to America's Future," *Huffington Post*, October 16, 2012, accessed October 26, 2012, www.huffingtonpost.com/jeff-faux/apples-lowwage-path-to-am_b_1970496.html.

10. Michael A. Levi et al., "How to Handle Oil Price Volatility," Council of Foreign Relations, March 19, 2012, accessed October 18, 2012, www.cfr.org/united-states/handle-oil-price-volatility/p27667.

11. Maria van der Hoeven, "Energy Price Volatility in Fossil Fuel Markets," in *The G20 Mexico Summit 2012: The Quest for Growth and Stability*, ed. John Kirton and Madeline Koch (Toronto, ON: University of Toronto, Newsdesk Media Group, and the G20 Research Group, June 2012), pp. 122–23, www.g8.utoronto.ca/newsdesk/loscabos/g20loscabos2012-07.pdf.

12. Foresight, *The Future of Food and Farming: Challenges and Choices for Global Sustainability* (London, UK: Government Office for Science, 2011), accessed October 18, 2012, p. 15, www.bis.gov.uk/assets/foresight/docs/food-and-farming/11-547-future-of-food-and-farming-summary.

13. Yash P. Mehra and Jon D. Petersen, "Oil Prices and Consumer Spending," *Federal Reserve Bank of Richmond Quarterly*, vol. 91, no. 3 (Summer 2005), p. 56.

14. Mark Cooper, *Excessive Speculation and Oil Price Shock Recessions: A Case of Wall Street "Déjà Vu All Over Again"* (Washington, DC: Consumer Federation of America, October 2011), p. i, www.consumerfed.org/pdfs/SpeculationReportOctober13.pdf; Office of Senator Jack Reed, "Reed Backs New Rules to Crack Down on Oil Market Manipulation," Jack Reed: US Senator for Rhode Island, April 17, 2012, accessed September 10, 2012, www.reed.senate.gov/news/release/reed-backs-new-rules-to-crack-down-on-oil-market-manipulation.

15. Barani Krishnan and Jonathan Leff, "Hedge Funds Bet on Oil Spike as Israel Attack Fears Grow," Reuters, August 17, 2012, www.reuters.com/article/2012/08/17/us-oil-funds-iran-idUSBRE87G03H20120817.

16. British Petroleum Press Office, "A Year of Disruption and Growth Proved Open Energy Markets Are Key to Stability," BP Global, June 13, 2012, accessed December 5, 2012, www.bp.com/extendedgenericarticle.do?categoryId=2012968&contentId=7075274. See also: British Petroleum Global, *BP Statistical Review of World Energy June 2012* (London, UK: BP Global, 2012), accessed October 18, 2012, www.bp.com/statisticalreview.

17. José Graziano da Silva, Kanayo F. Nwanze, and Ertharin Cousin, "Joint Statement from FAO, IFAD and WFD on International Food Prices," Food and Agriculture Organization of the United Nations, September 4, 2012, accessed September 10, 2012, www.fao.org/news/story/en/item/155472/icode/; Marco Lagi, Karla Z. Bertrand, and Yaneer Bar-Yam, *The Food Crises and Political Instability in North Africa and the Middle East* (Cambridge, MA: New England Complex Systems Institute, September 28, 2011), http://necsi.edu/research/social/food_crises.pdf.

18. Claire Schaffnit-Chatterjee, *Where Are Food Prices Heading? Short-Term Drivers, Trends and Implications* (Frankfurt, Germany: Deutsche Bank Research, March 10, 2011), accessed October 18, 2012, www.dbresearch.com/PROD/DBR_INTERNET_EN-PROD/PROD0000000000270746.pdf.

19. Marco Lagi, Karla Z. Bertrand, and Yaneer Bar-Yam, *The Food Crises and Political Instability in North Africa and the Middle East* (Cambridge, MA: New England Complex Systems Institute, September 28, 2011), http://necsi.edu/research/social/food_crises.pdf.

20. Marc Humphries, *Rare Earth Elements: The Global Supply Chain* (Washington, DC: Congressional Research Service, June 8, 2012), pp. 9-10, accessed October 18, 2012, www.fas.org/sgp/crs/natsec/R41347.pdf.

21. Robert J. Gordon, *Is US Economic Growth Over? Faltering Innovation Confronts the Six Headwinds*, Working Paper no. 18315 (Cambridge, MA: National Bureau of Economic Research, August 2012).

22. The Logic of Our Time in History

1. Center for Responsive Politics, "Business-Labor-Ideology Split in PAC & Individual Donations to Candidates, Parties, Super PACs and Outside Spending Groups," OpenSecrets.org, 2011, accessed September 13, 2012, www.opensecrets.org/bigpicture/blio.php?cycle=2010.

2. The 2012 Obama campaign made use of much more sophisticated voter identification and mobilization efforts than the Romney campaign—an imbalance that while significant in the short term is not likely to continue indefinitely. See: Sasha Issenberg, "Obama Does It Better," *Slate*, October 29, 2012, accessed January 4, 2013, www.slate.com/articles /news_and_politics/victory_lab/2012/10/obama_s_secret_weapon_democrats_have _a_massive_advantage_in_targeting_and.html; Karl Rove, "Rove: The Lessons of Defeat for the GOP," *Wall Street Journal*, November 14, 2012, accessed January 4, 2012, http://online.wsj.com/article/sb10001424127887324735104578118873224497426.html.

3. Christine Bogusz et al., ed., "The 2012 Long-Term Budget Outlook," Congressional Budget Office, June 5, 2012, accessed September 13, 2012, http://cbo.gov/publication/43288.

4. Adding state and local spending, currently around 11 percent of GDP, and even assuming no growth, this would bring total government spending to almost 50 percent of GDP. Christine Bogusz et al., ed., "The 2012 Long-Term Budget Outlook," Congressional Budget Office, June 5, 2012, accessed September 13, 2012, http://cbo.gov/publication/43288.

5. Thomas B. Edsall, "Limited War: How the Age of Austerity Will Remake American Politics," *The New Republic*, October 20, 2010, accessed November 2, 2010, www.tnr.com/article /economy/magazine/78564/austerity-economic-crisis-democrats-tea-party.

6. Jeff Faux, "The Hunger Games Economy," *American Prospect*, June 2012, accessed September 19, 2012, http://jefffaux.com/?p=254.

7. Ruy Teixeira, *New Progressive America: Twenty Years of Demographic, Geographic, and Attitudinal Changes Across the Country Herald a New Progressive Majority* (Washington, DC: Center for American Progress, March 2009), accessed August 20, 2012, www.americanprogress.org /issues/progressive-movement/report/2009/03/11/5783/new-progressive-america.

8. See: Christopher Chantrill, ed., "United States Federal, State, and Local Government Spending: Fiscal Year 1929 in Percent GDP," USGovernmentSpending.com, no date, accessed November 26, 2012, www.usgovernmentspending.com/year_spending_1929USpn_13psln _F0#usgs302. For 2011, see: Office of Management and Budget, "Table 15.3: Total Government Expenditures as Percentages of GDP 1948–2011," in *Historical Tables: Budget of the United States Government, Fiscal Year 2013* (Washington, DC: Government Printing Office, 2012), www.whitehouse.gov/omb/budget/Historicals.

23. The Prehistory of the Next American Revolution

1. Seymour Martin Lipset and William Schneider, *The Confidence Gap: Business, Labor, and Government in the Public Mind* (Baltimore, MD: Johns Hopkins University Press, 1987), p. 411.

2. Eyder Peralta, "Socialism, Capitalism: Merriam-Webster's Odd-Couple Words of the Year," *National Public Radio*, December 5, 2012, accessed December 17, 2012, www.npr .org/blogs/thetwo-way/2012/12/05/166579843/socialism-capitalism-merriam-websters -odd-couple-words-of-the-year.

3. Jane Mansbridge, *Beyond Adversary Democracy* (New York, NY: Basic Books, 1983), p. 289.

4. Alexis de Tocqueville, *Democracy in America*, vol. I, 7th ed. (New York, NY: Edward Walker, 1847), p. 62. Alternative translations replace "Municipal Institutions" with "Town meetings."

5. John Stuart Mill, "Tocqueville on Democracy in America (vol. I)," in *Essays on Politics and Culture*, ed. Gertrude Himmelfarb (Garden City, NY: Doubleday, 1962), pp. 200–201.

6. See: Paul Peterson, *City Limits* (Chicago, IL: University of Chicago Press, 1981).

7. Martin Buber, *Paths in Utopia* (Boston, MA: Beacon Press, 1958), pp. 13–14.

8. See: Gar Alperovitz, "Democracy: Inequality and Giant Corporations," chapter 4 in *America Beyond Capitalism: Reclaiming Our Wealth, Our Liberty, and Our Democracy* (Hoboken, NJ: Wiley and Sons, 2005), pp. 50–62.

9. For an overview of emerging experience in some areas, see: "Examples of PB," Participatory Budgeting Project, no date, accessed November 28, 2012, www.participatorybudgeting.org /resources/examples-of-participatory-budgeting.

10. An April 2009 Rasmussen poll found that among Americans under thirty, 37 percent favored capitalism, 30 percent favored socialism, and 30 percent were undecided. See: "Just 53% Say Capitalism Better Than Socialism," *Rasmussen Reports*, April 9, 2009. One year later, in April 2010, Rasmussen reported: "Adults under 30 are closely divided on the question." See: "60% Say Capitalism Better Than Socialism," *Rasmussen Reports*, April 23, 2010. In a December 2011 Pew poll, 49 percent of Americans under thirty had a favorable reaction to "socialism," compared with 46 percent who had a favorable reaction to "capitalism." See: "Little Change in Public's Response to 'Capitalism,' 'Socialism,'" Pew Research Center for the People & the Press, December 28, 2011.

11. See the conclusion of my *The Decision to Use the Atomic Bomb* for a discussion of culture and its role in limiting or not limiting the use of extraordinary military power. Gar Alperovitz, *The Decision to Use the Atomic Bomb* (New York, NY: Knopf, 1995).

12. Real GDP per capita in 1900 was $5,556.85 (in 2005 dollars). By 2000 it was $39,749.59. See: Louis Johnston and Samuel H. Williamson, "What Was the US GDP Then?" MeasuringWorth.com, 2011.

13. US GDP in 2011 was $14.958 trillion. US population was around 312.78 million people. Thus per-capita GDP was approximately $47,822 or $191,288 for a family of four. For GDP information, see: Office of Management and Budget, "Table 10.1: Gross Domestic Product and Deflators Used in the Historical Tables: 1940–2016," in *Historical Tables: Budget of the United States Government, Fiscal Year 2013* (Washington, DC: Government Printing Office, 2012). For population, see: Robert Schlesinger, "US Population 2012: Nearly 313 Million People," *US News & World Report*, December 30, 2011, accessed November 21, 2012, www.usnews.com/opinion/blogs /robert-schlesinger/2011/12/30/us-population-2012-nearly-313-million-people.

14. "Frequently Asked Questions About Mead/Bateson," Institute for Intercultural Studies, no date, accessed November 28, 2012, www.interculturalstudies.org/faq.html#quo.

Afterword: The Question of Long-Term Systemic Design

1. Gar Alperovitz, "Notes Toward a Pluralist Commonwealth," *Review of Radical Political Economics*, vol. 4, is. 2 (June 1972), pp. 28–48. Also available in: Gar Alperovitz and Staughton Lynd, *Strategy and Program: Two Essays Toward a New American Socialism* (Boston, MA: Beacon Press, 1973).

2. See also: Gar Alperovitz, "Local Democracy and Regional Decentralization," part 3 in *America Beyond Capitalism*, 2nd ed. (Takoma Park, MD: Democracy Collaborative Press, 2011).

3. See: David Harvey, *Rebel Cities: From the Right to the City to the Urban Revolution* (London, UK: Verso, 2012).

4. Staughton Lynd, *The Fight Against Shutdowns: Youngstown's Steel Mill Closings* (San Pedro, CA: Singlejack Books, 1982), pp. 42–44.

5. Center for Responsive Politics, "The Money Behind the Elections," OpenSecrets.org, 2012, accessed December 17, 2012, www.opensecrets.org/bigpicture/index.php.

6. George F. Kennan, *Around the Cragged Hill: A Personal and Political Philosophy* (New York, NY: W. W. Norton, 1993), pp. 143, 149.

7. Using 2010 data from the OECD, the US economy was $14.447 trillion (in current purchasing power parity measured in dollars). Germany was $3.079 trillion; France and Britain were

$2.229 trillion and $2.197 trillion, respectively; and the European Union as a whole was $15.94 trillion. See: "Frequently Requested Data: Gross Domestic Product," Organisation for Economic Co-operation and Development, no date, accessed November 8, 2012, http://stats.oecd.org.

8. The Social Security Trust Fund Board of Trustees' "high cost estimate" assumes an average annual real GDP growth rate of 2.25 percent from 2011 to 2021 as the economy recovers from the Great Recession. After 2021, they project that the growth rate will slow to approach around 1.4 percent by 2050. Using a baseline of $14.958 trillion GDP in 2011 (in chained 2005 dollars), this results in GDP of around $29.57 trillion in 2050. Using the "intermediate cost estimate," GDP would be around $37.01 trillion in 2050; and using the "low cost estimate," GDP would be around $46.39 trillion. Using the reported growth rates to 2090, then projecting them out to 2100, results in GDP estimates of $54.06 trillion (high cost), $102.49 trillion (intermediate cost), and $188.14 trillion (low cost). See: Social Security Trustees, *The 2012 Annual Report of the Board of Trustees of the Federal Old-Age and Survivors Insurance and Disability Insurance Trust Funds* (Washington, DC: Government Printing Office, 2012), p. 105.

9. William Bennett Munro, *The Invisible Government* (New York, NY: Macmillan, 1928), pp. 137, 153–54.

10. William Yandell Elliott, *The Need for Constitutional Reform: A Program for National Security* (New York, NY: McGraw-Hill, 1935), p. 193.

11. William Appleman Williams, *The Great Evasion: An Essay on the Contemporary Relevance of Karl Marx and on the Wisdom of Admitting the Heretic into the Dialogue About America's Future* (Chicago, IL: Quadrangle Books, 1968).

12. Alberto Alesina and Enrico Spolaore, *The Size of Nations* (Cambridge, MA: MIT Press, 2005).

13. Michael Keating and John Loughlin, eds., *The Political Economy of Regionalism* (London, UK: Frank Cass, 1997); Paul Balchin and Luděk Sýkora with Gregory Bull, *Regional Policy and Planning in Europe* (London, UK: Routledge, 1999); Yehua Wei, "Economic Reforms and Regional Development in Coastal China," *Journal of Contemporary Asia*, vol. 28, no. 4 (1998), pp. 498–517; Matthew Tempest, "Regional Government Around the World," *The Guardian*, June 16, 2003, accessed June 17, 2003, http://politics.guardian.co.uk /localgovernment/story/0,9061,978755,00.html; Klaus Konig, "Appraisal of National Policies of Decentralization and Regionalization," *International Institute of Administrative Sciences*, vol. 21 (1989), p. 3. James Manor has also noted that "nearly all countries worldwide are now experimenting with decentralization." James Manor, *The Political Economy of Democratic Decentralization* (Washington, DC: World Bank, 1999), pp. vii, 1.

14. James Wesley Scott, "Systemic Transformation and the Implementation of New Regionalist Paradigms: Experiences of Central America and Europe," in *De-Coding New Regionalism: Shifting Socio-Political Contexts in Central Europe and Latin America*, ed. James Wesley Scott (Surrey, UK: Ashgate Publishing, 2009), p. 20.

15. For some preliminary views on what this might require, see: William Greider, *Secrets of the Temple: How the Federal Reserve Runs the Country* (New York, NY: Touchstone, 1989); William Greider, "Dismantling the Temple," *The Nation*, July 15, 2009; Ellen Brown, *Web of Debt: The Shocking Truth About Our Money System and How We Can Break Free* (Baton Rouge, LA: Third Millennium Press, 2007); David Korten et al., *How to Liberate America from Wall Street Rule: A Report from the New Economy Working Group* (Washington, DC: NEWG, July 2011); Herman Daly, "From a Failed-Growth Economy to a Steady State," *Solutions*, vol. 1, is. 2 (February 2010); and work by John Fullerton, especially: John Fullerton, "Reimagining Capitalism in Post Sandy America," Capital Institute, November 6, 2012. See also my piece: Gar Alperovitz, "How Big Banks Run the World—at Your Expense," *Truthout*, June 8, 2012. For related work on monetary theory, see especially the work of L. Randall Wray and studies by other researchers working with the Levy Economics Institute of Bard College, NY.

Index

Affordable Care Act, 17–18, 85, 86
aggregate demand, 125
Ahn, Daniel P., 127
AIG (American International Group, Inc.), 93, 115
airlines, 104–7
    deregulation, 104
    government support for, 105, 107
    mergers and bankruptcies, 105
    public ownership of, 95, 107
airports, government operation of, 105
Alabama, Retirement Systems of, 63
Alaska Permanent Fund, 63
Alesina, Alberto, 153
Alliance to Develop Power, 36
alternative policies, 113
America Beyond Capitalism, 148–50
American values, 4–5, 140
antitrust actions, 77–79
Apple Inc., 126
Appleton company, 41
AT&T, 78
Austin, Texas, green development program, 56
Austin Energy, 59
auto industry bailout, 93, 102–3, 115

B Corp (benefit corporation), 39, 81
Baker, Dean, 125
Bank of North Dakota, 81
banks, 75–82, 89, 90, 93, 100, 115–16
    credit unions, 36, 80
    efficiency of, 94
    fiscal crisis and, 75–80, 94
    lobbying by, 76
    public operation of, 80–82, 95, 100
    regulation of, 76–79
    too big to fail, 77
Barber, Benjamin, 141
Bay Area Rapid Transit, 60
benefit corporation (B Corp), 39, 81
Bethel New Life, 38
Black Star Co-op, 36
Bookchin, Murray, 149
Boston, Fanueil Hall Marketplace developed by, 59–60

Brazil, publicly operated enterprises in, 95
broadband services, 60–61, 70
Buber, Martin, 144, 150
Bush, George W., 75, 119, 121
business groups, progressive, 134
businesses. *See* corporations

California
    CalPers state pension fund, 63
    universal health care legislation, 87
campaign spending, 4, 142
capitalism, 26, 141. *See also* corporate capitalism
Carris Reels Inc., 43
Carter administration, 30
CDCs (community development corporations), 37–38, 53–55
Champlain Housing Trust, 38
Chattanooga, Tennessee, broadband services, 61
checkerboard strategies, 65–71, 91, 114–17, 132
Chicago School of Economics, 78–79, 88, 107
China, 126, 128
Chiquita Brands International, 106
Chrysler Corporation, 93
cities. *See also* local governments; *specific cities*
    change in, 114–15 (*See also* checkerboard strategies)
    corporate relocations, effect of, 52, 100–102, 106, 143, 144
Citizens United decision, 130, 133
civil rights, 12, 19–20, 38
Clarke, Susan, 53
Cleveland, Ohio, 31–32, 54, 101, 102
climate change, xii, 4, 7. *See also* green development
    endless growth and, 108
    options to address, 133, 135, 144
    participatory planning process, 154
Clinton, Gill, 78
Commodity Futures Modernization Act, 78
community
    democracy and, 141–45, 149
    planning, role of, 154–55
community benefit strategies, 69–70

community-wide ownership strategies, 149–50 (*See also* public enterprises)

worker ownership, 29, 31–32, 150

community development corporations (CDCs), 37–38, 53–55

community stability, 102

corporate relocation, effect of, 100–102, 143, 144

planning for, 154

community sustainability, xiv, 91, 132, 134, 139–47, 154. *See also* ecological sustainability; green development

Connecticut health care legislation, 87

conservatives

affluence and, 90

free market view of, 51–53, 55

political contributions by, 130

Constitution, US, 156

consumer spending, 124–25

cooperatives, 35–37, 58

corporate capitalism, 6, 25–26, 46, 141, 143–44

corporate institutions. *See also* corporations

displacement of, 114, 135–36 (*See also* democratized ownership of wealth)

economic system dominated by, 2, 143

loss of belief in, 140

corporate state, 135

corporations. *See also* banks; corporate institutions

concentrated wealth, controlled by, 27

direct government investments in, 53–54, 64

economic development programs and, 91

efficiency of, 94–95, 99–101

government subsidies of, 52–57, 69, 105, 107

"grow or die" imperative, 104, 108, 145, 150

health care costs and, 86–88

political contributions by, 130

power of, 2, 113, 130, 142–43

relocations by, 52–53, 100–102, 106, 143, 144

too big to fail, 77, 94

countervailing power, 89–90, 114

Cowen, Tyler, 124

Cowie, Jefferson, 15

credit unions, 36, 80

crisis transformations, 89, 91, 92, 115–17, 132

auto industry bailout, 93, 102–3, 115

banks, 75–82, 89, 115, 132

big, 94, 115, 116, 132

health care, 83–89, 132

cultural and ideological hegemony, 46–48, 91

Dallas, Texas, hotel development, 61

Daly, Lew, 148, 151

decentralization, 107, 141, 143, 145, 149, 152–53

Dell Computer Corporation, 52–53

demand, aggregate, 125

democracy, 5, 135, 140, 145. *See also* democratized ownership of wealth

community and, 141–45, 149

large populations and geographic scales, effect of, 145, 151–53

wealth concentration, effect of, 142

Democratic majorities, increasing, 133

democratic socialism, 20–21

democratization strategies, 55–56, 92, 132, 145–46. *See also* checkerboard strategies; crisis transformations; emerging historical context for change; evolutionary reconstruction

democratized ownership of wealth, 27, 35–40, 46–47, 69, 114–15, 117, 132, 135–36, 141. *See also* democratization strategies; nationalization; wealth concentration, US; worker-owned companies

B Corp (benefit corporation), 39, 81

community and, 144

community development corporations, 37–38, 53–55

cooperatives, 35–37

crisis transformation and, 75, 89, 94

government's role in, 54

impact investment, 40

L3C (low-profit limited liability corporation), 40

land trusts, 38–39, 69

neighborhood investors, 40

single-payer health care, 88

social enterprises, 36–37

US socialism, 58–64

Denver Health, 62

Detroit, job losses in, 101

development socialism, 59–60

Dickey, Gerald, 29

discrimination, 19

Dodd-Frank Wall Street Reform and

Consumer Protection Act, 76–78
Durbin, Dick, 76
dynamic processes, 83

ecological sustainability, 4–5, 113, 140, 145, 149, 154. *See also* community sustainability; green development
economic development programs, 53–55, 91
economic inequality. *See* inequality
economic issues, planning for, 153–55
economic power, property ownership as basis of, 26–27
Economic Stimulus Act, 120
economy, democratizing. *See* democratized ownership of wealth
economy, US *See also* fiscal crisis; income inequality; wealth concentration, US
consumer spending, 124–25
corporate institutions, dominated by, 2, 143
federal spending as percentage of, CBO projections, 131
government stabilization programs, 119–21
health care spending, 83
military spending, 122
1945-70, growth during, 11–13
size of, 152
stagnation of, xiii, 34, 124–29
Edmonds Communitysolar Cooperative, 36
Edsall, Thomas, 131
efficiency, 104, 113, 154–55
airlines, 105, 107
corporate relocations, effect on cities of, 100–102
public *vs.* private enterprises, 94–95, 99–100
Eisinger, Peter, 53
elderly, as political constituency, 18
Elliott, Douglas, 80
Elliott, William Yandell, 153
emerging historical context for change, 116–19, 121–22, 130, 135
employee stock ownership plans (ESOPs), 41–43, 55, 63–64
employer-provided health insurance, 17–18, 86–87
employment. *See also* unemployment
corporate jobs, government subsidies of, 52
government incentives for, 102
military spending, supported by, 122

energy, renewable, 126
energy corporations, 108
energy prices, volatility in, 127–28
energy use, U. S., 108
entrepreneurial state, 53–54
environmental activists, 134–35
environmental legislation
labor, role of, 14
postwar, 12–13
environmental programs. *See* climate change; green development
equal pay for equal work, 6
equality, 4, 140
ESOPs (employee stock ownership plans), 41–43, 55, 63–64
Europe
health care, 84, 94
public airlines, 95, 107
public telecommunications services, 95
publicly operated banks and funding agencies, 95
Evergreen Cooperative Laundry, 32, 54
Evergreen Energy Solutions, 32, 54
evolutionary reconstruction, 35, 65–66, 91, 114–17, 132

Fanueil Hall Marketplace, 59–60
fascism, 26
Faux, Jeff, 131
Federal Aviation Administration, 105
Feldstein, Martin, 120
feminism, 19
feudalism, 26
financial stimulus, 119–21
fiscal challenges, future, 131
fiscal crisis
GDP and household net worth losses attributed to, 75
response to, 66, 68–71, 75–80, 93–94, 119–21
stagnation and, 124–29
unemployment attributed to, 75
food prices, volatility in, 127–28
foreign policy, development of alternative, 156
free market, 26, 51–53, 55, 121, 154–55
Friedman, Milton, 51, 79

Gaile, Gary, 53
Galbraith, John Kenneth, 89–90

gay rights, 19–20
gender inequality, 2, 6
General Motors Corporation, 93, 101–3, 115
GI Bill, 12
Gilbert, Richard, 103
Glass-Steagall Act, 78
global competition, US economy affected
   by, 125–28
Global Impact Investing Network (GIIN), 40
global peace, policies for, 146, 156
global trade, 113, 155
global warming. *See* climate change
Gordon, Robert, 128
government. *See also* local governments;
  state governments; US government
   airlines supported by, 105, 107
   businesses, direct investments in,
     53–54, 64
   corporations subsidized by, 52–57, 69,
     105, 107
   democratization strategy, role in, 55–56
Gramm-Leach-Bliley Act, 78
Gramsci, Antonio, 46
Great Depression, 8–10, 15, 119
Green City Growers Cooperative, 32, 54
green development, 32, 115
   businesses, 32, 54
   government programs, 55–57, 62
   landfills, methane captured from, 62
   public utilities, 59
Greyston Bakery, 37
Gross, Bertram, 135
growth, endless ("grow or die" imperative),
   104, 108, 145, 150

Harvey, David, 149
Hayek, Friedrich, 51
health care, US, 83–89, 100, 115–16, 131.
  See also Medicaid; Medicare
   Affordable Care Act, 17–18, 85, 86
   costs, 83, 86–87
   other nations compared, 83–85, 94
   outcome statistics, 83–84
   single-payer systems, 84–85, 87–88
   state universal health care plans, 87
health insurance, 17–18, 84–88, 90
hegemonic cultural and idea system, 46–48, 91
high-speed rail, 95, 103, 155
high-tech businesses, 109, 143

hospitals, government ownership of, 62
hotels, government construction and
   ownership of, 61
Hy-Vee company, 41

Imbroscio, David, 148, 155
impact investment, 40
incarceration rate, US, 4
income inequality, xii, 2–4, 12, 27, 125–26,
   133, 146. *See also* wages, US workers;
   wealth concentration, US
income per capita, US, 146
inequality, 113, 124–26, 150. *See also* income
   inequality; wealth concentration, US
institutions. *See also* corporate institutions
   community, challenge of, 141–44
   countervailing power theory, role in, 89
   development of, 34, 55, 132, 136, 155–56
   (*See also* systemic change)
   downward moving trends, 3–4
   institutional displacement theory of
     political power, 90–91
   loss of belief in, 140, 146
   political change, role in, 13–15, 156
insurance companies, 84–88, 90, 93
integrated system design, 99, 143, 155–56
International Association of Machinists
   and Aerospace Workers, 44
International Brotherhood of Electrical
   Workers, 44
International Brotherhood of Teamsters, 44
International Union of Electronic, Electri-
   cal, Salaried, Machine and Furniture
   Workers, 44
Internet service, 60–61, 70, 95
Interstate Highway System, 107
Israel, El Al airlines owned by, 95, 107
Isthmus Engineering and Manufacturing
   Company, 35

Japan Post Bank, 95
Johnson, Simon, 75, 77, 127
Josten, Bruce, 120

Kansas City, Missouri, green development
   program, 56
Kaptur, Marcy, 43
Kassoy, Andrew, 39
Kaufman, Ted, 77

Kazin, Michael, 19
Kelso, Louis, 42
Khan, Lina, 104, 106
King, Martin Luther, Jr., 20–21
King Arthur Flour, 39–40
Knight, Frank H., 79
Krugman, Paul, 126
Kucinich, Dennis, 43

labor unions, 12–16, 68, 78
    auto industry bailout role, 93, 102–3
    community organizing supported by, 69
    countervailing power role, 89–90
    employee ownership and, 30, 33, 42–44
    health insurance, support for, 18
    membership trends, 15, 113, 136
    new progressive movement,
        role in, 133–34
    political contributions by, 130
    postwar political change, role in, 13–14
    public sector, 69
land development, public, 59–60, 64
land trusts, 38–39, 69
landfills, methane captured from, 62
Landrieu, Mitch, 40
large populations/geographic scales, effect
    on democracy of, 145, 151–53
liberalism, 89–90, 113
liberty, 4, 113, 135, 140, 142, 145, 149
Lichtenstein, Nelson, 13
Lifetouch company, 41
Lilly Ledbetter Fair Pay Act, 6
Lipset, Seymour Martin, 140
Litecontrol Corporation, 43–44
lobbyists, 76
local democracy, 149
    community and, 141–44
    planning, role of, 154–55
local governments, 67
    banks and, 82
    corporate relocations and, 52–53,
        100–102, 143
    corporations subsidized by, 52–57, 69
    democratization strategy, role in, 55–56
    economic planning by, 53
    fiscal crisis, response to, 68–71
    hospitals owned by, 62
    hotel construction and ownership, 61
    land development, 59–60

landfills, methane captured from, 62
participatory lease arrangements,
    59–60, 70
public utilities, 58–59, 70
purchasing power, use of, 69
specific businesses, investments in, 53
telecommunications, investment in,
    60–61, 70
localist activists, 134–35
Logue, John, 31
Long, Russell, 42
Longman, Phillip, 104, 106
Louisiana Office of Social
    Entrepreneurship, 40
Louisville Biodiesel Cooperative, 36
Lynd, Staughton, 150

Madison, James, 151–52
Madison, Wisconsin, cooperatives, 35–36
Making a Place for Community, 148, 155
managed corporate capitalism, 26
Mannheim, Karl, 47
Mansbridge, Jane, 141
Market Creek Plaza, 40, 54
Marmor, Theodore, 14
Marriott Corporation, 52
Marx, Karl, 149
Maryland, Marriott Corporation
    subsidized by, 52
Maryland Brush Company, 44
Maryland Enterprise Investment Fund, 64
mass transportation, 60, 95, 103, 106–7, 155
Massachusetts health insurance plan, 87
McVeigh, Timothy, 135
Meadows, Donella, 7
Medicaid, 12–14, 18, 86
Medicare, 12–14, 18, 84–86, 88
medium-sized businesses, 109, 143
Miami-Dade Transit, 60
military spending, US, 11, 13, 122
Mill, John Stuart, 142
minimum wage, 7, 12
Mitchell, Lawrence, 108
Mobius, Mark, 75–76, 127
Mondragon Corporation, 33
monopolies, 77–79
Munro, William Bennett, 153

Namier, Lewis, 117

National Council of Senior Citizens, 14
National Industrial Recovery Act, 15
nationalization, 94, 132
    efficiency and, 94–95, 99–100
    during fiscal crisis, 93, 102–3, 115, 116
New Belgium Brewing Company, 43
New Community Corporation, 37–38
New Deal, 8–10, 15
New Economy Movement, 134
nontraditional businesses, funding of, 36
Norris, George W., 109
North Carolina, Dell subsidized by, 52–53
nuclear weapons, 122

Obama, Barack, 120
Obamacare. *See* Affordable Care Act
Oberlin, Ohio, green development
    program, 57
Occupy Movement, 134
Ohio, worker-owned businesses in, 28–32,
    34, 42, 150
Ohio Employee Ownership Center, 31, 63–64
oil production, 108
    price volatility and, 127–28
    publicly-owned enterprises, 95
Oklahoma City bombing, 1995, 135
OptiNet, 61
Organic Valley co-op, 36

Palley, Thomas, 124
Patagonia, 40
Paul, Ron, 43
pension systems, state, 63
Perl, Anthony, 103
Pioneer Human Services, 36–37
planning, role of, 153–55
pluralist commonwealth, 145
Point Loma Treatment Plant, 62
political action committees, 13
political change, 2–3, 113. *See also* democ-
    ratization strategies
    institutions, role of, 13–15, 156
    political theory of change, 3, 8
    strategies for, 116–17
political decision making
    current system of, 121, 125–26, 131
    demographic changes, effect of, 133
political power, 2–3, 6, 102
    of corporations, 2, 113, 130, 142–43

countervailing power theory,
    role in, 89–90
Democratic majorities, effect of
    increase in, 133
downward-moving outcomes and,
    3–4, 6–7
institutional displacement theory of,
    90–91
of institutions, 3–4, 13–15, 156
of low-income groups, 126
new constituencies, building, 91, 135–36
property ownership and, 26–27
wealth and, 142–43
political system
    communications, effect of national size
    on, 152
    trend shifts, contexts for, 7–16
political theory of change, 3, 8
populations, effect on democracy of large,
    145, 151–53
populism, 42, 109, 133–34
Portland, Oregon, green development
    program, 56
postwar economic boom, US, 11–16, 121
poverty, xii, 2, 4, 20
power, theory of
    countervailing power, 89–90
    institutional displacement theory of
    political power, 90–91
presidential elections, campaign
    spending for, 4
productivity, 125, 128–29
progressivism, 78, 89–90, 110
    business groups, 134
    emerging historical context for changes
    in (*See* emerging historical context
    for change)
    New Deal and, 8–10, 15
    options for change, 116, 133–36, 140–44
    political activism and, 19
    postwar economic boom and, xiv, 15
    race and, 16
    taxation and, 68
    traditional reform strategies and,
    133–34, 141
    union support for, 78 (*See also*
    labor unions)
projectism, 6, 55
property ownership

democratization of (*See* democratized ownership of wealth)

political and economic power based on, 26–27

public enterprises, 99–110, 113, 132, 155
  airlines, 95, 107
  banks, 80–82, 95, 100
  efficiency of, 94–95, 99–100
  "grow or die" imperative and, 108
  health care, 83–84, 94, 100 (*See also* Medicaid; Medicare)
  oil production, 95
  regional, 94, 109

public land development, 59–60, 64

public telecommunications services, 60–61, 70, 95

public utilities, 58–61, 70

punctuated stagnation, 127

purchasing power, strategic use of, 69

quasi-public entities, 69, 102, 115, 132, 154–55

racism, 16, 19–20, 113

railroads, 106–7. *See also* high-speed rail

rare earth minerals, 128

Reagan, Ronald, 34

Recology, 44

reform, 6–10, 113, 142, 145–46, 154
  evolutionary reconstruction and, 114
  limits of, 134
  progressive movement and, 133–34, 141
  through countervailing power (*See* countervailing power)

regional decentralization, 145, 149, 152–53

regionalized public enterprise, 94, 109

Reich, Robert, 15, 125

Reinhart, Carmen, 76

repression, 135

resources, limited, 127–28, 147

revolution, 117
  American, 139
  evolutionary reconstruction and, 114
  next American revolution, prehistory of, 139–47

Reyes, Carol Ann, 86

Riverview, Michigan, landfill project, 62

Rogoff, Kenneth, 76

Rohrabacher, Dana, 42–43

Roosevelt, Franklin Delano, 8–9

Roubini, Nouriel, 75, 127

Rouse Corporation, 59–60

Sacramento Municipal Utility District, 59

Salvatore, Nick, 15

San Diego, California
  Market Creek Plaza, 40, 54
  Point Loma Treatment Plant, 62

Sandhills Farm to Table Cooperative, 36

Schmidt, Eric, 120

Schneider, William, 140

schools, segregation of, 20

Schweickart, David, 155

segregation, 20

Service Employees International Union, 33

Simons, Henry C., 78–79

Singapore Airlines, 95, 107

single-payer health care systems, 84–85, 87–88

small businesses, 69, 109, 143

Smith, Adam, 51

Snell, Bradford, 101

Social Capital Markets (SOCAP), 40

social enterprises, democratized ownership of, 36–37

Social Security, 12

socialism, 26–27
  state, 26, 141, 143–44
  United States, socialism in, 58–64

Solow, Robert, 151

Southwest Key Programs, 37

Speth, James Gustave, 108

Spoloare, Enrico, 153

stagnation, xiii, 34, 124–29

stalemate, system in, 113

Standard Oil, 77–78

state governments. *See also* checkerboard strategies
  banks operated by, 81
  direct investment in businesses, 64
  ESOPs supported by, 63–64
  fiscal crisis, cuts in response to, 66
  pension systems, 63
  universal health care legislation, 87

state socialism, 26, 141, 143–44

Stein, Herbert, 85

Stigler, George, 79

Stiglitz, Joseph, 125

systemic change, 26, 75, 83, 132, 148–56.

See also checkerboard strategies; crisis transformations; democratized ownership of wealth; evolutionary reconstruction
 emerging historical context for (*See* emerging historical context for change)
 government role in, 55
 integrated system design, 99, 143, 155–56
 next American revolution, 140–41
 options for, 133–36, 140–47
 planning, role of, 153–55
 theory of change, 3, 8
systemic design, integrated, 99, 143, 155–56
systemic problems, overview of, 1–5
systemic trends, downward-moving, 3–4, 6–7

taxation
 corporate taxes, decline in, 4
 corporations, tax policies to subsidize, 52, 54–55
 employment incentives, 102
 ESOPs, tax benefits of, 42–43, 55
 fiscal crisis, tax increases as response to, 68
 top marginal rate, cuts in, 3–4
technological change, 125, 146–47
telecommunications services, public, 60–61, 70, 95
Tennessee Valley Authority, 109
Texas Permanent School Fund, 64
Texeira, Ruy, 133
Thatcher, Margaret, 25, 46, 94
thermonuclear weapons, 122
TINA (There Is No Alternative), 25, 46
Tocqueville, Alexis de, 142
transportation, 106–7. *See also* mass transportation
 airlines, 95, 104–7
 Interstate Highway System, 107
Transportation Security Administration, 105
Troubled Asset Relief Program (TARP), 80
22nd Street Retail Center, 55

unemployment, US, 75, 101, 119–21
 current rate of, xii
 economic stagnation and, 124–25, 127
 environmental laws, effect on passage of, 13
 during Great Depression, 10
 high unemployment areas, programs for, 102

Union Cab, 35–36
unions. *See* labor unions
US Constitution, 156
US Department of Health and Human Services Community Economic Development program, 54–55
US government
 airlines supported by, 105, 107
 auto industry bailout, 93, 102–3
 banks operated by, 80
 corporations nationalized by, 93
 economic development programs, 54–55
 health care programs (*See* Affordable Care Act; Medicaid; Medicare)
 military spending, 122
 projected federal spending, 131
 Troubled Asset Relief Program (TARP), 80
US Supreme Court, 130, 133
United Auto Workers, 93, 100
United Food and Commercial Workers Union, 33, 44
United Steelworkers, 30, 33, 44
Unity Council, 38
Unjust Deserts: How the Rich Are Taking Our Common Inheritance, 148, 151
urban unrest, 135
utilities, public, 58–61, 70
utopia, 47

Valley Transportation Authority, 60
van der Hoeven, Maria, 127
Vermont
 employee ownership center, 63–64
 universal health care legislation, 87, 90
Vermont Federal Credit Union Board, 36
Verone, James, 86
veterans, programs for, 12
violence, as change agent, 135
voluntary employee beneficiary association, auto bailout and, 93

wages, US workers, xii, 4, 12. *See also* income inequality
 minimum wage, 7, 12
 stagnation, 124–25, 131
Wagner Act, 15
wars, 121–22, 127. *See also* World War II
Washington Metropolitan Area Transit Authority, 60

wealth. *See also* wealth concentration, US
democratized ownership of (*See* democratized ownership of wealth)
power and, 142–43
wealth concentration, US, 27, 124–25, 133,
146. *See also* democratized ownership of
wealth
historically inherited knowledge and, 151
popular response to, xiii
traditional reforms, possibility of changing with, 142
trend in, xii, 3, 27, 113
Williams, William Appleman, 153
Williamson, Thad, 148, 155
W.L. Gore & Associates, Inc., 41
Woodridge, Adrian, 95–96

worker-community structural designs, 150
worker-owned companies, 28–34, 150
ESOPs (employee stock ownership
plans), 41–43, 55, 63–64
labor unions and, 30, 33, 42–44
Ohio, development in, 28–34, 150
state support for, 63–64
success of, 43
voluntary employee beneficiary association, auto bailout and, 93
World War II, 10–12, 19, 121
economic effects of, 11–12
veterans, programs for, 12

Youngstown, Ohio, 28–30, 32, 150
Youngstown Sheet and Tube, 28–30, 32

About the Author

Gar Alperovitz, Lionel R. Bauman Professor of Political Economy at the University of Maryland, is cofounder of the Democracy Collaborative. He is a former fellow of the Institute of Politics at Harvard and of King's College at Cambridge University, where he received his PhD in political economy. He has served as a legislative director in the US House of Representatives and the US Senate and as a special assistant in the Department of State. Earlier he was president of the Center for Community Economic Development, codirector of the Cambridge Institute, and president of the Center for the Study of Public Policy. Alperovitz's numerous articles have appeared in publications ranging from the *New York Times* and the *Washington Post* to the *Journal of Economic Issues, Foreign Policy, Diplomatic History*, and other academic and popular journals. His previous books include *America Beyond Capitalism, The Decision to Use the Atomic Bomb, Making a Place for Community: Local Democracy in a Global Era* (with Thad Williamson and David Imbroscio), and *Unjust Deserts* (with Lew Daly). He currently lives in Washington, DC.